The Historical Christ

The Historical Christ

A Cognitive Psychologist's Perspective

Bruce W. Behrman

RESOURCE *Publications* • Eugene, Oregon

THE HISTORICAL CHRIST
A Cognitive Psychologist's Perspective

Resource Publications
An Imprint of Wipf and Stock Publishers
199 W. 8th Ave., Suite 3
Eugene, OR 97401

www.wipfandstock.com

PAPERBACK ISBN: 978-1-6667-3784-4
HARDCOVER ISBN: 978-1-6667-9781-7
EBOOK ISBN: 978-1-6667-9782-4

JANUARY 30, 2023 1:24 PM

Contents

Preface

It has long been assumed, and it is probably true, that the thoughts and deeds of Jesus were for many years handed down by word of mouth. This is indeed a troubling likelihood. If the historical events reported in the Gospels are based on oral tradition, the so–called truths of the Gospels are based on human memory. And, as perhaps we all know, human memory is very fragile.

Nevertheless, little of biblical scholarship has turned to recent work in experimental studies of human memory, specifically conversational memory. It is likely that the testimonies of the early witnesses to the deeds of Jesus were conveyed through a conversational network. It is consequently helpful that experiments to simulate real-life memory situations are no longer solely based on laboratory studies in which subjects are instructed to retell events one to another through a chain of single person retellings. Rather, real-life conversations are held about events, then the subjects talk of these events to other groups, the participants of which retell these same events as best they can to others. This data is then gathered and analyzed. This process thus produces results that approach the situations we find in everyday life. This book utilizes the findings of conversational memory to assess the nature of the oral tradition surrounding Jesus.

Another aspect of recent memory work is that cognitive psychology has come to embrace clinical concepts of memory, in particular, the idea that memory is guided by individual desires and needs. I bring to the study of oral tradition Conway's self theory: the hypothesis that human memory retrieval is framed by the need to maintain self-coherence. That is, people seek to maintain a coherent life story when remembering; they write or rewrite their own history in such a way as to maintain self-integrity.

A third aspect of modern memory work has to do with collective memory. Hirst has shown that memory for conversations is generally slanted by a dominant individual in those conversations. Therefore, the memory resulting from a chain of conversations is primarily that of dominant individuals who are present not only at the original conversations but also are participants in later conversational retellings.

In this book, I use the above three aspects of cognitive psychology to assess the oral traditions concerning Jesus.

At this time, I would like to make one acknowledgement: it is to my wife, Rileyne. She spent hours going over my manuscript. For her work on this project, I am eternally grateful.

Abbreviations

CAT	communication accommodation theory
CBCA	criteria-based content analysis
DID	dissociative identity disorder
DSM	*Diagnostic Statistical Manual*
EBT	emotional broadcaster theory
IA	inattentional
LTM	*long-term memory*
PEM	*personal event memory*
RIF	retrieval-induced forgetting
SC	stereotype-consistent
SEM	*simple episodic memory*
SI	stereotype-inconsistent
SMS	*self-memory system*
STM	*short-term memory*
SVA	*statement validity analysis*
WM	*working memory*

1

Jesus Christ

The View from Cognitive Psychology

Most biblical scholars have agreed that after his death, many of the words and deeds of Jesus were handed down by word of mouth and that this was the case for many years. This is not to deny that the oral tradition was interlaced with written sources, perhaps even notebooks.[1] Still, it is likely that oral transmission played the predominant role in the formative years of the tradition. This book is not primarily concerned with the models of oral transmission as discussed in biblical literature;[2] rather, I will present experimental evidence concerning the generation and transmission of collective memory as it is pictured in the social/collective memory literature of cognitive and social psychology. Furthermore, the focus is not on what may be called the forensic memory literature, wherein memory is viewed as a reconstruction of the past, but on conversational memory, which considers recall as always guided by a host of personal and social goals. Overall, I cast oral tradition in terms of the social-interactionist approach.[3] The basic framework for this model includes a stimulus situation, a conversational format, and finally a network structure through which the information is conveyed. The social-interaction approach assesses how cognitive functions interact with the social systems in which they are embedded. In this

1. Bird, *Gospel of the Lord*, 47.
2. Eve, *Behind the Gospels*, ch. 1.
3. Vlasceanu et al., "Cognition in Social Context," 32.

model, it is assumed that individual cognitive functions have emergent properties in their social context. Individual cognitive operations not only affect individual behavior but produce social effects and are, in turn, influenced by social phenomena. This model has dealt with the emergence in the community of a variety of cognitive operations or processes—e.g., collective emotion, collective memory, and collective attention.

Specifically, I apply Hirst's model of collective memory,[4] which assumes that conversations generate cultural schema, false memories, and certain retrieval effects, which emerge in communities as constituents of collective memory. I view oral tradition as the transmission of collective memory, which is often, if not commonly, shaped by individuals who dominate conversations.[5] I view conversations as the originating engine of the collective memory of Jesus. These collective memories began during Jesus's lifetime and within days after his death. The more formal methods and processes of generating group memories such as envisioned by Bailey and Eve[6] would have developed later and then only after the tradition had solidified. Hirst's model does not tell us whether a witness is an eyewitness (although this is the common case) or whether the testimony is the result of eyewitness observation or a lengthy series of retellings. Many of Hirst's experiments involve a single conversational interaction. To determine whether a witness was an eyewitness I apply the findings of statement validity analysis (SVA), a form of statement analysis used to distinguish between experience based and non-experience-based testimony.[7] Further, I incorporate the 1932 Bartlett study[8] and the more recent Kashima studies,[9] as well as other experiments that investigate the qualitative changes in memory that occur over several retellings throughout a general network. We may then assess whether the Gospel records fit with the profile of serially produced retellings as demonstrated by the experimental results.

4. Hirst et al., "Of Sins and Virtues."

5. Cuc et al., "On the Formation."

6. Bailey, "Informal Controlled Oral Tradition," 5; Eve, *Behind the Gospels*, 66–68.

7. Steller and Köhnken, "Criteria-Based Statement Analysis"; Volbert and Steller, "Is This Testimony Truthful."

8. Bartlett, *Remembering*.

9. Kashima et al., "Maintenance of Cultural Stereotypes"; Lyons and Kashima, "Maintaining Stereotypes in Communication."

The Person of Christ

The early church believed in the divinity of Jesus. Jesus was considered a divine being.[10] He had descended from heaven and, upon his death, was taken back to heaven. This idea was not such a strange thing to people of this time. They viewed the supernatural as near and ready to break through at all times.[11]

The divinity of Christ was considered incontrovertible throughout the Middle Ages and even during the Protestant Reformation. Not until the Enlightenment, roughly 1650–1780, was Jesus thought of in purely human terms, although it was generally agreed that he exhibited an extraordinarily high level of moral consciousness.[12] At least this was the case for liberal, predominantly German, Protestant scholarship. Schleiermacher wrote that what uniquely defined Jesus was his constant and intense intimacy with God,[13] i.e., the "constant potency of his God consciousness."[14]

During this time, it occurred to some that a sane human, however much imbued with religious consciousness, would not have considered himself a divine being, unless he was mentally ill. In fact, Strauss wrote to William Lang that he feared that Jesus might have been mentally deranged.[15] For this reason, Strauss in his later years considered the apocalyptic "coming Son of Man" statements as secondary, i.e., products of the early church. This view, that the sayings of Jesus that speak of his divine status (for instance, the coming Son of Man verses) are secondary, has been promulgated by biblical scholars over the years and is perhaps the predominant view today, although it is subject to some debate.[16] The view that Jesus was gifted but otherwise quite sane is typical of modern biblical scholarship. Borg presents a representative view of Jesus. He writes: "Though the saints and Spirit persons are a bit crazy, when judged by conventional standards, they typically do not think of themselves in grandiose terms. I do not think people like Jesus have an exalted perception of themselves."[17]

10. Patterson, *God of Jesus*, 2.
11. Grant, *Saint Peter*, 7.
12. Dunn, *Jesus Remembered*, 25.
13. Schleiermacher, *Life of Jesus*, 88–104.
14. Dunn, *Jesus Remembered*, 36.
15. J. Miller, *Jesus at Thirty*, 105.
16. R. Miller, *Apocalyptic Jesus*, 1–13.
17. Borg, *Meeting Jesus*, 147.

But as we shall see, Jesus very much had an exalted view of himself. Recently, much literature has dealt with so-called portraits of Jesus in an effort to provide an assessment of what Jesus may have done or said.[18] In my view, the portrait of Jesus as the greatest wisdom poet in Jewish literature[19] but one who suffered from the constantly changing moods of manic depression best fits Jesus as described in the Gospels. We must right away dispense with the popular, or once common, view that bipolar I disorder portrays persons sequestered in the back wards of insane asylums. As Kay Jamison points out, manic depression is not a dementing condition but, rather, will often ignite extraordinary creativity in those who are already naturally gifted.[20] I think an investigation into the cognitive and phenomenological processes that are the inner world of manic depression, as opposed to the typical *Diagnostic and Statistical Manual* (*DSM*) delineation of behavior in such cases, will elucidate many of the issues concerning the Jesus of history. With this Byronic, Elijah-like Jesus in mind, it is possible to view the Gospel of John not as the creative work of a talented novelist and/or incredibly creative theologian but as a deeply insightful and talented messenger conveying the brilliant light of Jesus.[21] We need the writings of gifted poets, artists, and writers, to illuminate the mind of Christ.

I assert that John is a comparatively accurate picture of Jesus in that he is a first-order witness and portrays a Jesus who fits the schema of a poet who experiences the intense suffering and brilliance of manic depression.[22] This is to say that the grandiosity of John's Jesus becomes understandable within the profile of manic depression. The Johannine Jesus is the real Jesus. It is Jesus's mind we find in John; John rightfully captures Jesus's assertion of divinity. It is the Synoptics that are largely secondary in this regard, although Jesus's plea of divinity does break through at times. In my view, the Synoptics' focus on a messianic Jesus is due in part to Peter's need to maintain self-coherence[23] after Jesus's death. It is Peter's need for forgiveness that guides his memory to a Jesus who as Isaiah's suffering servant dies for the remission of sins. Peter is a dominant personality who shapes the early conversations about Jesus and thus shapes the subsequent collective

18. Borg, *Jesus in Contemporary Scholarship*, 18–43.

19. Barnstone, *Poems of Jesus Christ*, xxvii.

20. Jamison, *Touched with Fire*, 154, 54–56.

21. Kysar, *John*, 60.

22. Jamison, *Touched with Fire*, ch. 3.

23. Conway, "Memory and the Self."

memory processes displayed in the Synoptic Gospels.[24] In addition, the tenor of the Synoptics, with its focus on the scripts of Common Judaism, is due in large part to the overriding processes of culture as described by Bartlett and Lyons and Kashima.[25] These cultural demands tend to fit Jesus into well-known scriptural stereotypes and deemphasize his assertion of preexistence as a divine being.

It should be noted that the degree to which the Gospels are reliable is the subject of endless debate. Theories concerning oral tradition are for the most part speculative.[26] Consequently, I assess the reliability of the Gospels, as they describe Jesus, on the basis of seminal experiments in cognitive psychology. These empirical findings and experiments are presented in chapters 3, 4, and 5 of this book. Basically, I discuss the cognitive tools I will use to analyze the Gospels. Only then may we apply the hypothesis that Jesus suffered from manic depression to establish and elaborate the truths of Jesus's life.

This Book

Biblical Scholarship, Chapter 2

The second chapter of this book presents a brief discussion and critique of biblical scholarship from the perspective of cognitive psychology.

Memory and Emotion

In the next few chapters of this book—chapters 3, 4, 5, and 6—I discuss attention, memory, and emotion from the standpoint of conversational memory and the emergence of these concepts in collective memory.[27] I provide this overview of cognitive psychology to demonstrate the fragility of memory and its extraordinary selectivity, but more so to demonstrate its dependence on motivational properties of the individual personality. Memory is motivated; it operates at emotional/clinical levels. The retrieval process is even capable at times of throwing up screen memories that stand

24. Hirst et al., "Of Sins and Virtues."

25. Bartlett, *Remembering*, 118–77; Lyons and Kashima, "Maintaining Stereotypes in Communication."

26. Eve, *Behind the Gospels*, 66.

27. Vlasceanu et al., "Cognition in a Social Context," 32.

for other memories, which are usually of a very personal and emotional nature.[28]

Cognitive Psychology, Chapter 3

I discuss basic cognitive psychology but focus mostly on attention and the extreme selectivity of attentional mechanisms. I discuss experiments in attentional blindness, especially those that demonstrate that atypical, even shocking, statements or events may not be noticed; i.e., they may not be recalled even a few seconds after presentation. For example, in one experiment, a woman carrying an umbrella walked across a basketball court while players threw the ball to one another.[29] Participants were to note each time the ball was thrown. When asked two seconds later if they had seen anything unusual, they said that they had not seen anything odd. The woman was simply not part of the activated ball game. Out-of-schema events are either not brought into conversation or downplayed in conversation, as in "he just had a bad day," and at that point inhibitory processes take over. These processes cumulate over a series of retellings. I also discuss Conway's theory of self-maintenance as the goal of remembering.

Conversational Memory, Chapter 4

Since conversational memory is the basis for the social interaction model, I discuss seminal experiments in conversational memory.

Serial Retellings, Chapter 5

As noted here, I discuss recent evidence on qualitative changes in memory as information is told and retold.

Collective Memory, Chapter 6

In this chapter, I discuss Hirst's model of collective memory.

28. Conway, "Memory and the Self."

29. Simons and Chabris, "Gorillas in Our Midst."

Artists and Manic Depression, Chapter 7

I discuss Jamison's hypothesis that many great artists, poets, and musicians suffered from manic depression.[30] In addition, I discuss the major aspects of Jesus's words and deeds that fit the profile of manic-depressive disorder. However, I do not rely only on a *DSM*-like description of bipolar I behavior. I portray Christ through the lens of writers who suffer from manic depression and have described the inner world of their illness.

The Gospel of John, Chapter 8

In this chapter, I apply statement validity analysis (SVA)[31] and communication accommodation theory (CAT)[32] to the Gospel of John. These analyses indicate that the author of John is a first-order eyewitness to many of the events in Jesus's life. I consider the author of John to be the Beloved Disciple.[33] Because the Beloved Disciple was considered an intimate disciple of Jesus, chosen to deliver Jesus's message to humanity,[34] I suggest that he was able to accommodate to Jesus's speech[35] and thus was able to convey not only the content and meaning of Jesus's speech but in many cases his very words, his phraseology, his style of speech. Furthermore, the general features of manic depression, both the depressive and manic/hypomanic, provide convincing evidence that the portrayal of Jesus in the Gospel of John is a reliable one. My conclusion is that Jesus talked as he is portrayed in John and did consider himself God incarnate.

The Synoptic Gospels, Chapter 9

In this chapter, I apply cognitive mechanisms to the Synoptic Gospels. In my view, the style and content of the Synoptics is due in part to the influence and guidance of Peter whose memory of Jesus was subject to Peter's need for self-coherence and self-justification.[36] However, the militant,

30. Jamison, *Touched with Fire*, 54–56.
31. Volbert and Steller, "Is This Testimony Truthful."
32. Giles et al., "Accommodation Theory."
33. Bauckham, *Jesus and the Eyewitnesses*, 384.
34. Bauckham, *Jesus and the Eyewitnesses*, 393–96.
35. Giles et al., "Accommodation Theory."
36. Conway, "Memory and the Self."

apocalyptic focus of the Synoptic Gospels is also due in large part to the overriding processes of culture on serial retellings, as described by Bartlett, Lee et al., and Rubin.[37] The synoptic Jesus fits into well-known scriptural stereotypes that deemphasize the Johannine Jesus's assertion of preexistence as a divine being.

The Great Creeds, Chapter 10

In this chapter, I discuss the importance of my findings for modern scholarship and the Christian church. I have found that Jesus quite likely thought of himself as God incarnate, likely the wounded God portrayed in Zechariah. At times, he would wonder about it, but he could not shake the feeling that he was God. At times, he thought of himself an agent of God, God's *shaliach* or emissary,[38] perhaps the Son of Man, the Logos/Messiah.[39] But, as in many manic-depressives, the idea that he was identical with God was too compelling; and at those times, he would consider himself the great "I am" and then utter the "I am" sayings. It is likely that his most compelling identity was that of God incarnate; the "I am" sayings were not inventions of John, nor was the Nicene Creed an invention of the early church. It was the result of honest attempts to accurately interpret the Gospels and John in particular. The concepts of the Nicene Creed, clarified at Chalcedon, offer an accurate interpretation of John. But importantly, I suggest that cognitive psychology, through communication accommodation theory (CAT), and clinical psychology, through Jamison's recent portrayal of mood disorders in artists, combine to show that the great creeds reflect Jesus's own thought processes. CAT allows us to consider John as a close copy of Jesus's thought and verbal style. My hypothesis of manic depression allows us to propose that Jesus did, during manic episodes and also upon later reflection, consider himself to be God incarnate. For him, the *shaliach* and God incarnate are blended and combined into one concept.

Finally, I discuss whether the diagnosis of manic depression in any way diminishes Jesus. I argue that only if he is viewed in terms of the medical model is Jesus diminished as a poet and prophet of God. Does the diagnosis of manic depression diminish the beauty and profundity of the many

37. Bartlett, *Remembering*, 268–71; Lee et al., "Serial Reproduction of Conflict"; Rubin, *Remembering Our Past*, 281.

38. Witherington, *Christology of Jesus*, 270.

39. Dunn, "Let John Be John," 315.

artists discussed by Jamison, e.g., the beauty and truth of Blake's poetry? Nor does it the beauty and truth of Christ.

It may be argued that it is not appropriate to classify historical figures in terms of mental disorders. They are too distant in time, and we have too little information to make a credible diagnosis.[40] However, we are not making a medical diagnosis in terms of committing a person to a hospital or prescribing medicine. We are following in Jamison's and others' footsteps as they observed phenomenological patterns of inner processing and attempted to match those patterns with the behavior and thoughts of historic figures. In this case, we are matching patterns of manic depression (bipolar I) with those of Jesus as expressed in the Gospels.[41] This is simply a hypothesis testing procedure.

40. Capps, *Jesus*, 50–52.

41. Jamison, *Touched with Fire*, 102–47.

2

Biblical Scholarship *and* Cognitive Psychology

Since the Enlightenment, biblical scholars have pursued a historical Christ, a Christ that lay behind the Gospels and was not necessarily portrayed in them. Much of this scholarly endeavor has focused on problems stemming from the likelihood that most of what Jesus said and did was preserved primarily in human memory and oral tradition—and this for a period of at least several years and probably for decades.

Jesus Christ was crucified around 31 CE, but the Gospels were not written until sometime in the 60s CE or later.[1] Granted, some notes may have been taken, some sayings may have been memorized fairly well. But probably most of the information was discussed in various oral retellings and conversations. Slowly, these individual memories would have been translated into collective memory. A great deal of biblical scholarship has centered around the nature of this oral tradition. Scholars suspected that tradition changed the early memories and wondered to what extent this may have occurred. Thus, the primary goal of such scholarship was to assess the reliability of the Gospels. Although it was obvious early on that the reliability of human memory was very much an issue in the transmission of oral information, psychology as a science made little contribution to biblical scholarship. There was good reason for this: the scientific study of human memory did not blossom until the mid-twentieth century. In

1. McIver, *Memory, Jesus*, 1.

the 1930s, Bartlett wrote his famous work on remembering, which investigated the interior processes of recognition and recall, but his findings were scarcely touched by experimental psychologists, as they were laboring under the general behavioristic framework in vogue at the time. It wasn't until the cognitive paradigm shift led by Ulric Neisser and others that biblical scholars, at least a few of them, began to turn to psychology for help.

In this chapter, I discuss the works of some of the more influential biblical scholars who speak to issues surrounding oral retelling and tradition. I have included scholars who are representative of the various models of oral traditions discussed by Eve.[2] My purpose is not to summarize the approach of any individual scholar but rather to highlight biblical issues that are also examined in the conversational memory literature. I discuss biblical scholarship and evaluate it in terms of cognitive memory theory. I present critical evaluations where appropriate.

David Strauss

In David Strauss, we observe the placement of cultural stereotypes and schema onto the memory of Jesus.[3] It is surprising how modern Strauss is. Strauss maintained that Old Testament ideas over a long transmission process were slowly incorporated into memories about Jesus. Strauss called this process a myth-making process. By myth-making, Strauss meant the application of Old Testament ideas to the life of Jesus. This was at first an intentional process, but "without evil intent."[4] However, it soon became part of memory. For Strauss, the passage of a single generation would suffice to clothe Jesus in Old Testament stories and prophesies.[5] The legends of the messiah, already existing in the popular hope of the messiah, were simply transferred to Jesus. Certain things were characteristic of the messiah and had happened to him; therefore, they happened to Jesus.[6] For instance, the story of the cleansing of the temple may have arisen through the application of the Scripture "It is written, My house shall be called a house of prayer" (Matt 21:13). It is worth a lengthy quote to illustrate the insightful genius of Strauss:

2. Eve, *Behind the Gospels*, 15–86.
3. Strauss, *Life of Jesus*, 81–92.
4. Strauss, *Life of Jesus*, 85.
5. Schweitzer, *Quest of Historical Jesus*, 79.
6. Strauss, *Life of Jesus*, 89.

> In general, the whole Messianic era was expected to be full of signs and wonders. The eyes of the blind should be opened, the ears of the deaf should be unclosed, the lame should leap, and the tongue of the lamb should praise God. (Isa. 35:5f; 42:7; cf. 32:3, 4). These merely figurative phrases soon came to be understood literally (Matt. 11:5; Luke 7:21f) and thus the idea of the Messiah was continually filled up with new details. Thus, many of the legends had not to be newly invented, they already existed in the Old Testament and had merely to be transferred to Jesus and accommodated to his character and doctrines.[7]

These were unconscious processes. Strauss further noted that in the process of transmission, intentional fictions would likely be added to the unconscious myth-making processes. "In every series of legends . . . as soon as they become the subject of free poetry, or any other literary composition, some kind of fiction will be intentionally mixed up with them. . . . But a fiction, although not undesigned may still be without evil design. . . . In ancient times, and especially among the Hebrews . . . the line of distinction between history and fiction, prose and poetry, was not drawn so clearly as with us."[8] These ideas closely mirror Tversky and Marsh's 2016 finding that once-intentional elaborations later become memories.[9] Strauss did not talk in terms of modern conversational memory theory—indeed, no theory of memory was then available—but his ideas would easily fit into a model in which memory is shaped by the Old Testament schemata that are so much a part of Common Judaism.[10] I know of no recent scholar who has talked of psychological processes so close to those of modern cognitive and conversational memory as David Strauss. This myth-making process is a retelling process.

The life of Strauss spanned much of the nineteenth century. And it was during this time that biblical scholarship saw its greatest period of creativity. The picture of Jesus that arose was that of the liberal Jesus, a very human Jesus; Jesus was considered a man, rather than a divine being. But, he was considered an extraordinary person. Perhaps his personality was best expressed by Friedrich Schleiermacher: the uniqueness of Jesus was

7. Strauss, *Life of Jesus*, 84.

8. Strauss, *Life of Jesus*, 85.

9. Tversky and Marsh, "Biased Retellings," 33–34.

10. Dunn, *Jesus Remembered*, 280.

exemplified by "the constant potency of his God consciousness, which was a veritable existence of God in Him."[11]

Commensurate with this liberal view of Jesus was the belief expressed by many scholars of the day that the sayings about the coming Son of Man were inventions of the early church—that, in fact, however gifted, Jesus was a normal man, and as such, he would not have said such things. The liberal Jesus began to collapse when Weiss and Schweitzer maintained that the coming Son of Man statements indeed had been uttered by Jesus and that he did expect the imminent arrival of the kingdom of God as a real event, not just as a change in the human heart. In fact, Schweitzer thought that this eschatology was the primary theme of Jesus's life and thought. Schweitzer maintained that Jesus thought that he had been chosen by God to usher in the kingdom and that he was to accomplish this by his own suffering and death.[12]

Form Criticism

The form critics insisted that oral tradition began with certain ideal literary forms. Individual memory was quickly supplanted by stereotypical stories shaped by the community.[13] Memory was not critical or necessary to understand and elucidate tradition. The form critics maintained that oral tradition was the result of anonymous community influences; individual memory played no part in this. Tradition was shaped solely by community needs.[14] According to Bird, the commonly accepted list of forms was as follows: (1) individual sayings; (2) apothegms (short stories ending in moral admonishments); (3) parables; (4) discourses; (5) miracle stories; and (6) historical narratives, generally mythical in nature.[15] In addition, the form critics theorized that oral tradition followed certain laws of transmission. For instance, Joachim Jeremias outlined ten "principles of transformation" in his study of Jesus's parables.[16] These principles listed the ways in which the early church altered the parables and transmitted them from person to person and village to village. For instance, Jeremias noted that over time,

11. Dunn, *Jesus Remembered*, 36.
12. Dunn, *Jesus Remembered*, 46.
13. Bird, *Gospel of the Lord*, 117.
14. Eve, *Behind the Gospels*, 26.
15. Bird, *Gospel of the Lord*, 114.
16. Jeremias, *Parables of Jesus*, 23–24.

allegorical material and moral conclusions were added to the central core. Jeremias based this opinion on the fact that the Gospel of Thomas parables contain no or little allegorical material. Jeremias used these principles of tradition history to uncover what he thought might be the more primitive forms of each parable. More recently, Brandon Scott has used the insights of Jeremias and other form critics to determine the "originating structure" of the parables.[17] This approach has been roundly criticized, but the general idea that tradition would follow certain general principles is reasonable. The underlying idea of finding certain likely and constant errors in oral retellings was on target and commensurate with modern cognitive psychology.[18] The form critics did not overly concern themselves with whether the changes to tradition were intentional or due to unconscious memory processes. But form critics tended to view changes as deliberate and to serve present interests.[19] We shall see that recent experiments in conversational retellings have shown that these changes may at first be intentional, but they later become part of memory.[20]

VINCENT TAYLOR

Hengel has noted that a missing factor in the form criticism model was individual memory.[21] Vince Taylor in England was influenced by the German theorists,[22] but did bring the individual memory of the tradents into the mix. His famous quip: that "if the form critics are right, the disciples must have been immediately translated into heaven after Easter."[23] illustrates the point. Taylor, adopted many of the theories of form criticism, but with some major changes. For instance, Bultmann considered the pronouncement stories "ideal scenes" which illustrate a principle.[24] These forms were not memories of real events; they were formed by early church communities to maintain or promote community needs. But for Taylor, they are

17. Scott, *Hear Then the Parable*, 18.

18. Bartlett, *Remembering*, 171–85; Kashima et al., "Maintenance of Cultural Stereotypes."

19. Eve, *Behind the Gospels*, 124.

20. Tversky and Marsh, "Biased Retellings," 33–34.

21. Hengel, *Saint Peter*, 88–89.

22. Bird, *Gospel of the Lord*, 113–14.

23. Taylor, *Formation of Gospel Tradition*, 41.

24. Eve, *Behind the Gospels*, 22.

narrative forms of real happenings, forms in which oral tradition naturally clothes itself.[25]

Taylor writes a very credible scenario concerning the early formation of the tradition.[26] For Taylor, the first stage in the formation of the tradition was the rehearsal of the stories of Jesus without any organizing framework. In the first years after the resurrection, the tradition preserved cycles of connected sequences as shown in the passion narrative and as illustrated in the short connected cycles of Mark's Gospel (Mark 1:21–39; 4:35–41). According to Taylor, "this kind of recollection was in the nature of things."[27] Much fuller information lay behind these recollections. Not guided by biographical interest, the narratives soon began to decay. Within a decade, the Gospel, except for the passion story, became a collection of isolated stories and sayings. According to Taylor, there was no need for a "connected record. . . . The first Christians listened with deep interest to Peter and others as they told how one thing followed another; but if the succession of events had been for them a matter of great importance, it would be far better represented in the Gospels than it is."[28]

Note that here Taylor is positing a view of how the early memories were formed. He mentions a chronological recall of events as in Mark and suggests that this was a natural way of remembering. He notes that the eyewitnesses did repeat these stories but then goes on to suggest that chronological succession and narratives began to decay. There was for the most part no biographical/chronological interest. In Taylor's words, "Christian hands are full of jewels, but there is no desire to weave a crown."[29]

Taylor noted that the first followers of Jesus asked many practical questions of the disciples, e.g., when members of the church died before the parousia, what was their experience to be after death.[30]

According to Taylor, "the principal witnesses who shaped the tradition were eyewitnesses and others who had knowledge of the original facts."[31] These tradents traveled from one community to another. They told of Jesus's deeds and answered questions about him. In fact, for Taylor, the early

25. Taylor, *Formation of Gospel Tradition*, 29–30.

26. Taylor, *Formation of Gospel Tradition*, 168–89.

27. Taylor, *Formation of Gospel Tradition*, 169.

28. Taylor, *Formation of Gospel Tradition*, 174–75.

29. Taylor, *Formation of Gospel Tradition*, 174.

30. Taylor, *Formation of Gospel Tradition*, 172.

31. Taylor, *Formation of Gospel Tradition*, 170.

formation of the tradition seems to have been based not only on a preaching or teaching format but also on a conversational format wherein the people asked questions of the Christian leaders and in turn discussed the issues amongst themselves.[32] Thus Taylor, unlike the form critics, focuses on individual memory and a conversational format as the generating engine of tradition. All in all, Taylor's view is in accord with my view of eyewitness memory: at first, eyewitness memory is chronological; it later becomes shortened and stereotypical in nature, centering around short stories and important sayings.

Werner Kelber

The form critics based their entire foundation upon the idea that the Jesus tradition was oral in nature. However, for Bultmann, little distinction was made between conceiving tradition as a series of writings and oral tradition. That is, as Dunn would put it, Bultmann conceived of tradition, even oral tradition, as a series of layers and that one could therefore excavate through each layer down to the original.[33] For Kelber, the oral tradition has many characteristics that distinguish it from the literary paradigm. For Kelber, there is no original form, and there is no uniform evolutionary process behind the Synoptics. For Kelber, tradition need not always grow. It may forget. It may grow and diminish. It will forget when the community finds the information no longer useful. This process Kelber calls *preventative censorship*. But tradition is not limited to growth and loss. Tradition may be pared to its essentials, or it may be elaborated with additions and digressions. Themes may be substituted for one another; stock features may be shuffled.[34] Perhaps the most telling difference between oral and written tradition is that oral tradition is constantly tuned to the audience; it is communicative in nature. It is purposeful. For Kelber, the basic factor shaping oral tradition and memory is not the preservation of history but the maintenance of group identity.[35] This brings it, as we shall see, into agreement with newer ideas of conversational memory and the extended mind. Remembering is communicative, purposeful, and social.

32. Taylor, *Formation of Gospel Tradition*, 170–75.

33. Dunn, *Jesus Remembered*, 53–59.

34. Kelber, *Oral and Written Gospel*, 28–30.

35. Kelber, *Oral and Written Gospel*, 15.

As did the form critics before him, Kelber categorized the tradition into a number of forms: heroic (healing), polarizing (exorcisms), didactic (pronouncement), and parabolic stories. Each of the various types of tales or forms follows a set script or theme. Kelber lays these out for the major forms. For instance, for the heroic stories: exposition of healing, performance of healing, and confirmation of healing. He also lays out the basic scripts followed in the polarization and controversy stories. These stereotypical sequences are comparable to the various themes discussed by Perry and Lord in the Homeric epics.[36] Kelber maintains that folklore mirrors the basic tendencies of memory, in that it gravitates to the imagistic and stereotypical, as recent research in cognitive psychology has shown. "Orality's principal concern is not to preserve historical actuality, but to shape and break it into memorable, applicable speech."[37] Kelber insists that the Jesus tradition begins with the historical Jesus but that "once entered into speech the traditional Jesus yields to the call of the oral imperative. . . . The Jesus who is gathered into patterned episodes, is a simplified, heroized and visually impressive figure whose teachings emanate from controversies, and acts in a hostile world divided into hostile camps."[38] This description brings to mind the characters and scenes of epic poetry as delineated by Rubin: "Epic heroes are always on the move," moving from one place to another.[39] "Epic is composed of (1) agents, usually heroes or Gods, producing a series of actions; (2) that are particular, specific examples; (3) of a concrete, vivid, easy to visualize nature."[40] As Kelber observes, Mark's characters are not drawn as recognizable human beings, including Jesus. It is through their actions that the characters come alive. The most extensive portraits are those of Jesus and Peter; the rest remain nondescript.[41]

Kenneth Bailey

The models discussed so far have been theoretical, that is, based "on the writings of others or their own analysis of texts."[42] Kenneth Bailey's

36. Kelber, *Oral and Written Gospel*, 44–51.
37. Kelber, *Oral and Written Gospel*, 71.
38. Kelber, *Oral and Written Gospel*, 71.
39. Rubin, *Memory in Oral Traditions*, 62.
40. Rubin, *Memory in Oral Traditions*, 60.
41. Kelber, *Oral and Written Gospel*, 68–69.
42. Eve, *Behind the Gospels*, 66.

concepts were derived from observation. They were based on his personal experiences while working as a missionary in the Middle East.[43] Note that to this point, not much had been made of the issue of how information was controlled in oral societies. That changed with Bailey's introduction of a paper discussing his observations of Egyptian villages in the early part of the twentieth century. Bailey observed several methods of controlling oral tradition in the villages.[44]

For Strauss and later the form critics, the oral tradition was a long and uncontrolled creative process. Bailey's observations provided another model of how the tradition was handed on to others and brought to the field particular types of community processes. Bailey's model was based on his observations of villages in Egypt; but these may well have been what Galilean villages were like. Much of community life centered around the *hafalat samar*. According to Bailey, this term refers to a community gathering in which people may recite proverbs or poems and share stories of past events relevant to the community heritage.[45] The material presented at the gathering is usually of three types: (1) The first category consists of material not regarded as important for the life of the community, such as jokes or casual news. This material is not controlled or corrected by others at all. An identifiable teacher or tradent not required. Bailey refers to this process as informal and uncontrolled. (2) At the other end of the transmission spectrum are poems and proverbs. Here the transmission is considered formal. The material is memorized. A particular teacher is specified. (3) The third method of control is applied to parables and recollections of historical people and events important to the identity of the community. Here the material is subject to informal controlled processes. Some deviation is allowed, but any deviation to the basic thrust of the story will be corrected. There is no specified teacher, but he is usually an elder.

Bailey visited Egypt in the 1950s. He was told stories about John Hogg who had ministered to the villages in the late nineteenth century. He compared several of these stories of John Hogg, still circulating in the villages, with parallel stories reported by Rena Hogg in her 1914 book about her father.[46] Bailey reported a high degree of similarity between the stories

43. Eve, *Behind the Gospels*, 67.

44. Bailey, "Middle Eastern Oral Tradition," 364–65; Bailey, "Informal Controlled Oral Tradition."

45. Eve, *Behind the Gospels*, 67.

46. Hogg, *Master-Builder*, 215–17, as cited in Eve, *Behind the Gospels*, 69.

he heard and those reported by Rena Hogg. From these parallels, he concluded that the oral tradition had been quite stable over the nearly fifty-year interval between Rena Hogg's visit and his own.

It is not in the purview of this book to discuss the entire set of Bailey's data, but the transmission over decades of one of the stories, the robber story, of John Hogg and his companion being accosted by robbers well illustrates how retellings may change over time but nevertheless retain aspects of the original narrative.[47] While visiting Egypt in the early 1900s, Rena Hogg heard this story from a village elder, "a fine old patriarch," and reported it in her book. The elder told a story about Hogg's having been accosted by a gang of robbers late at night. However, Hogg told the robbers stories from the Bible, and in so doing was able to convert them to Christ. They returned his valuables and money and pledged to give up highway robbery. Hogg financed them until they could find credible employment. Bailey claims he heard the same story years later and that it was very similar to that told by the patriarch to Rena Hogg. However, Rena Hogg dismisses the story as a "romantic tale" and reports the same incident as told by her father, John Hogg.

John Hogg's version of this adventure as reported in his notes was much more mundane. John Hogg and a companion did run into a man with a gun, then heard swimmers in the nearby river, walked on, and encountered another group of men, all this late at night. Hogg took them to be farmers guarding their melon crop. They spent the night in a convivial manner and left in the morning. Hogg's companion, Shenoodeh Hanna, did read a Bible story to these men, which according to Hogg elicited a confession from one of the men that he had almost shot Mr. Hanna but that his brother had prevented him from doing so. Hogg and Hanna left in the morning and gave some money to the man who had accompanied them to their boat. The guard left the two preachers, "blessing their memory."[48]

The rather dramatic embellishment of the story reported by the old patriarch came early on. In fact, Rena Hoggs reports that Hanna gave a "thrilling" sermon two days later in the village of Assuit; thus, it is likely that the story immediately gained a dramatic interpretation but that thereafter it remained relatively stable. Years later, in the early twentieth century, Rena Hogg reported the dramatic version of the robber story told to her by the village patriarch; and then Bailey heard pretty much the same

47. Eve, *Behind the Gospels*, 69.

48. Eve, *Behind the Gospels*, 71.

dramatic version some forty years after that. The transmission of the old patriarch's version of the robber story over a period of over fifty plus years is consistent with Kelber's suggestion that transmission over many retellings and conversations follows a dramatic, heroic path. Modern experimental, conversational memory studies report a similar move to stereotypic form and memories based on emotional attitude.[49] The story had changed to a dramatic version by the time Rena Hogg had heard it, and that version did remain the same until Bailey heard it after another forty plus years. The same schematic frame that guided the story into its religious portrait early on kept it intact, once the basic schematic framework had been established.

A different scenario also recorded by Bailey provides evidence of the influence of community need in generating oral tradition. When analyzing Bailey's data, Weeden found evidence that the community would change sayings or events if the preservation of group identity called for it. Reverend Dagher, a recognized authority, the head of the Protestant Church in Lebanon, recited an old parable while lecturing to a large audience but dramatically changed the ending of the parable, so that the core meaning was changed.[50] It was this version that was then preserved until Bailey heard it during his investigation of the Egyptian community traditions. According to Weeden, this provided strong evidence that groups will change tradition if thought important for their identity as a group or, as Weeden puts it, to preserve the community's "present existential needs."[51]

Overall, Bailey's data is indicative that some aspects of an event may be preserved, although likely in an abbreviated and stereotypical manner. In the case of the robber story, the stereotypical schemata would have been that of a charismatic religious leader[52] who converts a group of vicious thieves to Christianity. Further, Bailey's study shows that a community may intentionally change material, should a dominant representative decide that the change is necessary to maintain group identity.

49. Bartlett, *Remembering*, 93–94; Kashima et al., "Maintenance of Cultural Stereotypes."

50. Weeden, "Kenneth Bailey's Theory," 28.

51. Weeden, "Kenneth Bailey's Theory," 28.

52. Lyons and Kashima, "How Are Stereotypes Maintained."

James Dunn

James Dunn was impressed by Bailey's work and impressed with the Egyptian villages' methods of preserving tradition. He was impressed with the activities of community members at various meetings, particularly church meetings and the *hafalat samar* (the evening talk). He noted that some degree of control was used to preserve traditions of the village and that the degree of control depended on the extent to which the information was important for the group's identity. Dunn suggests that the informal control method reported by Bailey seeks to retain the core of events and deeds when they are important to the preservation of group identity. For Dunn, however, the Christian communities aimed to control for historical accuracy.[53] Dunn maintains that the form of the tradition shown to be operating in the Synoptic texts is consistent with the use of an informally controlled method of the type used in Bailey's Egyptian villages.[54]

In fact, unlike the form critic's view that the tradition became increasingly remote from the historical Jesus, Dunn thought that his analysis of the Synoptics indicated that the impact that Jesus made and the historical core of events were preserved from the inception. It should also be noted that for Dunn, remembering is a communal process. As Dunn says, "It is not really possible to speak of tradition except as community tradition."[55] Dunn is quite emphatic on this:

> I simply do not believe that Peter, Mary of Magdala, and the like stored up many memories of Jesus' mission, which were only jerked into remembrance by "oral history inquiries" of a Luke or Matthew. They had already fed these memories into the living tradition of the churches as major contributory elements in the forming and shaping of that tradition.[56]

Richard Bauckham

For Richard Bauckham, the Gospels closely reflect eyewitness memories of Jesus's deeds and words. The dominant model of scholarship for many years, starting in the eighteenth century, was that a long series of retellings

53. Dunn, *Jesus Remembered*, 177–80.
54. Eve, *Behind the Gospels*, 83.
55. Dunn, *Jesus Remembered*, 481–82.
56. Dunn, *Jesus Remembered*, 483–84.

occurred between the original events and the final writings of the evangelists. Form criticism, the dominant mode of scholarship for many years, paid very little attention to the influence and fate of the first eyewitnesses. Vince Taylor quipped, "If the form critics are right, the disciples must have been translated to heaven immediately after the resurrection."[57] But many scholars continued to postulate that the tradition slowly changed through communal processes and needs, until Jesus was unrecognizable. Very little remained of the original material. As Bultmann said, "I do indeed think that we can now know almost nothing concerning the life and personality of Jesus."[58]

The idea that individual memory would be lost and replaced by anonymous community remembering did not sit well with Bauckham. Bauckham focused on historical research to the effect that antiquity held the reminisces of eyewitnesses in the highest regard. He used Brewer's 1995 theory of recollective memory as indicative that, at least for a few days or sometimes even weeks, autobiographical memory retained a partial copy of the initial event.[59] In addition, he cited studies in cognitive psychology as indicating that emotional events are better retained than everyday events.[60] He suggests that the memories of the original apostles lay not far behind the Gospels, perhaps only one link or two in the chain of retellings.

Bauckham discussed the Bailey model of oral tradition.[61] He noted that Christian communities might have operated something like Bailey's model suggests; however, Bauckham thought that a formal controlled model would have produced most of the material in the Synoptics and John, asserting that eyewitnesses would have been the preferred teachers of the tradition. He suggests that if the Bailey model obtains, the preferred approach to passing on the tradition would have been the formal controlled model, the control being provided by the original apostles. Bauckham, however, proposes a slight variation on Bailey's formal controlled model. Bauckham insists that the "known teacher" of Bailey's formal controlled model must be an eyewitness.[62] Further, for Bauckham, the sayings and

57. Taylor, *Formation of Gospel Tradition*, 41.

58. Bultmann, "History of Synoptic Tradition."

59. Bauckham, *Jesus and the Eyewitnesses*, 19–67.

60. Bauckham, *Jesus and the Eyewitnesses*, 319–57.

61. Bailey, "Middle Eastern Oral Tradition"; Bailey, "Informal Controlled Oral Tradition."

62. Bauckham, *Jesus and the Eyewitnesses*, 293.

events would have been memorized and preserved quite well; only minor distortions would have resulted from memory errors.[63] Any major variation would have occurred by intentional editing on the part of the eyewitnesses or established tradents.[64]

The major problem for Bauckham is that memory is much more unreliable than he asserts.[65] Further, memory is always motivated. It is not only subject to the classical "sins of memory"[66] but the conscious and unconscious motivations and strategies designed to preserve self-coherence.[67] Furthermore and most importantly, cultural metamemory and selective processes increase with the number of retellings.[68] First-order witnesses' memories do experience memory distortions, but they also can and do recall detail and context as described in the statement validity analysis and Pillemer's personal event memories (PEMs); but as retelling continues, especially from person to person, the retellings become more stereotypical and less specific and detailed, especially in terms of spatial and chronological features.

Bauckham was quite concerned with one of the major problems of collective memory: whether conversing with others in a social situation means the loss of individual memories. Bauckham insists that "individual remembering in a social context does not require us to dissolve the distinctiveness of personal recollection."[69] However, this is simply not the case. Hirst has shown that individual unshared memories may well be lost in group situations. In one study, almost half of all of the narrative units recalled by the group were not recalled by any member of the group prior to the group conversation. Thus, the group recall differed substantially from that of the separate memories of the individuals in the group as recounted prior to the group recall.[70] Individual memories may then be lost through inhibitory processes arising from induced forgetting.[71] Further, false memories of

63. Bauckham, *Jesus and the Eyewitnesses*, 286.
64. Bauckham, *Jesus and the Eyewitnesses*, 287.
65. Schacter, *Searching for Memory*, 98–133.
66. Schacter, *Searching for Memory*, 98–133.
67. Conway, "Memory and the Self."
68. Bergman and Roediger, "Can Bartlett's Repeated Reproduction."
69. Bauckhan, *Jesus and the Eyewitness*, 313.
70. Hirst and Manier, "Remembering as Communication," 280.
71. Coman and Hirst, "Cognition through Social Network," 321.

dominant individuals may be adopted by other members of conversations, as shown by post-group individual testing.[72]

McIver: Eyewitness Testimony and Pericope Form

As we have seen, many biblical scholars think memory works best when conveyed in short pithy sayings or brief episodes or stories like healing episodes or pronouncement stories. This was clearly stated by Johann Herder as early as the eighteenth century: "People more easily recall a parable, a saying, an apothegm, that they had found striking than connected discourses."[73] Further, Herder argued that the truth of the Gospels is attested by the fact that their content is structured around just such short pericopes. These episodes may be designated as the *pericopes* of the form critics or the heroic stories of the storyteller suggested by Kelber.[74] In a similar vein, as late as 2011, McIver was insisting that eyewitness memory was "granular,"[75] something like the personal event memories investigated by Pillemer.[76] McIver based this idea on Pillemer's concept of PEMs. It is clear that McIver equates Pillemer's PEMs with the pericopes of the Synoptics. Thus, we need to investigate the PEMs as described by Pillemer and compare them with the characteristics of eyewitness testimony listed by McIver.

In his research, Pillemer asked subjects, students at Wellesley, to describe important or salient events in their lives.[77] Based on the data gathered from his study, Pillemer was able to define five characteristics of a PEM.[78]

1. The memory represents a specific event that took place at a particular time and place, rather than a general event or an extended series of related happenings.
2. The memory contains a detailed account of the rememberer's own personal circumstances at the time of the event.
3. The verbal narrative account of the event is accompanied by sensory images, including visual, auditory, and olfactory images and

72. Cuc et al, "On the Formation," 760.

73. Dunn, *Jesus Remembered*, 193. See also Dibelius, *Tradition to Gospel*, 5.

74. Kelber, *Oral and Written Gospel*, 44–64.

75. McIver, *Memory, Jesus*, 127.

76. Pillemer, *Momentous Events, Vivid Memories*, 50.

77. Pillemer, *Momentous Events, Vivid Memories*, 203.

78. Pillemer, *Momentous Events, Vivid Memories*, 50.

bodily sensations that contribute to the feeling of "reexperiencing" or "reliving."

4. The memory details and sensory images correspond to a particular moment or moments of phenomenal experience.
5. The rememberer believes that the memory is a truthful representation of what transpired.

Pillemer was not interested in the accuracy of the events, nor did he test them for accuracy. Pillemer provides an example of a student's PEM as illustrative of the core qualities of PEMs:[79]

> I remember sitting in X's class on the day that a midterm . . . was handed back. I was a freshman and felt that I was in over my head. The professor gave a stern lecture on the value of good writing before she handed back the papers. . . . Suddenly she turned and looked directly at me, I thought I would die of humiliation. Then she said "But Y has answered the question well and has an unusual lyrical and personal style that enhanced her answer." I couldn't believe that she was talking about my paper, but she was. I can still envision that dimly lit little room in the bottom of Z and smell its peculiar musty odor. I can still picture her stern but kind face and feel the relief and pride that I felt at the moment.[80]

Note that the time and place are specific (not the date), the setting is specific and specifically described, even its location. The smell of the room is recalled, the look on the professor's face is distinctly recalled as it appeared at the moment the test was handed back: "I can still picture her stern but kind face." In addition, the student relives her feelings of "relief and pride" at that time.

The Synoptic Gospels are not nearly this specific or exacting. McIver recognizes this to an extent but then, rather surprisingly, suggests that the Synoptic Gospels reflect eyewitness memory and even suggests that eyewitness memory is particularly vague with respect to time and place.[81]

McIver provided a number of characteristics that he contends indicate the presence of eyewitness testimony. These were based, according to McIver, on Pillemer's listing of the features of PEMs. McIver suggests that eyewitness memory contains narratives of events, places, and people; is

79. Pillemer, *Momentous Events, Vivid Memories*, 51.

80. Pillemer, *Momentous Events, Vivid Memories*, 252.

81. McIver, *Memory, Jesus*, 124.

vague with respect to time and place; lacks further narrative context; takes place over a short time; and contains sensory information and, in some instances, irrelevant detail.[82] In fact, eyewitness memory is much more consistent with Pillemer than McIver. According to McIver, the essential features of eyewitness testimony are as follows:[83]

Contains narratives of events, places, and people. I agree that eyewitness testimony contains narratives of events, places, and people.

Vague with regard to place and time. This is clearly an incorrect assertion. One of the primary defining characteristics of eyewitness memory and PEMs is specificity with regard to location and spatial references. Statement validity studies repeatedly confirm the idea that detailed information, particularly that of time and location, are indicative of the presence of participants at the occurrence of an event.[84] The time need not refer to calendar time, e.g., July 10, 1689 CE. But the time should be specific. In the above example, the timing of the event is quite precise: the incident took place on the day the midterm was handed back. With regard to place, the PEM mentioned by Pillemer and given as an outstanding example of the characteristics of PEMs is extremely graphic with regard to place as well as time. As the participant says, "I can still envision the dimly lit little room, in the bottom of Z and its peculiar musty odor." This accords well with Johnson and Raye,[85] wherein it was shown that recollections of actual events showed higher imagery ratings and notably higher ratings for location and spatial arrangement of objects than imagined events.

Irrelevant detail. McIver also suggests that eyewitness testimony can and often does contain "irrelevant" details. The idea that eyewitness material contains irrelevant detail is widespread even in the scholarly literature.[86] This is an old idea, a popular opinion, and, as Brewer suggests, stems from the speculations of philosophers, but no evidence has been adduced to substantiate the theory.[87] And the studies that do exist indicate that irrel-

82. McIver, *Memory, Jesus*, 124–27.

83. McIver, *Memory, Jesus*, 124–27.

84. Steller and Köhnken, "Criteria-Based Statement Analysis"; Pillemer, *Momentous Events, Vivid Memories*, 50.

85. Johnson and Raye, *Reality Monitoring*, 67–85.

86. Dunn, *Jesus Remembered*, 687.

87. Brewer, "What Is Recollective Memory," 44.

evant detail does not predict eyewitness testimony. The SVA list of criteria[88] includes quantity of detail, and this is a significant predictor of actual observation of an event; however, also listed in the SVA criteria is *superfluous detail*, and this characteristic is not significant.

Length of narrative with context. McIver argues that eyewitness episodes lack "further narrative context." Lengthy narrative with characters moving from one context to another is common in eyewitness memory, as is chronological recall. As both Linton and Hoffman and Hoffman show,[89] chronological recall and ordering of events is the default configuration among eyewitness accounts. Chronological recall usually occurs by reference to some important event, e.g., "I remember it was about a week after Mark's graduation from high school," or "shortly after we had landed on Omaha beach."[90]

Brevity of report. McIver states that eyewitness memory is "granular,"[91] that is, brief. In fact, the structure and length of eyewitness testimony depends of the type of question asked of the witness. If the witness is asked to simply describe what happened, they will usually describe the event in order of the happenings. The series of events described may well be over several days. The brevity of the recall may increase over a series of retellings, as Bartlett and Lee et al. indicate,[92] but the initial eyewitness report may be quite lengthy. The PEMs were short because the participants were specifically asked to limit their recall to one instance. That eyewitness testimony generally consists of a series of unconnected, decontextualized events is simply not the case. In general, original eyewitness testimony will be of relatively lengthy, highly detailed narratives, described in the order of occurrence. This is not to say that the narrative is accurate, but it will contain graphic imagery, and often the characters move about from one place or location to another as the events unfold. The recall will not be like a modern cinematographic movie but more like a stage play, playing out an entire scene as it occurred, or as it is remembered to have occurred. And as SVA

88. Köhnken and Steller, "Evaluation of Credibility"; Steller and Köhnken, "Criteria-Based Statement Analysis"; Volbert and Steller, "Is This Testimony Truthful"; Vrij, "Critera-Based Content Analysis."

89. Linton, "Ways of Searching"; Hoffman and Hoffman, *Archives of Memory*, 154.

90. Hoffman and Hoffman, *Archives of Memory*, 151.

91. McIver, *Memory, Jesus*, 124.

92. Bartlett, *Remembering*, chs. 5 and 7; Lee et al., "Serial Reproduction of Conflict."

has it, the scenes will contain some degree of conversation or speech of the persons involved. "The moment my mother came into the room, he stopped smiling. And then he asked, Is that your coat?"[93] First-order testimony, testimony that is indicative that the witness was indeed present at the event, is not a shortened compressed report, that is, unless the situation calls for it. Subsequent retellings by others produce such a result.

Accuracy. McIver cites Yuille and Cutshall[94] to argue that overall eyewitness testimony is roughly 80% accurate with regard to the retention of event detail. Yuille's study is often cited to argue for the accuracy of eyewitness evidence. However, it is a special case. The case involved the attempted robbery of a store. The robber was shot by the owner. Witnesses gave their testimonies to the police within an hour after the event. Their testimonies were transcribed in written reports by the police. Several months later, the witnesses were again asked to recall details of the robbery. The 80% accuracy level was in great part due to the witnesses' memories of the report itself, the details of which were reported within a short time, within hours after the event.

McIver seems to be quite influential among biblical scholars. Craig Keener has written a recent, extensive work, assessing the Gospels as ancient biographies.[95] He concludes that the Gospels are generally reliable historical biographies, basing his conclusions in large part on McIver's review of experimental and empirical studies of human memory. Keener cites the characteristics of eyewitness memory that McIver lists in his book *Memory, Jesus and the Synoptic Gospels* and further relies to a considerable extent on the report of Yuille and Cutshall, discussed by McIver, concerning the reliability of witnesses to an actual robbery. This experiment, it will be recalled, reports an 80% accuracy rate among eyewitnesses. Referring to McIver, Keener argues that eyewitness testimony is generally reliable and that "biographic anecdotes from living memory more likely represent real events . . . than not."[96] Keener points out that ancient Mediterranean culture valued memory more than Western culture does and that, in general, the disciples of great men accurately preserved the core of their mentor's teachings. Keener argues that the Gospels fit within the genre of historical

93. Vrij, "Critera-Based Content Analysis," 6.

94. Yuille and Cutshall, "Case Study."

95. Keener, *Christobiography*, 369–400.

96. Keener, *Christobiography*, 447.

biography and that the Gospel writers, as well as Jesus's disciples, attempted to accurately recall and preserve Jesus's work.[97] The problem here is that Keener has based his conclusions to a considerable extent on an erroneous view of eyewitness memory.

Reports of Oral Historians

These testify to the length and indeed the frequent overall accuracy of the testimony of many who are asked to retrieve memories of their life experiences. There is a burgeoning literature collected by oral historians that presents evidence of thirty-to fifty-year-old memories that are quite detailed and are relatively accurate with regard to geographical and chronological features. One interesting case is that of Howard Hoffman, who was drafted at the age of eighteen to serve in World War II. His wife, an oral historian, interviewed him about his experiences in World War II. He was asked to recount his experiences as they had occurred. His memories compared well with the company log that recorded what had happened during the same period of time.

Howard was again interviewed some years after the first interview. During this second interview, Howard at first was asked to recount specific instances; i.e., Howard was asked to go out of chronological order and discuss the events connected with meeting the Russians at the Elbe River. Forcing the narrative out of sequence resulted in considerable confusion. This also resulted in a loss of a considerable amount of material. Omitted incidents were retrievable but only with considerable cuing. In addition, when forced out of sequence, Howard was confused regarding the location of the incidents. Specifically, he found it hard to recall whether the event had occurred in France or Germany. He was later allowed to tell his story on a chronological basis.

This second recounting proved to be very similar to the first. Howard recounted the events in the same order and often in the same words. In both cases, Howard's memory was better when events were taken in chronological sequence rather than in terms of subject categories, i.e., "incident when we were shelled."[98] Due to the striking similarity between the recall of first and second interviews, Alice Hoffman considered the memories part of an "archival" network, a network of memories retained in chronological order.

97. Keener, *Christobiography*, 448.

98. Hoffman and Hoffman, *Archives of Memory*, 154.

She considered the structure to be based on the significance of events and their constant rehearsal over time.

One of the most striking testaments to the tendency of eyewitnesses to recall a lengthy series of events in chronological order and with some detail, and indeed to recall the conversations of the participants, is that of David Faber. Faber's experiences are recorded in his book *Because of Romek*. Faber's publisher investigated the accuracy of Faber's testimony and found dates, places, and details to be corroborated. The investigators found extensive evidence to support Faber's account of incidents such as burning people alive in an "almost unheard of concentration camp, Krawinkel."

These witnesses' memories are illustrative of common types of recall of true eyewitnesses. Conversations as well as events are recalled. Conversations and dialogue may be displaced in time, shortened, extended, or forgotten. But the recall of this type, recalling a series of incidents in time, in successive places, is indicative of eyewitness testimony. And the fact is that the location changes enhance the memory contained therein, according to the *method of spatial loci*.[99]

The records of long-term memories of Hoffman and Faber and of similar witnesses of long past events, as Dunn rightly says, are not like those of the Synoptics. The Synoptics reflect the character of a lengthy series of retellings over many years. First-order eyewitness testimony is generally not granular. The PEMs of Pillemer were short and specific because the participants in his study were instructed to recall single specific events. Eyewitness recall of past events most often tends to form into lengthy chronological retellings. When asked to talk of specific events, eyewitnesses may, like Hoffman, become confused and omit important events. Most often when recalling events, eyewitnesses use a chronological format. Further, if an interested person asked an eyewitness to recall an event in Jesus's life, the memory of the eyewitness might be relatively dense in detail, but the recounting of the subsequent persons would continually become less full and more stereotypical.[100] It is only the Gospel of John that fits the profile of first-order eyewitness recounting.

In general, reading the examples given by Pillemer, one would be hard pressed to contend that the Synoptic Gospels present eyewitness memories or personal event memories as described by Pillemer. As Kelber points out

99. Berntsen and Rubin, *Understanding Autobiographical Memory*, 338.

100. Bartlett, *Remembering*, 171–76; Kashima et al., "Maintenance of Cultural Stereotypes."

so vividly, the Gospel stories in the Synoptics are stereotypically scripted and described. Many biblical scholars, especially Dennis Nineham,[101] attest to the stereotypic nature of the Synoptics; I simply note that stereotypic form is consistent with testimony that has been retold many times, as determined by cognitive experiments.[102] The cognitive literature thus supports Nineham in his assertion that the Synoptics reflect a long series of serial retellings.

Collective Memory

Concepts related to collective memory have been discussed by biblical scholars for some time, although the explicit use of the terminology of social and collective memory is only a relatively recent phenomenon. It perhaps goes without saying that concepts consistent with the ideas of collective memory play an important role in the thinking of many biblical scholars, particularly the form critics. For Kenneth Bailey and for James Dunn, to the extent that Dunn accepts Bailey's model, the group plays a major role in controlling the recall of past events. Collective memory, as opposed to individual memory, is usually said to generate tradition by relatively formal means.[103] In the early Christian communities, the tradition may have been solidified in preaching or in rituals such as the Lord's Supper. This is to say that while private remembering or reminiscing may and certainly does occur, collective memory occurs and is preserved in a wider social context.

These ideas do not exhaust the concepts usually put forth by social memory theorists and biblical scholars. One of the more important concepts used by social memory theorists is that of *framing*. This concept refers to the cultural frameworks or schemata that are used to interpret present events. Social memory of a particular person or group is thought to conform to the cultural framework of the community to which that person or group belongs. Another concept close to that of framing is *keying*. Keying refers to interpreting a particular event in terms of an earlier historical event. Thus, a particular story in the life of Jesus may be interpreted as the fulfillment of certain scriptural traditions of Israel.[104]

101. Nineham, "Eye-Witness Testimony, I," 14–16.

102. Kashima et al., "Maintenance of Cultural Stereotypes"; Bartlett, *Remembering*, chs. 5 and 7.

103. Eve, *Behind the Gospels*, 92.

104. Eve, *Behind the Gospels*, 96–99.

One of the more important questions concerns whether individual memory is reformed as it is transmitted to the group. For Halbwachs, the father of collective or community memory and tradition, it is. For Halbwachs, memory is reconstructive, not reproductive, and this memory is always maintained in a way that meets community needs. The primary goal of memory is to serve the interests of the community. Every act of individual remembering is social.[105] I shall address this issue in a later chapter of this book. As we shall see, these views are very much in line with those of modern cognitive/social psychology and indeed the social interactionist model of collective memory.[106]

105. Halbwachs, *On Collective Memory*, 53; Eve, *Behind the Gospels*, 93.

106. Vlasceanu et al., "Cognition in a Social Context," 369–77.

3

Classical Memory Theory *and* Conway's Self Theory

In this chapter, I discuss the basic concepts of human memory as delineated by cognitive psychology. I point out that what is probably the predominant level of memory analysis both by scholars and laypersons, the episodic level, provides only a very shallow, and at times simply inadequate, view of eyewitness memory. This approach focuses on particular episodes, such as a trip to Washington, a memorable dinner, or even a unique lecture given by a famous professor. Generally, it is asserted that while details of the event may be erroneously recalled, the core or gist of the event will be accurately recalled. In fact, memory is more fragile than that.

Even central events may be lost. Bartlett's work provides several examples. A more complete analysis of Bartlett than is usually done indicates that a particular story may be completely lost and replaced with something else. One of Bartlett's stories concerned an air raid over an English coastal resort during WWII. The story was well told in some detail. After only three retellings, the central core was lost, even the fact that the story took place during the war or that it involved an air raid and bombing of a seaside resort town.[1]

1. Bartlett, *Remembering*, 160–65.

Basic Concepts

Attention

I first assess the concept of attention and short-term or working memory. I focus on the degree to which our processing system is selective concerning the type of information taken in for further processing in memory. When brought to the fore, attention is often thought of as attending or not to an event or perhaps to a discourse or conversation; the general take is that the participant attended to the entire event or not at all. However, attentional processes are extremely selective. Generally, we attend to parts of an event, a central zone, really a central aspect of the event that fits a waiting schema in long-term memory. For instance, during a robbery, we may focus on a gun pointed at us but not on the robber's face, or on some other aspect of the robbery. The selection is not based on the environmental stimulus but rather the importance of the stimulus, and the importance is based on knowledge or prior experience. It is well known that a weapon produces a weapon-focus effect. The presence of a weapon in a scene reduces memory for other aspects of the scene.[2]

The workings of the attentional system are perhaps best illustrated by inattentional blindness (IA) experiments. These offer some surprising results. In what is arguably the most seminal IA experiment, a woman carrying an open umbrella or a person wearing a gorilla suit walked across a basketball court while participants were attending to a ballgame on screen during that time.[3] Thirty–five percent of the participants failed to see the woman, and 56% failed to notice the gorilla. The atypical events in these experiments are simply not selected for further processing. The degree of selectivity in perceptual processing is rather astounding. In another experiment, trained pilots using a flight simulator failed to notice a jumbo jet parked on the runway on which they were landing.[4]

What is subjected to deep processing depends not only on the presence of matching, narrative schema but also on the emotion linked to the schema. In one experiment, subjects were more likely to notice an unexpected face when it was congruent with subjects' mood.[5] This was

2. Loftus et al., "Some Facts."
3. Neisser and Becklen, "Selective Looking."
4. Haines, "Breakdown."
5. Becker and Leinenger, "Attentional Selection."

particularly true for the frowning face; a frowning face was noticed most exclusively by those in a sad mood condition.

Experiments on attention are extremely important for eyewitness memory. They illustrate that attention is extremely limited and depends on prior schema—and, importantly, that one's mood is linked to semantic schema. Several semantic experiments illustrate the selectivity of attention and its dependence on existing schemata. Unexpected words belonging to an already activated semantic category will be detected and recalled more often that those that are semantically unrelated to the category.[6] So if you are thinking about a particular semantic category, say, a particular poem, you will not notice even a rather startling or unexpected saying or assertion not fitting the concepts evoked by the poem. In the just-cited Koivisto and Revonsuo study, an unexpected visual stimulus semantically related to the observer's current interests was readily observed, whereas unrelated stimuli were not. The effect was larger when the unexpected stimuli were verbal stimuli than when they were pictures. *Cat* as a word was overlooked when attending to furniture, and the display showed pictures of furniture.

The consequences of selective attention reach far beyond laboratory experiments in perception. This selectivity may apply to the generation of collective memory[7] and thus the oral traditions concerning Jesus. An important hypothetical: Peter may have heard Jesus talk of his preexistence with the Father. Such assertions may simply have been too far removed from Peter's cultural schemata, which were likely based on the precepts of Common Judaism,[8] thus initiating inattentional processes (IA processes) for Jesus's claims of divinity. This process would lessen the accessibility of Jesus's assertions in memory, not only for one such instance but for all of Jesus's assertions of identity with God. In later conversations, Peter may well simply have omitted these ideas. Furthermore, the more often Peter discussed Jesus without discussing Jesus's preexistence or his "I am" sayings, the more likely the concept would have been inhibited, that is, made less accessible to retrieval. This inhibitory process is triggered by retellings that omit certain subjects linked to the story. Thus, as a rule in his conversations, Peter would likely not access Jesus's assertions of preexistent divinity. This process of inhibition (retrieval-induced forgetting or RIF) has been

6. Koivisto and Revonsuo, "How Meaning Shapes Seeing."

7. Hirst and Manier, "Remembering as Communication"; Vlasceanu et al., "Cognition in a Social Context."

8. Dunn, *Jesus Remembered*, 293–97.

demonstrated in the experimental literature. I will discuss this RIF process more fully in chapter 4.

Short-Term Working Memory

A long time ago, William James distinguished the memory of "the present moment," roughly commensurate with conscious experience, whether in perception or recollection, and a reservoir containing objects which may be recollected and "brought back" into this primary memory.[9] Today, cognitive psychology has greatly elaborated these concepts, but based on experimental evidence. The memory of the present moment is referred to as short-term working memory. It is often thought of as conscious experience, although we may not be aware of the processes underlying the percepts or concepts brought to attention. I will discuss these ideas only in so far as they enlighten us as to the basics of eyewitness memory and the retellings of oral tradition. There are four different processing systems to working memory, each with its own set of very limited resources: the executive control system, the phonological loop, the visuospatial sketchpad, and the episodic buffer.[10] Each has been identified by cognitive experiments and also by neuroimaging techniques. All in all, this fourfold group of systems offers a very limited capacity system, designed to ensure selective goal-directed processing of the environment. The central executive determines the importance of future goals and makes decisions, allocating attention to working memory components; the phonological loop is the speech-and-sound related component; the visuospatial sketchpad processes and retrieves visual images; and the episodic buffer integrates the sensory input and/or imagery with long-term storage—this is the locus of the very important process of *chunking*. Chunking works to overcome the short-term memory (STM) and working memory (WM) bottleneck by forming general categories of incoming information. Notice these processes occur within seconds, within thirty to forty-five seconds of receiving the information in sensory store. No copy is made of the sensory information. It is quickly taken up and placed into meaningful categories, however fuzzy and idiosyncratic they may be. This short-term process insures that, as Conway says, "there are no such things as autobiographical memories at least in the sense of discrete,

9. James, "Memory," 1:270–71.

10. Ashcraft, *Cognition*, 152–61.

holistic units in long-term memory."[11] If our brains made copies of sensory information, there would be no such thing as inattentional blindness; the umbrella woman of Neisser's experiment would have been retained and available in the visuospatial sketchpad for a substantial period of time following her presentation in sensory store. Given these findings, the idea of irrelevant detail as a mark of eyewitness memory should be dispensed with.

The limited capacity of short-term memory was vividly illustrated by Peterson and Peterson.[12] Subjects were presented with a three-letter trigram, e.g., MHA, and then asked to count backwards by threes from a large number, e.g., 728. The counting periods varied. At the end of the counting period, subjects were asked to recall the three letters. After only three seconds of counting, the subjects were able to remember an average of only 50% of the three letters. The average dropped to about 5% after eighteen seconds. The counting task knocked the letters out of the short-term store. Later, Waugh and Norman showed that it was not the duration of the store that limited performance but rather the capacity limit pertained to the amount of information the STM system could hold.[13]

The limited capacity of these systems is illustrated by having subjects process two tasks at one time, called the dual task method. The Turner and Engle experiment illustrates this nicely. The subject is read a list of arithmetic statements followed by one word, e.g., (6 x 2)–2=10? SPOT, and asked to recall the word at the end of the test. Subjects are able to recall only between two and seven words in this test, due to the capacity limit of working memory.[14]

Jefferies et al. illustrated the limited capacity of the episodic memory buffer as well as the power of chunking in the following experiment.[15] People were given a list of unrelated sentences and asked to recall them after hearing them. The subjects in the experimental group had to listen to the sentences and also press buttons on a keyboard when an asterisk appeared on the computer screen. For one group in the dual task situation, the sentences were unrelated to one another. For a different group, the sentences formed a coherent whole. The subjects who received the related sentences performed much better than those who had received the unrelated

11. Conway, "Autobiographical Knowledge," 67.
12. Radavansky and Ashcraft, *Cognition*, 138..
13. Waugh and Norman, "Primary Memory."
14. Turner and Engle, "Is Working Memory."
15. Jefferies et al., "Automatic and Controlled Processing."

sentences. When monitoring the appearance of the asterisks on the screen, the subjects were able to recall the sentences better when they formed a coherent story. The generation of a meaningful story reduced the demand on working memory sources for storing the sentences.

Retrieval from Long-Term Memory

Long-term memory (LTM) is generally considered to be a network of concepts, a network comprised of several levels above the episodic level. This network provides the groundwork for constructive processes in remembering.

At the structural level, it is Conway and Rubin's three-level hierarchical organization that has provided a theoretical structure consistent with the bulk of the experimental evidence.[16] In this theory, the deepest level (or highest) consists of periods of one's life that take place over years or decades (attending college). The second level consists of events that take place over weeks or months, say, vacationing in Florida or attending football games in one's freshman year in high school. This level consists of several similar basic-level episodes. The specific episodic level consists of single episodes, e.g., attending a particular game. It is important to note that the highest level, e.g., attending college, would contain generalizations made over the years from attending classes and going to college events. This thematic level contains highly elaborated information and thus is comprised of invariants generated over a period of years from similar specific episodes.

However important the structural aspect of memory is, it is the motivational aspect of memory that the present study is focused on. The fragility of memory retrieval from LTM has been illustrated time and time again in the laboratory. The susceptibility of retrieval processes to suggestive influences has been demonstrated in numerous studies, both in the laboratory and the field. People have recalled nonexistent broken glass or even a barn (nonexistent) in a large rural scene. Other examples include having been lost in a mall, having attended a wedding and breaking the punch bowl, and even having been rushed to a hospital.[17] None of these events took place.

But far more intriguing and important instances of false and distorted memories come from real-life cases. The ease with which the human mind is able to construct distorted and/or false memories is best illustrated by a

16. Conway and Rubin, "Structure of Autobiographical Memory."

17. Frenda et al., "Current Issues and Advances," abstract.

social epidemic especially virulent in the USA during the 1990s, an outbreak of events referred to by Daniel Schacter as the "memory wars."[18] In a typical case, an adult person recalls being sexually molested as a child by a parent or a close family member or some other authority figure, perhaps a teacher or priest. It was argued that this memory was a long-repressed memory, kept unconscious, repressed, because of its traumatic nature. The first publicized case of recovered memory was the George Franklin case. Eileen Franklin, George Franklin's daughter, suddenly recalled a bloody scenario that occurred twenty years prior to her recollection. Her memory was vivid and specific: she recalled seeing her father rape and kill a friend of hers. She was only eight years old at the time of the crime. She testified that her memory of the murder and rape suddenly surfaced when she observed her own daughter behave in a particular manner. This murder took place in 1969. She did not recall the event until 1989. The jury found George Franklin guilty of both the rape and murder solely on the basis of the recovered memory of Eileen Franklin. The theory was that Eileen had repressed the violent memory but that it had come to light in true Proustian manner while she was talking with her daughter. This case was widely publicized. Soon cases of sexual abuse similar to the Franklin case began to appear.

Allegations of sexual abuse became pervasive among American families. A bitter debate occurred between family members and professionals from psychology, medicine, and law on both sides of the issue.[19] Many times, the forgotten memories would appear in the wake of psychotherapy, individual and/or group. Further, books were written on the subject, even outlining specific symptoms that were indicative that a person had been abused as a child. Probably the most widely read book at the time was *The Courage to Heal*, written by two psychotherapists, Bass and Davis. This book provided readers with a list of possible abusive activities "ranging from the relatively benign (e.g., being held in a way that made them uncomfortable), to the unequivocally abusive (e.g., being raped or otherwise penetrated)."[20] It went on as follows: "If you are unable to remember any specific instances, like the ones mentioned above but still have a feeling that something abusive happened to you, it probably did."[21] And later, the authors write:

18. Schacter, *Searching for Memory*, ch. 9.

19. Schacter, *Searching for Memory*, 248–79.

20. Loftus, "Reality of Repressed Memories," 525.

21. Bass and Davis, *Courage to Heal*, 21.

> Often the knowledge that you were abused starts with a tiny feeling, an intuition. . . . Assume that your feelings are valid. So far no one we've talked to thought she might have been abused, and then later discovered she hadn't been. The progression always goes the other way, from suspicion to confirmation. If you think you were abused and your life shows the symptoms, then you were.[22]

What were the symptoms? The authors listed low self-esteem, suicidal or self-destructive thoughts, depression, and sexual dysfunction, among others. A survey of several hundred families accused by recovered memories revealed that the book was implicated in "almost all cases."[23] The book has been revised and now is in its third edition, but the basic ideas remain the same. The new edition speaks of how abuse affects the survivor in six basic ways: how abuse affects self-esteem, feelings of intimacy, the body, sexuality, parenting, and family relationships. More specifically, Bass and Davis point out, for instance, that some survivors have strained relationships with their families, find it hard to set boundaries, struggle with anxiety, feel compelled to feel perfect. The list is long. The first basic category alone, self-esteem, contains twenty-one different characteristics indicative of abuse. The other categories each contain lengthy lists. It would be difficult to find any person who would not be characterized by several of these features found in survivors of abuse. In sum, this book presents an extremely suggestive diagnostic system.

Most importantly, these cases certainly show the delicacy of memory and the power of suggestive cultural schemata to distort memory and even to generate new memories that are not true, at least not true in a factual sense. *The Courage to Heal* only reflected the spirit of the times. Bass and Davis's book was only one of many. Psychotherapists enthusiastically recovered false and repressed memories of abuse. Loftus, who argued that many of these recovered memories were false memories, was roundly hated by many of the psychology community.

But then, it was not just the books. They were only a symptom of the emotional overtones prevailing in the culture. In the 1990s, the accusations of abuse by one's daughter or son were so predominant that a counterattack arose and an association, the False Memory Syndrome Foundation (FMSF), gathered to counter these accusations. The FMSF brought suits to counter those brought by the accusing children, after which many accusers

22. Bass and Davis, *Courage to Heal*, 22.

23. Wakefield and Underwager, *Accusations of Child Abuse*, 486.

retracted their testimony. Many of those who had brought suit against their families later retracted and filed suits against psychologists. Dan Schacter, a well-known and respected memory researcher, suggested that the memories were indeed in many, if not most, cases false. He listed several factors that buttressed this idea: experimental evidence that false memories can be generated in the laboratory settings; the fact that many accusers retracted their accusations; the fact that many of the accusers had been in psychotherapy.[24]

It is generally thought that only plausible fictions produce false recall.[25] However, it was not logical plausibility that was the major factor responsible for the production of these false memories of abuse. It was emotional plausibility that centered around the emotional turmoil experienced by the children when growing up among their families.

Most likely, these memories of child abuse were screen memories.[26] The memories of abuse provided a screen for the sometimes painful experiences of childhood. These memories provide clear-cut distinctions between good and bad parents, as opposed to the more confusing feelings associated with their upbringing. Therapists who are not convinced of the authenticity of the reports acknowledge and are impressed by the honesty and emotional turmoil of the accusers. Further, the essential material of the memories may have been transported and elaborated from the accounts of others, celebrities, movies, and television.[27] These observations are consistent with the idea that recall may be guided by a person's personality, goals, and emotions, not merely the cultural narratives active during this period.

Another event illustrative of these points is John Dean's testimony before the Senate Watergate Committee.[28] Dean recalled many separate discussions with White House personnel and talks with President Nixon. His recall covered episodes spanning several years. He was often in error at the lowest episodic level. He was very confident in his recall of certain meetings with Nixon but often made major mistakes even as to the gist of conversations. For instance, the March 21 meeting with Nixon consisted of two parts: first, Dean warned Nixon that the cover-up was in danger of becoming unraveled; in the second part of the meeting, Nixon, Haldeman,

24. Schacter, "Illusory Memories."

25. McIver, *Memory, Jesus*, 80.

26. Ganaway, "Some Additional Questions."

27. Loftus, "Reality of Repressed Memories," 525.

28. Neisser, "John Dean's Memory."

and Dean discussed the possibility of offering a one-million-dollar bribe to one of the conspirators to keep him quiet. However, Dean left the bribery discussion completely out of his recollection of the March 21 meeting, placing a very abbreviated discussion of bribery at an earlier meeting.[29] In his article on Dean's memory, Neisser points out that several complex concepts enter into the workings of memory retrieval. One's personality may guide recall. He viewed Dean as a very ambitious and self-centered person; the March 21 meeting was Dean's chance to play a larger role among Nixon's advisors and be the first to warn him of the true state of affairs in the investigation. Thus, the only theme of the meeting in Dean's mind was his talk with Nixon regarding the fragility of the present situation. Neisser suggests that "his ego got in the way" of accurate retrieval.[30]

The false memories of child abuse during the "memory wars" and John Dean's testimony point to a deeper level of processing underlying the generation of false memory than mere plausibility. *Episodic memory*, based on the generation of communalities among repeated events, is not sufficient here. The cognitive theories of memory that omit the more clinical/emotional aspects of processing are not sufficient. A more recent model of autobiographical memory that takes into account the motivational aspects of memory retrieval is Conway's self-memory system.[31] For Conway, it is a basic tenant of cognitive psychology that memory is motivated, not just at a conscious, intentional level but more commonly at a clinical/Freudian level. False memory is not merely a plausible memory derived from a general narrative category of events (i.e., a year of basketball games) but often based on unconscious aspects of personality.

Conway's Self Memory System

Conway has proposed a self-memory system (SMS) for autobiographical memory.[32] Here the overriding structure in long-term memory is the conceptual self. This self system comprises an individual's life story and its beliefs, values, and attitudes. The long-term structure consists of lifetime periods and general events. This is the knowledge framework. Subsisting within this framework is episodic memory, consisting of various degrees

29. Neisser, "John Dean's Memory," 112.
30. Neisser, "John Dean's Memory," 108.
31. Conway and Pleydell-Pierce, "Construction of Autobiographical Memories."
32. Conway and Jobson, "On the Nature," 154.

of specific memories, complex episodic memory, and specific episodic memory, partitioned into episodic elements. The self system is dependent on the cultural milieu. Here Conway distinguishes between individualistic cultures and collectivistic cultures. In individualistic cultures, the self is conceived as a unique autonomous individual entity, comprising personality traits, motives, values, and feelings. In collectivistic cultures, the self is conceived as interdependent with the surrounding social structure. All people have both self systems, but one of them dominates, depending on the surrounding culture. The United States is an individualistic culture, while Asian cultures are collectivistic.

Conway and Jobson present an additional concept, the working self, which is essentially the conceptual self as it encodes, evaluates, and retrieves information commensurate with either individual or cultural roles and goals. Either an autonomous or relatedness hierarchy of goals functions to shape behavior into culturally appropriate ways of thinking and operating in the culture.[33] The dominant working self as a hierarchy of either individualistic or relatedness goals is activated and then used to encode and integrate memory into the autobiographical knowledge base. In this regard, the role of the working self is analogous to that of working memory of classical cognitive psychology.[34] These two different cultural/working selves influence remembering according to their basic set of goals. Persons from individualistic cultures provide lengthy self-focused autobiographical memories that focus on individual experiences, with more references to internal states and feelings, whereas people from collectivistic cultures provide only general accounts that focus on collective activities and routines, and emotionally neutral events and social interactions. They tend to recall the behavior of significant others and focus on the roles of other people, family, community. People from individualistic cultures focus on their own achievements, status, and emotions.

Simple episodic memories (SEMs) become attached to the more enduring conceptual knowledge structure, which forms a frame for the SEMs.[35] Knowledge is gradually abstracted from the episodic memories and becomes part of the more general periods or indeed lifetime periods. The working self is used to encode, organize, and retrieve autobiographical memories. This process allows for the elaboration of the memories in

33. Conway and Jobson, "On the Nature," 62.

34. Baddeley, "Working Memory."

35. Conway and Jobson, "On the Nature," 65.

culturally sanctioned ways. And in turn, these memories express and maintain the cultural, expected self.[36]

As discussed above, the working self is a concept akin to the working memory of classic cognitive psychology. This system's main function is the management of goals. Importantly, the working self supervises the construction of memories, creatively redesigns their meaning, and determines their accessibility. This is all done with the idea of preserving self-coherence, i.e., maintaining reasonable links between life goals and historic reality. The link with history may be lost when self-coherence is threatened, resulting in false or heavily edited memories designed to protect the integrity of the self. The self is conservative; it aims to avoid life-goal changes.[37]

The most enlightening instances of the working self's attempts to preserve life goals are provided by post-traumatic stress patients. It is common that those who survive stressful events report difficulties with memory and intrusive thoughts after the event. A good example is given in Conway's seminal 2005 article "Memory and the Self."[38] A man who drove cars for a living was a backseat passenger in a car that was involved in an accident that consisted of a high-speed collision with another car. His wife lost consciousness after the collision, and he thought at the time that she might have died. He anticipated the collision at the time but he did not cry out. Later, he experienced intrusive thoughts to the effect that he should have cried out a warning to the driver and that had he done so, he could have prevented the collision. With these thoughts, he experienced extreme guilt. He often reexperienced the guilt he felt right after the collision, when he thought that his wife had died and that he could have prevented the accident had he cried out. He underwent cognitive therapy. He revisited the site. He was shown police records, which indicated that he had in reality no time to utter a warning and that he could not have prevented the collision. His memory had increased the time before the impact, as Conway says, to maintain his feeling of control as a professional driver, even though this produced extreme guilt. The working self had operated to maintain his self-coherence. The accident, combined with cognitive therapy, showed him that he was not always in total control when driving. Realizing this, after a time, his intrusive thoughts began to dissipate. He did not return to his career of professional driving. In fact, he would not even sit in a car

36. Conway and Jobson, "On the Nature," 66.

37. Conway, "Memory and the Self," 597.

38. Conway, "Memory and the Self," 598.

for some time after the accident. He realized that he had entered a career of driving because of his need for control. A change of life career is not unusual with patients. In fact, as Conway notes, one of the most common comments from PTSD patients after therapy is that they are a "new person," and many do change life careers and become new persons, i.e., adopt new life goals.

Barclay, the Life Story

Barclay's views interplay nicely with Conway's self theory. For Barclay, a person throughout his life generates a life story, a narrative that is fashioned according to various purposes. Autobiographical memory is not a replay of historical events or a reconstruction of history, but rather has its own purposes and products. Perhaps the dominant purpose is a coherent meaningful narrative.[39] Two major purposes of autobiographical memory are creation of a coherent life story over time and establishment of meaningful relationships. It thus has both an individual and social set of goals. Remembering is constructed with these two purposes in mind, intrapsychic and interpsychic. Autobiographical memory is constructed primarily within a contextual, narrative framework; this narrative consists of spatiotemporal, causal, and evaluative or emotional aspects. Narratives are constructed and reconstructed with the purpose of creating and maintaining a coherent life story. The most important aspect of the narrative involves the evaluative function, i.e., the meaning of events. Eyewitnesses attempt to construct a narrative that contains spatial and temporal memories, causal sequences, and evaluative statements, all of which combine to form coherent narratives. As Barclay puts it, "an important property of a life story is that it must be both linguistically and psychologically coherent."[40] The push to create coherence may account in part for the errors that occur with autobiographical recall and eyewitness testimony in general. Narratives offer a structure that enhances memory, especially spatial structure, but the push for coherence in stories or narratives may also lead to false memories. Especially in the case of traumatic events is this a problem. People who have experienced trauma may have incomplete narratives, which in turn may hamper memory. People who have experienced trauma—e.g., Holocaust victims, victims of long-term abuse, rape victims—may not have a temporal sense

39. Barclay, "Autobiographical Remembering," 99.

40. Barclay, "Autobiographical Remembering," 112.

or sense of location to aid their memories, Barclay notes.[41] Fabrications of experience occur to make actual events or sequences of events sensible and meaningful. War veterans and victims of extreme trauma, such as the Holocaust, are capable of producing detailed spatial and temporal narratives. Generally, the memories are consistent with the written records, but also there are errors, sometimes quite surprising ones. These distortions of memory occur when a narrative lacks coherence or when it is inconsistent with reality and needs revision. Traumatic events such as rape or even ongoing traumas such as the Holocaust may generate narratives which lack coherence. Many Holocaust victims' stories were very fragmented; there was simply no narrative to explain such evil. For particular events, facts may be revised to conform to a more meaningful, coherent life story or personal narrative. Barclay theorizes that personal narratives are constantly being improvised to meet self-coherent goals and that this process is one of the major reasons that eyewitness reports may be in error.[42] For instance, Wagenaar and Groeneweg asked the prisoners who survived Camp Erika, a WWII German prison camp, to recount their experiences. After long periods of time, prisoners often recounted interactions with guards or other events as less aversive or violent than they had earlier reported them to be.[43]

I hope we have illustrated the extreme fragility and suggestibility of long-term memory retrieval, how needful and susceptible to cultural override it is. The ease with which the Old Testament concepts and stories might have been incorporated into the memories of Peter and other disciples of Jesus cannot be overestimated in light of modern memory studies. As memories of child abuse were false, so too entire sequences of the Gospels, particularly those of the Synoptics, might have been. The culture of the Old Testament was surely as powerful as that which generated the accusations of child abuse during the "memory wars."

Both Conway's and Barclay's ideas are applicable to Peter and other disciples of Jesus. With the crucifixion, their entire life narratives were destroyed. However, their culture provided an explanatory frame to create, and indeed continue in a different form, their life story. Their memories most likely were reformed to accommodate the death of Jesus. From the standpoint of recent findings in memory research, Scripture provided not only an intellectual explanation but also the suggestive power to bring their

41. Barclay, "Autobiographical Remembering," 113.

42. Barclay, "Autobiographical Remembering," 95.

43. Wagenaar and Groeneweg, "Memory."

memories in line with its predictions. Scripture had the suggestive power equal to or greater than that of the book *Courage to Heal* or psychotherapy in the culture wars. We shall return to this topic in a later chapter. In this regard, I may suggest that Isaiah provided an explanation for Jesus's death and even exonerated Peter from his guilt for having betrayed Jesus. Thus, Peter recalled Jesus as taking on the persona of Isaiah's man wounded for our sins. In Peter's mind, Jesus went to the cross to live out Isaiah's predictions (Isa 53). This scenario would have allowed Peter to assign coherence and integrity to his life story.

In addition, it is likely that these considerations account for the discrepancies among the Synoptics and especially between the Synoptics and John. It is important to note that the influence of suggestive forces is multiplied when the eyewitness testimony is repeated innumerable times throughout a lengthy network. They operate on first-order eyewitnesses but to a lesser degree. As I will argue, the author of John is an eyewitness to many events in Jesus's life. And consequently, the stories in John are closer to the historical Christ than are those of the Synoptics.

4

Conversational Memory

The model of remembering I shall apply to the Gospel tradition is the social interaction view expressed in Vlasceanu et al.[1] This model focuses on cognitive functions, e.g., emotional processes and memory as they emerge into and influence social phenomena. More specifically, I focus on Hirst's collective memory model.[2] The social interaction approach is experimentally based and focuses on conversations as the communicative mechanism that affects emergent social cognition. Closely linked to conversational remembering is collective memory, in that individual memories tend to show a greater degree of overlap after a conversation than before.[3]

When people converse, they tell of things that have happened to them; they exaggerate, they omit aspects of the event. Their talk is purposeful, they talk differently to different audiences. But carrying on such conversations about events is then retold to others, forming a broad network for maintaining and transmitting information among people. Such conversational retelling results in a substantial agreement among individuals. It is this collective memory that produces the framework of oral tradition.

Since conversations form the basis of collective memory within the context of social interaction theory, we look next at conversational memory. It may be best to portray conversational memory by distinguishing it

1. Vlasceanu et al., "Cognition in a Social Context," 369.
2. Hirst et al., "Of Sins and Virtues," 141.
3. Vlasceanu et al., "Cognition in a Social Context," 369.

from the classic recall memory of cognitive psychology. This latter memory theory is the memory theory referenced by biblical scholars, e.g., McIver, Crossan, or Allison.[4]

As noted in chapter 2, recent biblical scholarship has attempted to include the findings of cognitive psychology in the quest for modeling the formative processes of the oral tradition. A good number of scholars have brought the findings of experimental memory research to bear on the problems inherent in oral transmission. Crossan early on noticed the importance and relevance of the theory of constructive memory.[5] Others, including Bauckham, Allison, and McIver,[6] have addressed the reliability of the Gospels in terms of memory theory. To date, the memory theories discussed by biblical scholars have been forensic in nature. The goal of these experiments was to assess memory for accuracy. Participants in the experiments cited in the biblical literature, those comprising classical cognitive psychology literature, were instructed to recall the facts as accurately as possible. These experiments were designed to uncover the mechanisms of human memory, but always under the guiding principle that the purpose of memory was to determine and recall what was really said or what really happened.

The classical experiments in cognitive psychology are only remotely relevant to the real-life oral tradition. The participants in the experiments operate under the assumption, explicit or implicit, that their performance will be judged for accuracy of recollection. As Dudukovic et al. put it, "most laboratory memory studies encourage the veridical rehearsal of information."[7]

Conversational memory is non-forensic. That is, when remembering an event, people are not under the impression that they will be somehow judged for accuracy. In conversational memory literature, the focus is on retelling experiments. What are called retellings in the cognitive literature are instances of remembering that reflect real life and are not elicited under what we may call classic laboratory or forensic conditions. In classic memory experiments, participants are instructed to recall events as accurately

4. McIver, *Memory, Jesus*, 21–40; Crossan, *Birth of Christianity*, 1–68; Allison, *Constructing Jesus*, 381, 460–61.

5. Crossan, *Birth of Christianity*, 1–68.

6. Bauckham, *Jesus and the Eyewitnesses*, 240–63; Allison, *Constructing Jesus*, 381; McIver, *Memory, Jesus*, 21–40.

7. Dudukovic et al., "Telling a Story," 125.

as possible. In experiments involving retelling, participants define accuracy in their own way. Explicit or implicit instruction to be as accurate as possible is not given. The content of retellings vary with their purposes; these purposes vary greatly and range from entertainment to persuasion. Conversational memory often tends to be based on emotional aspects of the event. Subjects tend to center their recounting on evaluations and interpretations.[8] They tend to access metamemory, that is, to try to understand the happenings of the past from the standpoint of knowledge exterior to the event. Retellings are goal directed and very audience related. When asked to recount people and events as accurately as possible, the recall tends to center on narrative facts. Retellings in conversational memory are evaluative and generally have a purpose other than factual recounting, and as we shall see, memory is reshaped accordingly. In retellings, individuals want to persuade, to promote, to convince, perhaps to paint a person in a certain way.

Marsh and Tversky

At this point, we turn to retelling/conversational remembering experiments. In the retelling literature, subjects are asked simply to retell stories. They are not asked to recall as accurately as possible but simply to retell the stories. Participants are sometimes told that the person hearing the story will simply retell it to others and that no one will assess their stories for accuracy. Conversational memory includes both retellings by single persons and actual conversations between people. The representative study in this genre is that of Elizabeth Marsh.[9] This experiment illustrates many of the characteristics of conversational remembering and retelling.

In this experiment, participants simply described and recorded their retellings of personal events over the course of one month. No other instructions were given. They were given a recording form for each retelling. They described their memories and recorded whether the goal was to convey facts, convey pride of accomplishment, entertain, avoid conflict, or elicit sympathy, or whether they had another purpose in mind. They were then asked to indicate whether any of four types of distortions had occurred in each of their retellings. Subjects reported that each event was retold an average of 2.7 times. Subjects reported that the retellings were distorted

8. Hyman, "Conversational Remembering."

9. Marsh, "Retelling Is Not Same."

in some way: 36% were selective, 26% were exaggerated, 25% minimized, 13% contained information that was added to the actual event. Viewing these distortions as inaccuracies, 61% of the retellings containing distortions were inaccurate, but the participants judged only 42% of their retellings as inaccurate. One-third of the retellings containing distortions were judged as accurate. The audiences varied. Eighty-eight percent of the retellings were told to peers; 7% to authority figures parents, coaches, etc.; 5% to other audiences. Stories were told for various purposes, and some were told for multiple purposes: to convey facts, entertain, elicit sympathy, avoid conflict, recount a personal achievement out of pride, share information. A majority of the events were considered emotional. Seventy-two percent of the events were labeled as somewhat intense or very intense. The types of distortion depended on the characteristics of the event. Intense events were more likely to contain minimizations and omissions than exaggerations and additions. Participants were more likely to distort social and academic events than job-related events. Further, social events were the most likely type of events to be labeled as inaccurate. The purpose of the retellings had a large effect on distortions. When the purpose was to convey facts, there were fewer exaggerations and additions; when the primary purpose was to entertain, there were more exaggerations and additions. When the goal was to elicit sympathy, the subjects reported more exaggerations than other types of distortions. Participants did report changing their retellings. The most common reason for changing their retellings was a change of audience. For instance, students often omitted details when talking with their parents.

The Marsh 2007 experiment illustrated that natural retellings operate against a background of conscious bias.[10] The conversations are motivated, have a purpose. Whether the major purpose is to convey facts or is more personal, e.g., the elicitation of sympathy, the results show that people consciously add, omit items, or otherwise spin them to satisfy various motives. These may not be cultural but personal in nature. In addition, people often do not think they are distorting the truth. This experiment is not alone in its indictment of conversational remembering. Several diary studies indicate that in everyday conversation, people tell lies and admit to doing so.[11] In Feldman et al.,[12] subjects interacted with a new person for ten minutes.

10. Marsh, "Retelling Is Not Same."

11. DePaulo et al., "Lying in Everyday Life."

12. Feldman et al., "Self-Presentation."

Immediately afterwards, they indicated the truth value of their statements made during the conversation. Over 60% of the subjects indicated that they had distorted the truth during the conversation. People are quite willing to tell lies in ordinary conversation. As the Marsh study indicates, distortions are acceptable and are frequently regarded as accurate in everyday conversation.[13]

If retelling operates with intentional distortion, the question arises: what is the effect of conscious bias on subsequent memory? We shall see that conversations that at first may operate with intentional bias, i.e., contain intentional exaggerations or omissions, soon result in memories coincident with these initial biases. Thus, I find that Strauss was right in determining that the transmission of myth may have been at times intentional, although it later becomes unconscious.[14] Our additions and exaggerations, as well as our omissions, become true for us. This process accounts for much of the variation in eyewitness recall. The subjects in experiments on conversational memory are often consciously aware that their retelling is biased but later recall the biased information as true.

Conversation and Bias

There are several studies that illustrate the effect of conscious bias on both retelling and later recall. We have studies that show that after witnessing or experiencing an event, the bias chosen in conversing afterward affects retelling and later recall in the direction of the adopted perspective. It is well known that prior perspective can affect encoding and retrieval. Pichert and Anderson is a case in point.[15] The subjects were asked to read a story about two boys playing in a house. They were asked to read the story from the perspective of a burglar or a home buyer. After reading the story, the participant was asked to recall the story from one perspective; then, after recalling the story, he was asked to recall the story from the other perspective. Both recalls reflected the adopted perspective: the home buyer perspective resulted in recall of details relevant to a future owner; the burglar perspective recalled details important to a thief, e.g., the house contained expensive works of art.

13. Marsh, "Retelling Is Not Same."
14. Strauss, *Life of Jesus*, 82–85.
15. Pichert and Anderson, "Taking Different Perspectives."

The Tversky and Marsh[16] set of experiments nicely illustrates this important concept: intentionally fabricated events, additions, or omissions may later become honest memories. The Tversky and Marsh study consisted of four experiments, in each of which participants read a story and then wrote a biased letter about one of the characters in the experiment. In the first experiment, the story was about the participant's two college roommates (both imaginary). In the second experiment, the story involved two suspects in a murder mystery. For the roommate story, the participants were asked to write either a letter recommending one roommate to a fraternity or sorority or a letter to the office of student housing complaining about the roommate's behavior and requesting reassignment. For the mystery story, the participants were to write a letter to the jury that urged conviction of one of the suspects.

In the roommate story, each roommate did both annoying and prosocial things (David's alarm wakes you up, David met new people by sharing a table); in the murder mystery, both suspects did incriminating and exonerating things (Walters often argued with the victim, Walters held back tears when he learned of the victim's death). In both experiments, a recall test was administered after the letters had been written. The third experiment repeated the first experiment, except memory was assessed via a recognition test rather than recall. The fourth experiment was particularly interesting. It repeated the first, except the participants were asked not to include specific behaviors (Rachel talks loudly on the phone) in their letters but rather to refer only to generalities (Rachel is messy). The letters complaining about roommates contained many more annoying items (David's alarm wakes you up) and coincident elaborations (generalities that were not specified in the text, e.g., David is a slob) than did the control group, which was simply asked to remember and write out the story. This trend was evident in the murder mystery study also. The perspective taken in the letters affected the direction of the recalled items in both the roommate and murder mystery experiments. In both experiments, the participants recalled more perspective-related items for the character they wrote about than for the non-discussed character. The fourth experiment, the evaluative retellings experiment, provided evidence that the activation of schema by the imposed perspectives was as important in generating these results as selective rehearsal. Further, according to a Tversky and Marsh 2000 study, the perspective at retelling imposed an integrated theme on an otherwise

16. Tversky and Marsh, "Biased Retellings."

list-like structure and allowed interpretive elaborations that linked the facts in each of the experiments.[17] These schemas not only organized the retellings but guided retrieval at a later time. These experiments clearly show particular perspectives adopted in conversations are able to reorganize the factual information, elaborating important events and omitting others according to a given theme. The authors assert that what happened in these experiments is quite close to natural storytelling, wherein the storyteller uses and reorganizes information to dramatize a certain goal. This is what we all do in real life when engaged in natural conversations, but our memories pay the price.

The importance of retelling goals was brought to the front in an experiment by Dudukovic et al. As the researchers put it, "when testifying in court or supplying evidence to a police officer people usually try to be as accurate as possible. However, when relating an anecdote to friends, people often focus on entertaining (exaggerating, dramatizing the story) their audience rather than on accuracy."[18] Participants read a story describing a particularly hectic night at a bar. The story contained interesting events and mundane events. One group of participants were asked to retell the story in an amusing, entertaining manner. They were to imagine that they were telling the story to a group of friends who had never heard the story. A second group of participants were asked to retell the story as accurately as possible and to imagine that they were telling the story to a policeman or lawyer who needed to have as accurate an account as possible. In all, there were three retellings of the story. Each group retold the story under the same instructions. The stories were retold two days apart. Linguistic analysis indicated that, in general, the entertainment group used comparatively more emotion words, present tense verbs, and words indicating certainty; the accuracy group used more sensory words and words that indicated tentativeness (e.g., maybe or perhaps). The study suggested that the entertainment group used "the language of storytelling," i.e., words indicating emotion, certainty, and present tense.[19]

The entertainment script changed not what was told so much as the way it was told. The subjects in the entertainment group included the same basic events as did the accuracy group but exaggerated them and added their own details. The amusement group imported many more events that

17. Tversky and Marsh, "Biased Retellings," 31.

18. Dudukovic et al., "Telling a Story," 125.

19. Dudukovic et al., "Telling a Story," 140.

had not happened than the accuracy group. Some of the intrusions were plausible, e.g., Mrs. Makeup putting on more lipstick; some were not so predictable, e.g., bringing a dog into the bar. The entertainment participants inserted an average of 12.6 events that did not appear in the original story in any form (intrusions), whereas the accuracy group inserted only 3.4 intrusions. As the researchers put it, "a good story is not necessarily accurate but is told with certainty."[20] The researchers' main interest in the experiment was whether an "entertainment script exists."[21] They concluded that, at least in the current study, the retellings of the group given entertainment instructions reflected a top-down schematic storytelling organization given to exaggeration, certainty of speech, and emotional expression. Reflecting on the results of the experiment, the exaggerations and dramatizations of the storyteller will likely influence later memory.

Affective Impact

Conversations focusing on single goals are likely a rarity. Natural conversations sometimes have a single purpose, sometimes a combination of purposes. But perhaps the most common initiating format for conversation is the immediate personal emotional reaction to an event. In fact, Bartlett maintains that upon witnessing an event the first reaction is an attitude towards the event, awakened in the perceiver.[22]

After witnessing an emotionally intense event, a person may talk to others primarily in terms of their emotional reactions. A 2005 study by Marsh et al. provides evidence that talking primarily about emotional reactions to an event can initiate schemas resulting in selective recall, emphasizing reactions and emotions, to the detriment of narrative recall.[23] In this experiment, all subjects saw a violent film scene. One group was asked to described their emotional reactions to the film as they might when talking to a friend; another group was asked to describe the scene in a factual way, as if they were talking to the police. The group asked to talk about their personal reactions later made a greater proportion of major errors (reporting the wrong person as having been shot) in a later recall task than did the group asked to recount the scene as a narrative. The difference in

20. Dudukovic et al., "Telling a Story," 132.

21. Dudukovic et al., "Telling a Story," 127.

22. Bartlett, *Remembering*, 207.

23. Marsh et al., "How Eyewitnesses Talk," 41–42.

proportions was striking (.23 vs .45). Tversky suggests that the personal reaction group generated a general schema that guided retrieval of the attitudes and feelings experienced during the film, resulting in a diminished retrieval of narrative facts. Certainly, in real life, people are not instructed to focus only on their emotional reactions; but after witnessing a violent scene, it is likely that emotional reactions would be at the forefront of any later conversations about the event.

Perhaps the most important experiment defining conversational memory as opposed to forensic memory was conducted by Hyman.[24] In this experiment, subjects talked about a short story, they had read, Maupassant's "The Legacy." They discussed it with either another student (dyadic, conversational condition) or with an experimenter (individual memory condition). In addition, the instructions differed in terms of the instructions given the subjects. The subjects were asked either about their memories, i.e., to recall the stories and report what they "remember about the story," or they were asked about their personal reactions to the story, i.e., what "you got out of the story."

The recall data was coded for narrative units, interpretations and summaries, metastory remarks, and evaluations. The narrative details described the scenario and plot of the story; interpretations included attributions of thoughts and feelings to the characters, speculations about what might have happened before the story and what might yet happen, and even alternative actions the characters might have taken to achieve their goals. Metastory statements included comparing contemporary society and values to the events in the story. Evaluations included emotional reactions, e.g., "I liked or disliked," or "I felt pity," or "I felt bad."

The conversational (dyadic) subjects who operated under personal reaction instructions organized their response around the evaluative, metastory comments, whereas the subjects under the memory instructions responding to the experimenter gave much more detailed narrative responses. The memory subjects and the experimenter-based subjects used more narrative-related details as opposed to what the dyadic subjects used. The experimenter-based subjects gave typical story recalls; they structured their memories in a narrative form and gave many details. The dyadic subjects gave more evaluative and metastory-laden recall protocols.

As Hyman notes, "Traditional memory experiments demonstrate one aspect of the contents of memory—narrative organization and attention

24. Hyman, "Conversational Remembering."

to detail . . . . Conversational remembering however allows a different view of the contents of memory and the conversational mode appears to be an equally natural way for people to remember. By conversational mode I mean a certain way of structuring remembering around information beyond the story—such as evaluations and metastory comments."[25] Dyadic subjects discussed "applications of the story to their own lives and in terms of society at large."[26] Conversational remembering (dyadic) focused on evaluations as opposed to narrative. Some of the dyadic subjects gave no narrative at all. Hyman further concluded that this study provided strong evidence for schema-based reconstruction. This was shown by the inclusion in the recall protocols of knowledge beyond the story and by the subjects' incorporation of "their understanding of literature, society, and themselves."[27]

Note that in both Marsh et al.'s experiment on emotional impact and Hyman's work on conversational memory,[28] emotional and evaluative recall predominates in the retellings. When emotions are in play, mood-dependent retrieval becomes one of the more important guiding principles in remembering. While not a retelling experiment per se, an important study that explores the effects of mood dependence on memory is that of Reisberg and Heuer.[29] Two groups of subjects saw a story depicted on slides. The stories began and ended in the same way. The central portion of both stories depicted a boy watching his father at work. In one story, the neutral story, the father was a mechanic. The story depicted the boy watching his father as he worked on a car. In the other story, the arousal story, the father was a surgeon, and the boy watched him perform an operation on an accident victim. When tested two weeks later, the arousal subjects generally performed better, that is, they recalled more central information (everything directly relevant to the plot) and peripheral detail information. However, the interesting finding for our purposes is how people think about emotional events. As Heuer and Reisberg state, "one thinks about emotional events in more personal, more psychological ways, and less in schematic or abstract ways, relative to how one thinks about neutral events."[30] This is

25. Hyman, "Conversational Remembering," 63.

26. Hyman, "Conversational Remembering," 63.

27. Hyman, "Conversational Remembering," 63.

28. Marsh et al., "How Eyewitnesses Talk"; Hyman, "Conversational Remembering," 63.

29. Reisberg and Heuer, "Remembering the Details."

30. Heuer and Reisberg, "Vivid Memories," 180.

dramatically shown in the Reisberg and Heuer study (1992) when the intrusion errors, information reported that had not taken place, are analyzed. In the neutral story, for instance, subjects recalled that the mother brought the child to school or went grocery shopping afterward (neither of which happened). The nature of the intrusion errors changed for the arousal story. Here the errors concerned the character's emotions to events. Here, for instance, subjects reported "vivid recollections of hearing the mother was upset that the child saw the medical procedure or that she was angry that the father allowed his son to view the surgery." Neither of these reactions was mentioned in the story. Most importantly, as Heuer and Reisberg indicate, emotion creates mood-congruent recall. That is, factual detail may be created to fit the emotion. This idea fits the hierarchical structure posited by Bower,[31] wherein emotional mood is a high-level cue connected to a variety of lower-level events. The emotion itself cues an event that, although it did not happen in the story, is nevertheless logically related to the emotion.

Communication Accommodation Theory

In line with viewing memory as communication are concepts involved in communication accommodation theory (CAT). In this theory, individuals may accommodate to each other's speech skills and do so in several ways. They may either converge or diverge to or from each other's style of speech or even accommodate to the content of speech. Commonly, this theory speaks to a dyadic situation, wherein one speaker is in a perceived superior relationship to the other. The major proponent of CAT is Howard Giles.[32] In this theory, which is based on empirical data, people may converge on the speech or thought forms of a more dominant figure—a boss in the corporation, a therapist, a teacher, anyone in a position of authority over the more subservient person. These instances of convergence have been empirically substantiated. In addition, the opposite may occur. People or groups may diverge from a dominant figure or other group when that entity becomes threatening to their identity or self-esteem. However, in the present study, I am more interested in the concept of convergence of speech patterns, ranging from syntactic skills to higher level forms of communicative skills, especially between people in intimate relationships such as Jesus and his disciples.

31. Bower, "Mood and Memory."

32. Giles et al., "Accommodation Theory."

Early studies focused on speech and stylistic behaviors. Convergence included such behaviors as speech rates, vocal intensity, pausing frequencies and length, and response latency. Later studies incorporated higher level linguistic and communicative analyses operating at the discourse level. These communicative acts included speech content, opinions, and self-disclosures.[33]

Selective Retelling and Retrieval-induced Forgetting

It is common knowledge, at least when pressed, that we are all biased in some fashion or other; the biased-retelling experiments not only indicate that we retell the stories in line with our biases or purposes, but they provide evidence that the effects are long lasting. Subsequent memory is spun in accord with these biases, corroborating the notion that saying is eventually believing. Generally, the distortions will fit the biases. A witness retelling the story will likely change the story even more to accord with the original attitudes.[34] This need not be in the form of embellishment or additions, however; it may also take the form of omissions. It is to this deleting or minimizing process that we now turn.

As I have noted, a relatively long chain of retellings likely occurred before the Synoptic Gospels were committed to writing, and these consisted of both one-on-one retellings and conversations. Thus, it is not unlikely that some stories were left out or that some parts were omitted along the way. What happens when one retells a story but leaves out certain incidents in the story? A body of literature in social and cognitive psychology has been produced that attempts to answer this question. The concept embodied in this literature is called retrieval-induced forgetting (RIF). In the seminal study on RIF,[35] subjects were presented with word pairs, consisting of category-exemplar pairs, e g., animal-dog, animal-cat, vegetable-broccoli, vegetable-pea. Next, the subjects received retrieval practice by which they completed cued exemplars, e.g., animal-dog. In the retrieval practice phase of the study, subjects were presented with some of the categories, e.g., animal, but no other categories, e.g., vegetable. In the presented categories,

33. Giles et al., "Accommodation Theory," table 1.

34. Bartlett, *Remembering*, 53–55; 205–8; Bergman and Roediger, "Can Bartlett's Repeated Reproduction."

35. M. Anderson et al., "Remembering Can Cause Forgetting."

only some of the target exemplars were cued, e.g., animal-dog. But other exemplars were omitted, e.g., animal-cat. In the final recall phase, the subjects were asked to recall all the exemplar words of each category. The practiced words in the presented categories are labeled Rp+, the unpracticed words are labeled Rp-, the words in the unpracticed categories (all of the words in the unpracticed categories are unpracticed) are labeled Nrp. A practice effect occurs when the number of Rp+ words recalled is greater than the number of Nrp words. RIF occurs when Rp- is greater than Nrp. That is to say, when unpracticed words are related to a practiced category, they are less likely to later be recalled than when the unpracticed words are not related. So in this case, more unpracticed animal exemplars would be forgotten than unpracticed vegetable exemplars. The theory here is that recalling words in a practiced category inhibits competing, i.e., related words, words in the same category, animal words; but the inhibitory process does not reach across to other categories, to vegetables.

RIF has been observed with many stimuli; its effects have been proven robust across many types of experiments. Of importance to recalling in everyday life, the RIF phenomenon has been reported for stories and autobiographical memories. Further, the RIF phenomenon has been reported both in persons reciting the edited story (WI-RIF) and in persons who had only listened to the story (SS-RIF).

In a study by Cuc et al., participants are told a story about going to Coney Island.[36] The story included these events: eating a hot dog, going on a roller coaster, and swimming in the ocean. The narrator tells the story a second time but leaves out eating a hot dog. The next time he tells the story, he would forget the hot dog incident, i.e., it would be inhibited (WI-RIF). He would be more prone to forget the hot dog incident than had he heard the entire story only one time. The same RIF process would also apply to one who had only listened the second time (SS-RIF).

The RIF processes also obtain for more abstract concepts. Here is an example of SS-RIF: suppose a president wants to inform people of his struggles to push a health bill through Congress. He tells people about the program and the difficulties of getting his program enacted into law. But he wants people to forget the compromises he made to get it passed. To do this, he would tell the story a second time but omit the compromises

36. Cuc et al., "Silence Is Not Golden."

he made at the time.[37] People would forget those compromises to a greater extent than would those who had simply heard the entire speech one time.

It may prove enlightening to briefly discuss a study exploring the retrieval-induced forgetting of autobiographical memories within conversations.[38] In this study, short autobiographical memories were collected for several categories, e.g., happy, tragic. Subjects in pairs were told to read the events; one read them, the other listened. Then, the pairs were told to talk about the events. The subjects were allowed to converse until they reached a natural stopping point. The conversations between participants were transcribed and sorted into categories. Events left out of the mentioned categories in a later conversation were recalled less often than events from categories that were never discussed in the original conversation. This was so for both speaker and listener, demonstrating both SS-RIF and WI-RIF. Regarding the present results, Stone et al. assert: "What it shows is that even something as personal as an autobiographical memory can be changed through social interactions."[39] Furthermore, the effects were substantial. For instance, for the speaker recalling his own memories in free-flowing conversation, the proportion of memories recalled when the categories (e.g., happy events) were mentioned during the conversation was .34, whereas the proportion was .70 when the category was not mentioned during the conversation.[40]

I must also point out that the transmission of the RIF effect would not have ended with only one transaction. It would probably have continued throughout a network involving not only one-on-one retellings but a series of conversations among disciples and villagers. The effect of transmitting practice and RIF effects through successive social interaction was studied by Coman and Hirst. In this study, subjects heard arguments, pro and con, about the legalization of euthanasia. They then were presented with a series of slides that presented half of the arguments in favor the euthanasia. Next, they were given a recall test for all of the original arguments, pro and con. The next phase consisted of a conversation about the arguments between pairs of participants. After that, the participants were again given a final recall test of the initial arguments. The practice effects and RIF were

37. Hirst et al., "Of Sins and Virtues," 152.

38. Stone et al., "Forgetting Our Personal Past."

39. Stone et al., "Forgetting Our Personal Past."

40. Stone et al., "Forgetting Our Personal Past," table 5, 11.

propagated through the network.[41] In fact, both the practice and induced forgetting effects were amplified through the social network. For example, RIF percentages (percent of participants omitting particular arguments) were substantially greater in the final recall than in the initial recall and conversation. Thus, we see that RIF effects are extremely important for shaping the content of oral information as it is transmitted throughout a network of retellings. I will address this again later as it applies to the Jesus traditions.

Conversational memory is the caldron responsible for the formation of the New Testament Gospels. Conversations among witnesses occurred long before more formal rituals or sermons were advanced. The traditions concerning Jesus would have set in and hardened via the principles of memory observed in the conversational memory studies. Of prime import is the occurrence of metamemory in conversational data.[42] This provides evidence that Jesus's disciples and other witnesses could easily have accessed Old Testament sayings and stories in conversation and discussed them as applicable to Jesus.

They would then have imported them into their memories of Jesus. It matters little whether these Old Testament stories accurately reflect the events in the life of Jesus; the witness's memories would have been judged as accurate.[43]

41. Coman and Hirst, "Cognition through Social Network," 330.

42. Hyman, "Conversational Remembering."

43. Marsh and Tversky, *Spinning*, 491–503.

5

SERIAL RETELLING *and* DISTRIBUTED MEMORY

IN THIS CHAPTER, WE investigate the propagation and maintenance of stories and events through a network of retellings and conversations. Of the recent biblical scholars, it is the Jesus Seminar that has most provocatively argued that the Gospels are the result of memories that were continuously edited over the years. The Jesus Seminar has speculated rather extensively about the workings of memory as memory is transmitted from one person to another over lengthy periods of time.[1]

The Jesus Seminar and other severe critics of the Gospels have asserted that very likely Jesus was an itinerant sage, much in the like of the Greek Cynics, a wise and even holy man, who ran afoul of the established religious authorities and was thereby sentenced to death. After Easter, the followers of Jesus began to imagine that he had been truly a unique being who had a special relationship with God, indeed, that he was the Son of Man figure portrayed in Dan 7, and the Son of God, endowed with the ability to forgive sins. Others assert that Jesus was a progressive Pharisee, a shaman, or spirit person.[2] According to many of the more conservative scholars, the Jesus Seminar and others of the more fervently critical scholars represent only the outmost fringe of recent scholarship.[3] That may be, but I think that their

1. Funk, *Acts of Jesus*, 1–40.

2. Capps, *Jesus*, 3–45.

3. Blomberg, *Historical Reliability of Gospels*, 16–17.

arguments will not soon fade. The reason is that the seminar's arguments are based in part on a rational and well-thought-out, although a comparatively speculative and somewhat naïve, view of human memory.[4] Note that the Jesus Seminar does not quite accuse the evangelists of outright lying when drawing a picture of their historical Christ but instead asserts that they imagined and invented much of the Synoptics and nearly all of John. Really, these arguments are founded on their view of how human memory works. In *The Acts of Jesus*, the contributors maintain that the evangelists did not willfully distort the truth, but rather that their faith overcame the truth.[5] The evangelists might have imagined scenes, using Scripture as a predictive framework. For instance, John 19:33–36 states that the soldiers did not break Jesus's bones on the cross. It is arguable that John recalled this because Exod 12:46 states that the Passover lamb's bones should not be broken before it is served at the Passover meal: "Christian imagination as prompted by Scripture."[6] The Jesus Seminar maintains that the apostles did not willfully distort the past but goes on to say that they simply adapted reality to their own imaginations and perspective. As the Jesus Seminar puts it, "for many . . . it is incomprehensible that the evangelists would have recorded stories that were the product of Christian imagination, that well-intentioned believers would have invented tales about Jesus, but they seem to have done so." The authors explain that "memory does not operate like a videotape recorder, but memories are constantly edited, deleted, augmented . . . as one calls them to mind. And when one adds the element of fear, paranoia, or conviction, or nostalgia, those memories become more vivid and powerful than everyday life. These imaginative stories suffered both embellishments and omissions over time. The oral tradition is in large part based on folklore, which means that it's wrapped in memories that have been edited, augmented, and combined over the years."[7] The Jesus Seminar makes it clear that the evangelists "did not willfully distort the truth; rather they were merely indulging the human proclivity to adjust inherited oral traditions to their own controlling perceptions born of faith."[8]

It appears that the Jesus Seminar is saying that anyone in the chain of oral transmission may have inadvertently (unconsciously) edited the

4. Funk et al., *Five Gospels*, 27–29; Funk, *Acts of Jesus*, 1–41.

5. Funk, *Acts of Jesus*, 6.

6. Funk, *Acts of Jesus*, 8.

7. Funk, *Acts of Jesus*, 6.

8. Funk, *Acts of Jesus*, 7.

message, from the original eyewitness to later believers, including the evangelists who wrote the Gospels. These ideas appear to be similar to those authored by David Strauss some hundred years earlier.[9]

It should be noted that in the early chapters of *The Acts of Jesus* (6–7), the seminar indicates that this editing process was largely the work of unconscious memory processes; later in the book, the contributors seem to indicate that the changes or inventions were quite willful. What does the experimental literature have to say concerning the validity of the idea that much of the evangelists' writings were based in such edited memories? The Jesus Seminar did not back up its ideas of memory with experimentally derived data. However, recent work in memory can mount an imposing defense of the seminar's assertions. Recall the Tversky and Marsh study,[10] finding that intentional additions and distortions may well become confidently retrieved memories during later retellings.

The Jesus Seminar may be overly optimistic. The seminar suggests that the disciples remembered the core or gist of what Jesus said.[11] However, memory is much more beholden to emotion than meaning. Further, the seminar thinks that it can detect Jesus's style.[12] This would not follow from Bartlett's work, wherein style is lost within a few retellings.[13]

Sir Frederic Bartlett

Most of the experiments in chapter 4 dealt with one conversation or retelling, or data averaged across retellings. However, in chapter 5, we are interested in the processes of extended oral tradition, i.e., the way memory changes over a series of conversational interactions or retellings. The way a story is retold by the same person may be included in such an analysis. A growing body of literature speaks to these issues. The most well-known groups of studies were carried out by Sir Frederic Bartlett.[14]

In the 1930s, Bartlett used folktales, ordinary stories, passages using ordinary prose, and pictures. The stories used by Bartlett and discussed in this book are contained in the appendix. In one set of studies, studies that

9. Strauss, *Life of Jesus*, 75–91.
10. Tversky and Marsh, "Biased Retellings."
11. Funk et al., *Five Gospels*, 28.
12. Funk et al., *Five Gospels*, 30.
13. Bartlett, *Remembering*, 93.
14. Bartlett, *Remembering*, 63–95; 118–85.

used the method of *repeated reproduction*, Bartlett had a person study the material for a time, then asked the same person to recall it, once after fifteen minutes, and again later, at various times. In another set of studies, studies that used the method of *serial reproduction*, Bartlett had one person read the story or passage and after a short time write it down. Each participant read the story to himself twice. Bartlett then asked another person to read the first person's reproduction. Then another person would read this reproduction. The stories subjected to this process of serial reproduction were repeated a large number to times. For example, one story, "The Son Who Tried to Outwit His Father" continued for at least twenty reproductions. The subjects did not know the purpose of the experiments. If a participant asked, they were told that the study was about the accuracy of recall.[15]

Bartlett has been criticized for his lack of rigor. He did not worry about conducting his research in terms of repeatable, experimental design.[16] In fact, Gauld and Stephenson argued that Bartlett's subjects may have taken their task to be one of retelling rather than remembering; and that approach would account for the degree of reconstruction obtained in his work.[17] Of course, even so, his studies fit quite well with recent work in conversational remembering. Bartlett's work has been found to be replicable. Roediger conducted a study that followed the procedures Bartlett used in the method of repeated reproduction.[18] Subjects read "The War of the Ghosts," then reproduced it fifteen minutes later, and again after one week. A follow-up test was administered after six months. The proportion of major distortions increased with the retention interval. The proportion of major errors after six months was .58 out of the total number of propositions recalled. The total number of propositions recalled decreased over time. Thus, after six months, most of the story that was recalled was distorted in some fashion. These findings are in line with Bartlett's.

Bartlett found that, over time, his stories were greatly abbreviated and subjected to considerable distortion.[19] Over several reproductions, both in the repeated reproduction series and the serial reproduction series, there were many omissions. The reproductions were abbreviated. Certain trends in handing down traditions appeared to be dependent on cultural practice.

15. Bartlett, *Remembering*, 65.

16. Kintsch, "Introduction."

17. Gauld and Stephenson, "Some Experiments."

18. Bergman and Roediger, "Can Bartlett's Repeated Reproduction."

19. Bartlett, *Remembering*, 63–95; 118–85.

In all cases, additions, intrusions, and elaborations fit more general cultural schemas. For example, in "The War of the Ghosts," the original phrase "the people began to fight" became "he had been fighting in a great battle."[20] In general, the poetic style of the folk tales was transmuted into conventional, hypotactic English.

One criticism of Bartlett's research that might be mounted by biblical scholars is that Bartlett's research is based on writing, not oral communication. However, I think that unless the message is memorized, Bartlett's findings would apply to the transmission of messages presented briefly and then later conveyed to another person, whether the format were written or oral communication. The format—serial reproduction through written retelling or oral conversation—seems to make little difference. Kashima et al. have found that stereotypes set in whether subjects engage topics via oral dyadic conversations or via single-person written retellings.[21]

The story almost exclusively cited when discussing Bartlett is "The War of the Ghosts." This folktale is cited in many journal articles and in almost all texts on cognitive psychology. However, in his book *Remembering*, Bartlett discussed eight passages. These consisted of two folk tales and six other examples, including four stories and two rather essay-like passages. These latter six passages were written in literary English. Bartlett notes that what is presented in his book represents only a small portion of the amount of data he had collected. It appears that some of his conclusions were based on the non-presented data as well as the presented. Bartlett notes that he included the folktales precisely because they were from another culture and did not follow the grammatical structure or thought patterns of European culture. One of the folktale series was "The War of the Ghosts."[22] It comes from a culture very different than that of most English college students. Bartlett wanted to know what happens when a story travels about from one culture to another. He wanted to cast some light upon the general conditions of transformation. Several of the incidents in "The War of the Ghosts" had no clear interconnection. Bartlett wanted to see how sophisticated subjects would deal with the "lack of rational order." "The War of the Ghosts" has a "surprising, jerky" form. It lacks subordinating clauses typical of Western grammatical structure and leaves the reader "puzzled and uneasy." Bartlett considered the story to be "like that which would confront the spectator

20. Bartlett, *Remembering*, 74.

21. Kashima et al., "Maintenance of Cultural Stereotypes."

22. Bartlett, *Remembering*, 65.

of one of the early cinematographic films with the usual explanatory connecting tags omitted."[23] The story also has a supernatural element. Bartlett wanted to see how subjects would deal with the supernatural aspects of the story. For instance, one is never quite sure whether the two men from Egulac are ghosts themselves.

Reviewing the reproductions of the eight passages, both in the repeated reproduction and serial reproduction series, and in many more passages not presented in *Remembering*, Bartlett found evidence for the existence for what he called schema or schemata. Many scholars today, including even those in the field of cognitive psychology think of schemata as equivalent to the jist of a passage or core or central plot of an event or story. Radvansky and Ashcraft write that "A schema is a mental framework or a body of knowledge about some topic."[24] Referring to "The War of the Ghosts," the authors note that while memory is certainly subject to error, only the details are lost; the narrative plot and/or sequence of events is left, although material may be added via preexisting relevant schemata.[25]

That a basic plot or central idea of stories or events remains after a series of retellings is not what Bartlett emphasized. It is the "affective reaction" to the event, the attitude that persists. As Bartlett says, "It is this attitude which accounts for the persistence of sameness of repeated reproduction."[26] Bartlett takes pains to contradict the idea that this all is simply finding a good fit to preexisting knowledge. Rationalization is only partially an intellectual process. It is an affective bias that determines the relation of the old to the new. Rationalization, the search for meaning, is partly intellectual but also, perhaps predominantly, emotional, so much so that the reconstructive process is primarily dependent on one's emotional biases.[27] Bartlett talks of "pattern" or a "set of organized reactions."[28] He uses the term *schema*, but at the same time he is uneasy with the term. He emphasizes that the patterns are always changing. Bartlett notes that attitude is generally the first thing mentioned after subjects read the passages and is referred to in terms like "exciting," "adventurous," or "like what I read when I was a boy."[29] Thus

23. Bartlett, *Remembering*, 86.
24. Radvansky and Ashcraft, *Cognition*, 237.
25. Radvansky and Ashcraft, *Cognition*, 236–37.
26. Bartlett, *Remembering*, 207.
27. Bartlett, *Remembering*, 85.
28. Bartlett, *Remembering*, 201.
29. Bartlett, *Remembering*, 207.

the first reaction to an event is an attitude, an evaluation of it in emotional terms. The attitude comes first. Remembering is an attempt to justify the original attitude.

For Bartlett, memory is personal.[30] Attitude is an effect of the organism's capacity to turn round on its own schemata. It is a conscious process. The outstanding details that are recalled are the result of an evaluation of items that "begins with the functioning of appetite and goes much further with the growth of interests and ideals."[31] We should not forget that Bartlett's main idea is rationalization, the quest for meaning. Bartlett does not talk of "gist" or "plot"; he does refer to "patterns" and "organization" but, far more frequently, "impression" or "attitude."[32] When asked to define their general impression of a story, subjects most commonly spoke of their "attitude" to the story.[33] All experiences are connected by a common interest. This seems to be primarily an evaluative response. As noted above, the event may be labeled with terms such as "exciting" or "adventurous."[34] Bartlett considers the quest for meaning to be an attempt to relate the event or story to something else, either to an individual idea or to a social, conventional habit or behavior. For example, one subject on reading "The War of the Ghosts" abruptly exclaimed, "This is clearly a murder concealment dream." Another: "This is not an English tale."[35] These are both efforts after meaning.

All of these interpretations reflect the "peculiarities of individual attitude," according to Bartlett.[36] Bartlett considered the reconstructive activity to form out of the relation between attitude and schema, out of "the whole active mass of organized relevant past experience," and out of some outstanding detail or details of the story. Memory is personal.[37] Schemas are interconnected and form an "order of predominance among themselves." Bartlett refers to this organization of schema as "temperament" or "character." He considers remembering to "take on a peculiarity of the temperament" or personality of the person remembering the event. Thus,

30. Bartlett, *Remembering*, 213.
31. Bartlett, *Remembering*, 213.
32. Bartlett, *Remembering*, 201–8.
33. Bartlett, *Remembering*, 206.
34. Bartlett, *Remembering*, 207.
35. Bartlett, *Remembering*, 84.
36. Bartlett, *Remembering*, 71.
37. Bartlett, *Remembering*, 212–13.

recall depends on the interrelations of "appetites, instincts, interests and ideals of the person."[38] In other words, remembering is in part a function of the whole personality of the individual. In general, Bartlett emphasized both the social character of remembering and its dependence on human personality.

"The War of the Ghosts" (the story is recorded in its entirety in the appendix) is particularly interesting to discuss, in part because its style is quite different from that of Western culture. Further, its changes illustrate many, if not most, of the important distortions Bartlett found in his data set. This story is a North Pacific Indian folktale. In the original story, two young men from Egulac go to the river to hunt seals. Then they are confronted by five men in a canoe. The men in the canoe invite the two young men to join them and go to fight "the people." One of the men from Egulac was hit during the fight. At that point, the young man who had been hit said "Oh, they are ghosts." He went home. He died the next morning. When the method of repeated reproduction (same person recalls the story at successive times) is used, the ghosts assume a more and more prominent aspect of the story as time goes on. For example, one subject after fourteen days changed the two young men from Egulac to ghosts. "There were two ghosts. They went on a river. There was a canoe on the river with five men in it. There occurred a war of ghosts."[39] In general, the story generates a strong supernatural impression in the participants. This impression clearly guides retrieval at later times and becomes stronger as time passes.

When the story was passed from one person to another using the method of serial reproduction, distortions again ensued, but their nature had changed. The general atmosphere of the story had moved from the supernatural to the secular. Here it is important and rather striking that using the serial reproduction approach (one person to another person), the ghosts completely disappear within a few trials. All trace of the supernatural or religious feeling is slowly subtracted out. Such was the case with three separate chains of serial reproduction of "The War of the Ghosts." This certainly is quite at odds with the situation involving one person's repeated reconstructions over time. The initial impression of the uncanny or supernatural is greatly diminished and disappears when the story is passed from one person to another. The original story was written in a poetic form that conveyed emotion and an overlying impression resonant with supernatural

38. Bartlett, *Remembering*, 212–13.

39. Bartlett, *Remembering*, 76.

tones. However, as Bartlett notes, style is difficult to transmit.[40] The supernatural impression was lost within one or two transactions when the story was recalled and reproduced through a series of different people. The secular, conventional, Western culture predominated.

In general, Bartlett was impressed with the extraordinarily creative nature of the changes incurred as the stories were passed from one person to another. He refers to the "radical nature" of the changes. Incidents and events are added, omitted, or transposed; opinions and epithets are changed into their opposites; and conclusions are reversed. There is a loss of setting and context.[41] As perceptual details are lost, the stories undergo a loss of spatial and topographical detail. As Bartlett says, "Setting is a peculiarly mutable element." It determines interpretation, then ceases, although interpretation continues. The "attitude continues to function but through all this the subjects are satisfied with their efforts, believing they have passed on the important features with little or no change but merely omitted unessential matters."[42] The order of incidents in the story may be changed. And any part of the story may be changed, beginning or end. "Where the opinions expressed are individual they appear to tend to pass over into opposed conventional views."[43] Only the impression remains. As long as what can be built around it can be given a reasonable setting, the subject is content to think that it was at least for the most part correctly recalled. In many cases, the original would hardly ever be connected with the later reproductions. The whole atmosphere of the original is changed in serial reproduction. "Human remembering is normally exceedingly subject to error."[44]

Certain additional findings of Bartlett are particularly relevant and important for our purposes:

1. Rationalization

This is the tendency to connect the story or items in the story to something outside of the story. Bartlett refers to this as an "effort after meaning."[45] He gives as an example the woman who after reading "The War of the Ghosts"

40. Bartlett, *Remembering*, 81, 173.
41. Bartlett, *Remembering*, 172.
42. Bartlett, *Remembering*, 175.
43. Bartlett, *Remembering*, 173.
44. Bartlett, *Remembering*, 175–76.
45. Bartlett, *Remembering*, 84.

suggested that "this is very clearly a murder concealment dream."[46] This process is similar to the generation of metamemory during conversations as described by Hyman.[47] This process involves connecting to cultural existing scripts and individual needs. As Bartlett puts it, it is at this point that "individual interests and peculiarities come most clearly into play."[48]

2. The Conventionalization of Language

Bartlett describes the style of folktales as similar to "early cinematograph films with the usual explanatory tags omitted."[49] English subjects supply the linking, explanatory participles, e.g., "as" and "so." Some further examples: "The young man did not feel sick (wounded) but nevertheless they proceeded home"; "Evidently the opposing forces were quite willing to stop fighting."[50]

Other good examples of the adoption of existing cultural schemata when recalling "The War of the Ghosts," in this case, the phrases and ideas stemming from WWII, follow. One subject, after reading "The War of the Ghosts," said the war party was "heard to advance"; after three months, this subject recalled that they "marched forward." A different subject in his later versions described the warriors as "a land force."[51] This same participant in his first reproduction wrote that the Indian had been shot; in a later reproduction, that "he was struck by a bullet." As Bartlett maintains, language changes towards the "general communication habits of a community."[52]

3. Loss of Individuality and Style

The style of the original story is lost after a time. This finding is a particularly pervasive feature of retellings based on the serial reproduction method.

46. Bartlett, *Remembering*, 85.
47. Hyman, "Conversational Remembering."
48. Bartlett, *Remembering*, 87.
49. Bartlett, *Remembering*, 86.
50. Bartlett, *Remembering*, 86.
51. Bartlett, *Remembering*, 92.
52. Bartlett, *Remembering*, 87.

"The descriptive passages lose most of the peculiarities of style and matter that they may possess."[53]

4. Abbreviation and Development of Stereotypical Form

Interestingly, according to Bartlett, most of the signature elements of cultures disappear as they pass to culturally different groups. This process proceeds in tandem with the development of stereotypes. As Bartlett puts it, "with frequent reproduction the form and items of remembered detail very quickly become stereotyped and thereafter suffer little change."[54] This finding accords well with the more recent experimental findings of Kashima, to the effect that retellings lose atypical items and generate cultural stereotypes as stories pass from person to person.[55] As we will see, these observations of Bartlett are consistent with the assessment of biblical scholars that the Synoptic stories are particularly vague regarding setting, time, and location, and embody narratives that demonstrate rigid stereotypical patterns. As Kelber noted,[56] the various story forms in the Synoptics follow set scripts. Mark's characters are not drawn as recognizable human beings, including Jesus. It is through their actions that the characters come alive. The most extensive portraits are those of Jesus and Peter; the rest are faceless.[57] This stereotypical narrative arises from the quest for memorability in the face of diminishing memory as the tales are told and retold. Kelber's analysis is consistent with Bartlett's finding, that memory lapses into stereotypical forms as it is conveyed over serial reproduction transactions.

5. Personality vs. Gist

The concept of "gist" was briefly discussed above, but the concept is so pervasive in discussions of remembering that I need to address it more thoroughly. These results do not indicate (nor is it Bartlett's take on the data) that the gist of any one passage is preserved, although that is a popular view of Bartlett and of memory in general. This commonsense view of

53. Bartlett, *Remembering*, 81, 93, 173.

54. Bartlett, *Remembering*, 93.

55. Kashima et al., "Maintenance of Cultural Stereotypes."

56. Kelber, *Oral and Written Gospel*, 51–55.

57. Kelber, *Oral and Written Gospel*, 51–65, 68; Nineham, "Eye-Witness Testimony," I, II, and III.

memory is not Bartlett's. Bartlett's focus is on rationalization as a search for meaning, and this meaning is found by reference to either individual needs or cultural mandates.

Neisser expresses similar ideas in his article discussing John Dean's memory of his various meetings with President Nixon. Of Dean's testimony, he says, "Dean never reproduces the real gist of anything. . . . His testimony has much truth, but not at the level of gist."[58] Dean's memory for a particular event may actually represent a series of repetitions, a prototypical pattern. He remembers his Sept. 21 lecture to the president because he planned it, then presented it, and no doubt went over it again and again in his mind. He is not remembering the gist of a single episode by itself but the common characteristics of a whole series of events. His many meetings with Nixon constituted a "repisode."[59] The invariants are: Nixon wanted the cover-up to succeed; he was pleased when it went well; he was troubled when it began to unravel; he was perfectly willing to consider illegal activities if they would extend his power or confound his enemies. Dean recalled the whole theme of his conversations with Nixon and expressed it in different events.[60]

However, Neisser also cites individual needs and clinical/psychological processes, even Freudian concepts, when discussing the operation of remembering. He attributes Dean's failure to recall the bribery discussion between Haldeman, Nixon, and himself on Sept. 21 to Dean's narcissistic tendencies. The Sept. 21 meeting was recalled exclusively in terms of his lecture to Nixon about the fact that the situation was about to unravel. A large, if not the main, portion of the Sept. 21 meeting with Nixon was, in fact, given over to a three-way conversation between Nixon, Haldeman, and Dean about the possibility of offering a bribe of one million dollars to certain parties involved in the cover-up. But later, the bribery discussion was relegated in Dean's memory to a different meeting and there accorded only a small paragraph. According to Neisser, Dean's "ego got in the way."[61] The omission of the bribery discussion from the Sept. 21 meeting was not simply a matter recalling the wrong date: rather, the bribery talk was cut off from Dean's all-important (in his mind) lecture about the "cancer growing

58. Neisser, "John Dean's Memory," 114.
59. Neisser, "John Dean's Memory," 114.
60. Neisser, "John Dean's Memory," 114.
61. Neisser, "John Dean's Memory," 114.

on the Presidency."[62] This discussion of individual psychology fits well with Bartlett's focus on attitude as formed in conjunction with basic feelings and interests and ideals of the person.[63] It is this impression or attitude that will guide remembering an event. Neisser maintains that memory operates from high levels of abstraction and general themes; but he cites the power of personality as the primary factor in guiding the recall of events.[64]

Many biblical scholars tend to assert that memory preserves the central meaning or core of sayings or events. By this, they generally mean the rational narrative schematic aspects, rather than the emotional. The Jesus Seminar seems to resonate with this idea.[65] That is, if anything is preserved, it is the meaning of the saying or parable, although their interpretations seem to indicate the preservation of nearly the same wording as the original source. Dunn theorizes that it is the historical (factual) core of events that communities preserve. Dunn does not say so explicitly; rather, Dunn attempts to show that tradition preserves the gist or core of events. He does this by showing that the wording of New Testament parallels varies but that the central idea designated by the parallel verses remains the same; the core is stable. This is due to the impact that Jesus made. For Dunn, the oral tradition provides the continuity, the "living link" back to Jesus himself.[66]

Certainly, the processing system abstracts the gist or meaning of words or sentences. This has been known since the work of Sachs and others.[67] But the memory system is much more dependent on individual processes operating at a clinical, psychoanalytic level than classical cognitive psychology might support. This has been made evident from Bartlett's work and more so from the work of Conway.[68]

6. Changes Generally Occur Slowly

The changes that occur as information is passed from one person to another generally occur slowly and in small steps. This is true even if information is repeated by the same person. An excellent example of a slow but

62. Neisser, "John Dean's Memory," 114.

63. Bartlett, *Remembering*, 207–8.

64. Neisser, "John Dean's Memory," 114.

65. Funk, *Acts of Jesus*, 1–41.

66. Eve, *Behind the Gospels*, 13; Dunn, *Jesus Remembered*, 239.

67. Sachs, "Recognition Memory."

68. Bartlett, *Remembering*, 205–14; Conway, "Memory and the Self."

seemingly inevitable shift of information is illustrated by the sequential shift from what may be considered a primitive symbolic description of the death of the Indian in "The War of the Ghosts," to a modern Western description of his death. This is the series of transformations undergone by the "black thing" emerging from the dying man's mouth as this incident is retold over a series of retellings. In the original tale, the death of the Indian as he opened his mouth is described thus: "When the sun rose, he fell down. Something black came out of his mouth. His face became contorted." In succession, the Indian's death was portrayed as follows: a black thing rushed from it; a black thing rushed out of his mouth; a great black thing flew out of his mouth; his soul fled black from his mouth; at sunset, his soul fled black from his mouth; his soul passed out of his mouth; the Indian died and his spirit fled; his spirit had left this world; his spirit left the world.[69] This example nicely illustrates Bartlett's statement to the effect that elaboration is a stage in a process, the end of which is a form of rationalization. First, the unfamiliar is elaborated by a mixture of familiar and unfamiliar; then, the unfamiliar fades away. This type of finding, more than any other, provides support for the form critic's assertion that the Synoptic Gospels are the result of a lengthy series of anonymous retellings.

7. Dominant Individual

As counterpoint to the fact of slow change, Bartlett notes that often one creative person would consciously attempt to introduce changes to a story. As a rule, the changes occurred slowly, but Bartlett also noted that at times the attitude of one person could change the direction of the retellings. He notes that, in one case, a subject asked if he could add something. He was told to relate the tale as it had been told to him, but he nevertheless proceeded to introduce a number of elaborations. These carried through the series. Another student made a special note that a certain story was not connected and that therefore he would add something. Later reproductions became increasingly elaborate and detailed.

69. Bartlett, *Remembering*, 127.

8. Maintenance of the Initial Impression

Participants in the repeated reproduction group kept their original attitude or emotional response to the end. Of course, in this condition the same person repeated the story again and again. Participants in the serial reproduction condition did not. This same diversity may be observed with the supernatural aspects of "The War of the Ghosts." Ghosts become a predominant theme when the same person repeats the story. However, the ghosts soon disappear completely in the serial reproduction condition.

9. Loss of Setting

"The War of the Ghosts" in its original form specifies locations and names the towns involved in the story. The two young men are said to be from Egulac. The story specifies that "the warriors went up the river to a town on the other side of Kalama." The people came down to the water to fight. The wounded warrior went back to Egulac. "So the canoes went back to Egulac, and the young man went ashore to his house and made a fire." The towns are named. The characters are constantly moving from one place to another. More exacting locations are not specified, but one gets a sense of spatial location even from this material. These concepts are lost in later reproductions. One might argue that these names and locations are strange. But the same loss occurs in the air raid story; the setting there was an English resort town.[70]

Yoshihisa Kashima

The most important group of recent studies aimed at transformations that occur as information is passed through a social network are those of Kashima and his associates concerning stereotype maintenance over a series of retellings.[71] Generally, these studies indicate that stereotype-consistent (SC) material is maintained and elaborated, whereas atypical, stereotype-inconsistent (SI) information is removed from the series. This effect is particularly strong when retelling instructions are utilized, rather than recall.

70. Bartlett, *Remembering*, 172.

71. Lee et al., "Serial Reproduction of Conflict"; Lyons and Kashima, "How Are Stereotypes Maintained"; Kashima et al., "Maintenance of Cultural Stereotypes."

The Jamayans

In one study,[72] a set of stereotypic characteristics of a fictitious group called the Jamayans was created, and a story about a member of the group containing both stereotype-consistent and stereotype-inconsistent behaviors of the person was written. Subjects were provided the information defining the group and a copy of the story. They were asked to read the story and retell it in writing to another person. The story was retold through four retellings. The students were told that another student would read their story but would never know what the original was like. The students were further told that the second person would retell the story to a third student who would do the same. Each student was told that it was up to them as to how they wrote the story and what they chose to say. When all the participants were provided with a list of characteristics typical of the Jamayans, the proportion of stereotype-consistent clauses remained at over 90% throughout the reproduction chain, whereas the proportion of stereotype-inconsistent clauses in the retellings fell from over 70% in the first retelling to less than 40% in the last. Thus, when participants in a series of retellings are aware of certain stereotypes of a group, inconsistent information is rapidly filtered out of the retelling series.

Gender Stereotypes

An important study explored the effect of gender stereotypes on memory.[73] This study described the events at a dinner party held by James and Sarah. The story was transmitted through a chain of five participants. The results indicated that for plot-relevant information, the SI information was reproduced more often in the early parts of the transmission chain, but later, the SC information gained the advantage. For background information, SI information and SC information were degraded as the story was retold, but the proportion of SC information retained remained substantially greater at all points in the chain. This experiment again illustrated the degradation of SI information over time. The experiment consistently exhibited the loss of SI clauses as information is conveyed from one person to the next. Both plot-relevant and background information were degraded to a greater

72. Lyons and Kashima, "How Are Stereotypes Maintained."

73. Kashima, "Maintaining Cultural Stereotypes."

extent for SI information than for SC information during the later part of the reproduction chain.

Kevin the Politician

Lyons and Kashima[74] constructed a story about a politician, Kevin, who enters a fun run and finds that his opponent also entered the run. Kevin decides to cheat and take a bus for part of the run. When boarding the bus, he noticed a dog caught in a fence, got back off of the bus, tried to help the dog, and missed the bus. After several minutes, he tried to catch the bus again but again missed the bus. He gained publicity for helping the dog. There were two conditions, a memory condition and a retelling one. The participants in the retelling condition were simply told to retell the story; they were not told, nor was it implied, that they would be checked for accuracy. Those in the memory condition were told that they should try to recall the story as accurately as possible.

The story was reproduced through four-person chains using the method of serial reproduction. The stories were reproduced in writing; the next person read the retelling and in turn reproduced the story from memory. The differences in the percentages of stereotype-consistent and -inconsistent items observed in the retellings was large, 87% vs. 34%. Over the four trials, the percentages of both SC and SI information retold decreased significantly.

As the story was retold (retelling condition) the subjects developed a theme of publicity and linked various statements and events, originally theme-irrelevant, with it.[75] In the memory condition, the recollections of the participants tended to render relatively disjointed versions: the various sayings and events remained separate and not related to a central theme. However, in the retelling condition, the participants developed a coherent whole, centered around the quest for publicity. After several reproductions, a defining modification of the story occurred. The decision to cheat because Kevin "was shy about competing with his political opponent" was omitted. He now realized that he would have to win the fun run, in that this would gain publicity for him. It was to gain publicity that he decided to cheat. This strong publicity theme ran throughout the retelling series but not throughout the memory series. Further, in the communication/retelling condition,

74. Lyons and Kashima, "Maintaining Stereotypes in Communication."

75. Kashima et al., "Maintenance of Cultural Stereotypes."

the dog rescue became tied to the central theme; in the original story, it was treated as a sideline. In this study, political stereotypes were not provided to the participants. The characteristics of politicians were not listed in the materials, nor were they presented to the subjects; these were simply inferred from the present cultural milieu. Over time, the subjects formed a coherent picture of a typical politician. They then linked theretofore neutral clauses to the stereotype.

In general, in these experiments, the SI clauses drop out. When the target group shares and endorses the stereotypes, the SC information remains at a high level throughout the transmission. Serial reproduction often results in a coherent story. The atypical events drop out, or they are changed and gathered into a coherent, culturally representative theme.

It is important to emphasize: most of the studies that have investigated the production and maintenance of stereotypes have used forms of written communication; however, Kashima et al. examined the maintenance of stereotypes through the use of oral conversations. In this study, the stereotype-inconsistent information attracted more attention in the early conversations than stereotype-consistent information. However, this greater attention did not result in the maintenance of SI information. The major character in the story, a politician, was portrayed in stereotypic form even after the second retelling. It is important and worth noting that in conversation, attention to stereotypic inconsistencies was noted but downplayed: "That's quite strange, maybe he was just having a bad day." This kind of odd behavior was then omitted in future retellings. Further note that these omissions would have set the stage for inhibitory processes (RIF) in subsequent conversations.[76]

It is obvious that major changes occur when information is transmitted from one person to another. The Kashima experiments make it clear that the predominant information shift consists of removing SI information from the stories. Thus what is left is a general stereotype, most often generated by the culture. This was clearly the case in the Kevin-the-politician experiment and a number of similar experiments.

Finally, how do these findings from Bartlett and Kashima compare with the layout and pattern of the finished Synoptic Gospels? Biblical scholars are best equipped to provide an analysis of the New Testament structure. For this we turn to a well-known biblical scholar, Dennis Nineham. In a series of articles, Nineham argues that the internal evidence taken

76. Kashima et al., "Maintenance of Cultural Stereotypes."

from the Synoptic Gospels themselves points to a lengthy development of oral tradition that formed the final product as we have it. He points to the "formal stereotypic character of the separate sections, the absence of individual particular details" as strong evidence that the Synoptic Gospels were not the direct product of eyewitnesses.[77] This certainly accords with the findings of cognitive psychology. The work of Bartlett and Kashima et al.[78] is consistent with and supports Nineham's view that the Synoptics' lack of perceptual and geographical particulars indicates that they are the result of a long series of retellings passed from one person or community to another. We now need to examine the formation of collective memory and the interplay of individual and community remembering.

77. Nineham, "Eye-Witness Testimony, II," 245.

78. Bartlett, *Remembering*, 63–95; Kashima et al., "Maintenance of Cultural Stereotypes," 61.

6

The Formation *of* Collective Memory

Collective memory commonly refers to memories that a group forms and preserves that are important for its continued well-being.[1] Generally, the terms *social* or *collective memory* refer to those recollections preserved by relatively formal means. Many scholars refer to the actions of society in shaping collective memory. High-level authorities construct monuments, establish rituals, and oversee the content of textbooks to preserve memory. Today, this list might include writings in history books or government documents. In ancient oral societies, commemorative ceremonies were used; in the early Christian church, worship rituals were created. Eve maintains that the Jesus tradition was not formed and passed on by individuals conversing with one another; "while such reminiscing may have occurred, the recollection that was significant for the transmission of the Jesus tradition occurred in wider social contexts, such as the worship and teaching of the primitive church."[2]

The clearest and most incisive presentation of individual, collective, and cultural memory as these concepts are used by social memory theorists is given by Huebenthal.[3] Note that individual memory is not overlooked in the social memory literature. Huebenthal finds it productive to separate

1. Eve, *Behind the Gospels*, 92.
2. Eve, *Behind the Gospels*, 92.
3. Huebenthal, *Reading Mark's Gospel*, 170.

what she terms *social memory* into three separate categories: social, collective, and cultural memory. *Social memory* as a category of broader social memory is formed in the cauldron of conversation. It is based in individual memories; its character is similar to what is designated as conversational memory. It is not official; it is generated in small groups such as families. It is limited in time. It ends when witnesses pass away. *Collective memory* is formed in groups larger than families; the members may not know one another. Memory is maintained through participation in common meals, feasts, or anniversaries. It is somewhat official in character. One perspective prevails here. *Cultural memory* is the third type of memory referenced by Huebenthal. It is not limited in time; it lasts as long as it preserves the group's identity. It refers to one perspective and is concerned with the remote past—mythical, primordial past. It shares memories with everyone at the national level or of particular religions. It is imposed from the top down and is official in nature.[4]

Another perspective is taken by Kirk. Unlike many social theorists, Kirk directly addresses the issue of the transmutation of individual memories into cultural memory.[5] He refers to tradition as an abstraction or representation of individual memories. These abstractions are collective and cultural memories. Individual memories are shaped by already existing cultural memories and may be further elaborated or partially deleted by the newly generated tradition. The original individual memories are not destroyed but become increasingly irrelevant.[6] Tradition may be thought of as an autonomous cognitive system. Thus, tradition becomes a "symbolic mediation of the past: it subsumes normative elements of the past freed of all but the barest spatio-temporal contextualization."[7] Free from original contexts, this new set of symbolic representations may be mobilized to meet any new challenge that arises for the community. This ensures the transmission of cultural identity into the future.[8] Importantly, Kirk maintains that this approach does not mean that the Synoptic tradition has dissolved all contact with the past. Rather, tradition may be viewed as a "commemorative representation of historical events."[9] It is pivotal to realize

4. Huebenthal, *Reading Mark's Gospel*, 170.
5. Kirk, *Memory and Jesus Tradition*, 84–89.
6. Kirk, *Memory and Jesus Tradition*, 84–85.
7. Kirk, *Memory and Jesus Tradition*, 86.
8. Kirk, *Memory and Jesus Tradition*, 86–87.
9. Kirk, *Memory and Jesus Tradition*, 202.

Kirk insists that the Gospels are not to be regarded "in their relative brevity as very incomplete records preserving just traces of events" but that they should be thought of as "symbolically concentrated mediations of the aggregate of events."[10]

A quite different model of collective memory, one based in experimental psychology, and the model I apply in this presentation, may be seen in the social interactionist approach taken by Hirst et al. and also by Vlasceanu et al.[11] This approach has three aspects: 1) Social contagion, based on the operation of schemata as the organizing principles of memory. This often incorporates cultural scripts as the guiding schema for memory. It is through conversation that these scripts are generated and incorporated into memory. As Hyman has shown,[12] conversations produce metamemory or references to concepts outside of the events in question, often cultural scripts. 2) The presence of a dominant individual. This greatly facilitates the emergence of shared memories among individuals. 3) A general network underlying the transmission of data. Let's elaborate these three factors in order.

Conversation and Social Contagion

We have seen in the previous chapters that the conversations that are constantly occurring in everyday life have the potential to reshape our memories of past events. Hirst et al.[13] claim that it is this malleability of memory, its apparent fragility, its "sinful" nature,[14] especially apparent in conversations, that generates a high degree of agreement among individuals. When individuals in a group come to share individual representations of past events, the result is collective memory. This collective memory is generated through the so-called memory failings, particularly the constructive processes producing cultural schemata, social contagion, and retrieval-induced forgetting.

Collective memory based on conversations may be quite different than that imposed by established governing bodies of nations—or of any

10. Kirk, *Memory and Jesus Tradition*, 70.

11. Hirst et al., "Of Sins and Virtues"; Vlasceanu et al., "Cognition in a Social Context," 32.

12. Hyman, "Conversational Remembering."

13. Hirst et al., "Of Sins and Virtues," 142.

14. Schacter, *Searching for Memory*, 98–133.

group, for that matter. And thus, these conversational collective memories belong more to the rank and file of an organization than to its officers.

Generally, biblical scholars take a top-down approach to collective memory, at least as the concept applies to oral societies.[15] As with Halbwachs, for most biblical scholars, collective memory resides with authorities. As Fentress and Wickham said, in ancient preliterate oral societies, the hallmark of historical truth is dictated by group leaders.[16] It is this view of collective memory that we see exemplified in Weeden.[17] There is a strong tendency in a community for the truth of a matter to be congruent with the exigencies of the present. Weeden further notes a correlation between truth and rank. What was declared truth by a former elder in the past may be declared false by an elder authority in the present.

Hirst et al. view conversations between individuals as the generator of a level of memory that often runs counter to the more official community line[18]—or perhaps, in oral, more primitive cultures, counter to an elder's interpretation of an event. This distinction between social and conversationally founded collective memory may prove useful in assessing memory in oral societies. Rather than investigate the mnemonic practices that are based on and derived from governmental authorities, Hirst et al. investigated the conversations everyday persons have about past events. They cite modern examples of this two-level view of collective memory. They note, for example, that the Lithuanian people construct their collective memories around Lithuanian historical events rather than those mentioned in Russian textbooks.[19] These cultural memories are handed down from generation to generation. Collective memories of smaller groups or villages may operate in a similar fashion. The collective remembering of Jesus was probably much more of the vernacular, conversational type—at least, at first.

Surely, Jesus and the early followers of Jesus—Jesus and his itinerant disciples—would have sat down with families and answered many questions in a give-and-take conversational format. As Patterson observes, many ideas were in the air at the time. Jesus and his disciples "thought, argued, and lived in a complex world, full of ideas."[20] And it is at this

15. Eve, *Behind the Gospels*, 92.

16. Fentress and Wickham, *Social Memory*, 82.

17. Weeden, "Kenneth Bailey's Theory," 34–35.

18. Hirst et al., "Of Sins and Virtues."

19. Hirst et al.,"Of Sins and Virtues," 143.

20. Patterson, *God of Jesus*, 146.

conversational/evaluative level of memory that the recall and retelling of events, especially life-changing events, occurs. Further, emotional events quickly expand throughout the social network. This was demonstrated by the recent Egyptian uprising, wherein people learned about the demonstration in Tahrir Square and quickly showed up in large numbers.[21] The more emotional and/or significant, the greater the spread through the network.[22] This distinction between the traditional, top-down view of collective memory and the social interactionist view is in some ways similar to Horsley's distinction between the great tradition and little tradition in ancient Israel.[23] The little tradition contains the prophetic scripts in the Bible. These are the messianic and prophetic cultural scripts, e g., the resistance of Elijah to Ahab and Jezebel, popular among the peasantry.

Dominant Individual

Cognitive psychology furnishes evidence that changes to oral tradition may be more complex than suggested by biblical scholars. Both Kelber and Weeden[24] suggest that change will occur when a community's existential identity is threatened. This is an anthropological approach.[25] However, since a dominant individual in the community may change the interpretation of a community's memory, we must take into account the complexities of individual processing to understand the flow of oral tradition. Experimental psychology has it that distortions of memory—willful distortions or unconscious ones—occur as a function of individual motives and purposes.

Hirst and his associates have found that conversation is often dominated by a single person, usually an eyewitness and/or one who is a ranking individual in the community or is considered an authority in the subject at hand. Thus, collective memory is often dependent on the recollection of a single dominant narrator.[26] This, interestingly, places the development of collective memory in the hands of one person. It brings individual memory into play as precedent to the development of collective or social memory. Thus, collective memory may reflect the personality of one person as much

21. Hirst et al., "Of Sins and Virtues."
22. Harber and Cohen, "Emotional Broadcaster Theory," 382–93.
23. Horsley, "Oral Tradition."
24. Weeden, "Kenneth Bailey's Theory," 33–34.
25. Weeden, "Kenneth Bailey's Theory," 36.
26. Cuc et al., "Silence Is Not Golden."

as the needs of the community. This accords with the idea that a high-ranking individual may form collective memory, but the motive may be much more complex than merely preserving community identity.

General Network: The Emotional Broadcaster Model

Hirst assumes that information is propagated though a general social network, in which the retellings may flow back to the originator and to others earlier in the network. Thus, an individual may be influenced by many other people in the network, not just the one person preceding them in a chain. This system allows a great amplification of the effects of social contagion, as well as other frailties of memory, such as RIF and schematic referencing. Short paths between members can be found even in a very large network. Harber and Cohen[27] found that after only three exchanges of information, 881 people knew of an event, from an original group of 33. Thus, the social contagion of cultural schemata may be spread quickly from one person to many others. This system amplifies the formation of shared memories and thus forms collective memories in a short time.

In the Harber and Cohen 2005 experiment, a class of 33 students were taken on a field trip to the city morgue. They then kept track of how the news of the class field trip spread. They kept a list of their friends whom they had contacted. The students also kept a list of the friends of the friends that had been contacted. Friends of the first and last friend on the friends of friends list were also counted. This final level constituted the tertiary level of sharing. In the end 881 people knew of the event from a class of 33 students. The information was transmitted within a week.[28] The emotional broadcaster theory (EBT) is based in large part on the "emotional discrepancy" theories of emotional arousal.[29] This theory predicts that high emotion occurs when expectations about how the world works are violated. Janoff-Bulman posited that news is highly transmittable when basic schemas constituting assumptions that the world is just, well ordered, and nonchaotic and that the self is good are breached.[30] Harber and Cohen note that

27. Harber and Cohen, "Emotional Broadcaster Theory," 390.
28. Harber and Cohen, "Emotional Broadcaster Theory," 394.
29. Mandler and Watson, "Anxiety and Interruption."
30. Janoff-Bulman, "Assumptive Worlds."

intense emotions increase the range of travel throughout the network.[31] In this case, they hypothesized that a visit to the morgue brought students into contact with a world that was the opposite of a reasonable, just world and that the news would travel quite quickly, as indeed it did.

Emotional Impact of Events

Another point about Hirst's view of collective memory: conversational memory is generally emotional and evaluative in nature[32] and, in great part, derives from impressions of events more than from analytic aspects of events. The focus of classical top-down social memory theory based on Halbwachs's views seems to reside in memories sanctioned by administrative institutions or authorities. For instance, the memories of wartime events carried by conversations of individual persons are bound to be quite different from the information contained in company records, with regard to the emotional impact suffered by the individuals who experienced the events. The underlying emotions and intentions are removed from the everyday conversations of people. As we have seen, conversational memory tends to deal with evaluations, emotions, and impressions taken from the event. And as I have shown, it is the emotional impression that persists.[33] Thus, as in the case of the Lithuanian traditions vs. the official Russian texts, the conversations of the people may preserve the emotional impact of an event or person better than top-down social memory. And as we have seen, emotions are themselves cues to retrieval; therefore, they may and do produce memories not available under emotionally neutral conditions. Further, the intensity of the emotion will increase with the number of retellings in conversational reproductions.[34] This finding is especially telling in that emotion itself works to expand the reach of the broadcasted message.[35]

31. Harber and Cohen, "Emotional Broadcaster Theory," 382–93.

32. Hyman, "Conversational Remembering."

33. Bartlett, *Remembering*, 207.

34. Lee et al., "Serial Reproduction of Conflict."

35. Harber and Cohen, "Emotional Broadcaster Theory," 392–93.

Collective Memory Experiments

It is Hirst's idea that it is the collective thrust of the "sins of memory,"[36] the very fragility of human memory, that produces shared memories among participants in networks of communicating individuals. Since the time of Bartlett, researchers have regarded the processes of constructive memory in a negative way, as giving rise to errors and distortions of fact. Certainly, this is true when viewed from a forensic standpoint. Hirst, however, suggests that these "sins"[37] may have contributed to the survival of our human species, in that they make collective memory—in the sense of shared, agreed-upon memories—possible. These mechanisms, then, facilitate the formation of group cohesion. The memories may be distortions or confabulations, but they generate agreement among group members.

One of the more compelling and significant studies in the conversational memory literature concerns individual and conversational memory of an Indian family for several past events that involved the entire family. The family had immigrated from India two years prior to the study. Each family member was first asked to recall several events that they had all experienced, e.g., a trip to Coney Island. In this first phase, they were asked to recall the events separately from one another. After the initial individual recounting, the participants were brought into a single room and asked to recall the events as a family. It was found that 45% of the pre-group narrative units came from one individual. Only 2% of the pre-group narrative units came from all four family members. Thus, each family member told a different story prior to the group conversation. A few basic facts were told by all four: that they went to an amusement park, the aquarium, or the beach. In other words, each family member individually recalled a relatively different story.[38]

A second finding of the Hirst and Manier study was that the conversational memory of the family was substantially different from individual memories. Almost half of the group narrative units did not appear in any of the pre-group recountings. Thus, the group memory differed considerably from that told by individuals. The group memory that emerged from the family conversation contained only half of the pre-group units. Further, the memories of a single person, the daughter, contributed 58% of the total

36. Schacter, *Searching for Memory*, 98–133.

37. Hirst et al., "Of Sins and Virtues."

38. Hirst and Manier, "Remembering as Communication," 280.

group narrative units and over 75% of the unshared group narrative units.[39] It is not uncommon for the memories of a single dominant person to make up most of the memories of a group or community.

Hirst and others[40] suggest that informal, nonregulated conversation is the primary engine of vernacular collective memory. This is not idle speculation on Hirst's part. A growing body of literature supports this hypothesis. An informative experiment is that of Cuc et al.[41] In this study, participants consisting of Romanian families first read stories, then recalled them individually (pre-group recall). Then, in a second phase, they recalled them as a group (conversational remembering) or as individuals (control). In the third phase, the participants again recalled the stories individually (post-group recollection). Cuc et al. found a greater degree of overlap among memories after the group conversation (post-group memories) than before it. This increase in shared memories did not occur after the individual recall of the control group. The greater convergence after conversational recall occurred primarily in those groups having dominant narrators, i.e., those narrators who contributed substantially more to the conversation than others. Thus, Cuc et al. attribute the emergence of collective memory in this experiment to conversational recall. They also found that greater degrees of overlap between ideas occurred in the experimental groups who had dominant narrators. Further, they found that the collective memories consisted primarily of the dominant narrators' ideas.

In the second experiment of the Cuc et al. study, it was found that the false memories of critical details that were discussed in the conversation by a dominant narrator were adopted by participants in the post-group recall. Clearly, Bauckham's idea that individual memories would be preserved in the collective is simply not correct.[42] In fact, the Hirst experiments clearly indicate that individual memories may be changed by community conversations, especially memories (including false memories) contributed by a strong participant.

We see that collective memory is often the memory of a dominant person, who, like everyone, is subject to errors of his own memory but whose errors will be picked up by others in post-group recall. "Critical false

39. Hirst and Manier, "Remembering as Communication," 281.

40. Hirst et al., "Of Sins and Virtues," 143.

41. Cuc et al.,"On the Formation."

42. Bauckham, *Jesus and the Eyewitnesses*, 313.

recalls were more likely to have as their source the strongest narrator rather than another group member."[43]

In the absence of a dominant narrator, post-group collective memory will likely consist of the core and central elements of the original story. The post-group memories consist of the shared pre-group recollections, which in turn should consist of the central parts of the story.[44]

As Hirst et al. have pointed out,[45] both practice effects and retrieval-induced forgetting may operate to form and solidify collective memories as information is conveyed through a successive reproduction network. Practice operates to reinforce stereotypes.[46] People may intentionally omit events, setting up induced forgetting.

As previously mentioned, the effect of transmitting practice and RIF effects through successive social interactions was studied by Coman and Hirst. In this study, subjects heard arguments, pro and con, about the legalization of euthanasia. They then were presented with a series of slides that presented half of the arguments in favor of euthanasia. Next, they were given a recall test for all of the original arguments, pro and con. The next phase consisted of a conversation about the arguments between pairs of participants. After that, the participants were again given a final recall test of the initial arguments. The practice effects and RIF were propagated through the network.[47] In fact, both the practice and induced forgetting effects were amplified through the social network. For example, RIF percentages (percent of participants omitting particular arguments) were substantially greater in the final recall than in the initial recall and the conversation.

We see that practice and RIF effects are extremely important for shaping the content of oral information as it is transmitted throughout a network of retellings. Collective memory becomes solidified around stereotypic forms as information is transmitted via serial reproduction networks. I will address this again later as it applies to the Jesus traditions.

43. Cuc et al., "On the Formation," 760.

44. Cuc et al., "On the Formation."

45. Hirst et al., "Of Sins and Virtues."

46. Lee et al., "Serial Reproduction of Conflict."

47. Coman and Hirst, "Cognition through Social Network," 330.

Network Structure

Recent experiments have assessed the effect of the structure of networks on the degree of mnemonic convergence among participants. For instance, Coman et al. assessed the effects of two types of networks, clustered and non-clustered, on the degree of mnemonic agreement.[48] Participants first studied information about Peace Corps volunteers. Participants were then broken into pairs forming either a clustered or non-clustered network. The participants in each pair then conversed about the volunteers. The degree of separation, defined as the number of links in the shortest path between two nodes in the clustered (two clusters) and non-clustered conditions, was calculated. The degree of separation ranged from one to five in the clustered condition and one to three in the non-clustered. The clustered condition contained two clusters. The mnemonic convergence—the degree of agreement, the number of items remembered in common—was greater for the non-clustered condition than the clustered.

The non-clustered condition may be akin to the social situation in Jerusalem after the death of Jesus. There was, as Cullman has it, at least two major groups among Jesus's disciples at that time: the Johannine circle and the Galilean, Petrine group.[49] Based on the experimental data, there would have been a greater degree of separation between the members of these different clusters than between those of a hypothetical single group.[50] This could have accounted for the relatively small mnemonic agreement between these groups as compared with a single socially compatible community. It is important to note that the two groups in the Coman et al. experiment were not initially differentially biased regarding information provided them. As the authors say, future research might assess the interaction between network structure and sociocultural conditions or differences as they affect mnemonic convergence. However, this experiment showed that clustering alone affects collective memory. There might have been neutral events perceived by both the Galilean and the Johannine groups; but the grouping factor itself would have affected the degree of convergence on those subjects. So, the weaknesses of human individual memory may be seen to promote the generation of collective memory. These mnemonic errors often occur in the midst of social interaction, particularly in

48. Coman et al., "Mnemonic Convergence."

49. Cullmann, *Johannine Circle*, 93.

50. Coman et al., "Mnemonic Convergence."

the midst of conversations, and are then enhanced and elaborated as the memories are discussed and transmitted throughout a general network. As these interactions occur, once-unique memories of individuals become more similar. Thus, the group members form a common identity. For Hirst and colleagues, the human memory system seems designed to produce the benefit of social cohesion.[51] These conversational effects would have been very much in play among Jesus's disciples, both during Jesus's life but particularly in Jerusalem after his death.

51. Hirst et al., "Of Sins and Virtues."

7

Manic Depression *and* Jesus

A substantial number of portraits of Jesus have emerged in the past few years.[1] These portraits have presented a wide range of behavioral constellations. Jesus has been portrayed as a healer, a magician, a sage, a cynic; there are many others. Other scholars have assessed Jesus in terms of psychiatric categories. In the early twentieth century, several psychiatrists presented Jesus as emotionally unstable and diagnosed him as manifesting the symptoms of dementia praecox. Albert Schweitzer countered these clinical assessments by arguing that Jesus was simply adopting and identifying with various cultural scripts fitting his intense religious feelings.[2] Later, Anton Boison, a chaplain in a mental hospital, noted that many patients who presented psychotic disorders exhibited an intense relationship with God and thought that they had been sent to somehow save the world. Boison referred to this schema as "messianic consciousness."[3] Boison presented Jesus as one who experienced psychotic episodes but who had conquered their debilitating aspects and emerged with a better understanding of the human condition. Since then, the personality of Jesus has been discussed in terms of a variety of psychological models. Several practitioners and scholars have analyzed Jesus in terms of psychoanalytic theory; others have discussed abnormal aspects of psychotic disorders and found many

1. S. Davies, *Jesus the Healer*, 7.
2. Schweitzer, *Psychiatric Study of Jesus*, 60–62.
3. Boison, *Exploration of Inner World*, 134.

of them present in behavior of Jesus. More recently, Raymond Lloyd diagnosed Jesus as manic-depressive.[4] It is beyond the scope of this book to evaluate all of these psychological perspectives, at least extensively. I intend to present a psychological theory that constitutes a more comprehensive fit to the evidence than those presented to date. I am not excluding the more sociological, political perceptions of Jesus. But it is psychological theory that offers the best hope of fitting the data presented by the Gospels, if we include the Gospel of John.

I am most in line with two views of Jesus: Borg's concept of Jesus as a spirit person and Davies's idea that Jesus suffered from identity disorder and was subject to possession by the Spirit of God. Both of these theories incorporate the characteristics of altered states of consciousness or, as it is often called, cosmic consciousness.[5] But these theories do not explain the extreme mood changes of Jesus, nor do they explain the depth and extent of his empathic understanding and love for his fellow human beings. Further, these views involve amnesia for the feelings of grandiosity or contact with God and speaking the things of God. This is not true of manic depression.

I view Jesus as a gifted poet who suffered from what is now called manic depression in its extreme form, bipolar I. This places him in the category of many famous artists, poets, writers, and other artists cursed or blessed with the mood shifts of manic depression. In bipolar disorder, people experience a wide range of moods, ranging from clinical depression of the darkest sort; benign normality (euthymia); hypomania, a condition wherein one feels highly energetic and creative; and mania, wherein one experiences extreme manic states. These so-called mood shifts consist not only of changes in feeling and emotion but changes in cognitive processing. A person may move from a depression wherein they experience extreme lethargy of thought and often cannot recall the beginning of their own sentences to a state of experiencing extreme creativity, quick thinking, and feeling that they are many steps ahead of others. When one experiences an elevated hypomanic mood, thoughts and associations come quickly; the hypomanic/manic phase is a phase of high energy and carries with it a sense of the visionary. Often, these feelings are religious and messianic in nature.

This elevated mood may develop and reach a phase that involves bizarre associations, hallucinations, and extreme delusional grandiosity. The

4. J. Miller, *Jesus at Thirty*, 118–207.

5. James, *Varieties of Religious Experience*, 217.

moods may become raging, full of hate, and occasionally bring bouts of "madness." As Jamison says, these moods "appear to the world as mercurial, intemperate, volatile, brooding or stormy. In short they form the common view of artistic temperament." These moods also comprise the moods and thought patterns of manic-depressive illness.[6] These moods change over time, and the duration of any one mood ranges from days to weeks to months, even years. The moods generally come on slowly. Cheney notes that she can tell when she is moving into hypomania as she cannot contain her words and perceives herself as very fast and witty in conversation.[7] She notes that she has a hard time waiting for others to get their words out. Black depression may also last for extended periods. In fact, Jamison reports that she lived through a suicidal depression that lasted for about one and a half years.[8] I suggest that Jesus moved throughout the bipolar spectrum and at different times experienced all of these states.

This book is predicated on the idea that "madness" (defined as manic depression) and artistic greatness are related. The idea that madness and artistic greatness are related is a very old one and should come as no surprise. The ancient Greeks thought priests and poets communicated with the gods through a type of inspired madness. Socrates spoke of a divine madness in Phaedrus: "So according to the evidence provided by our ancestors, madness is a nobler thing than sober sense . . . madness comes from God, whereas sober sense is merely human."[9] It is this creative, divine madness that was said by Plato and Socrates to be a necessary prerequisite to the generation of great art.[10] The relationship between madness and creative thought was again observed during the Renaissance. Michael Drayton, writing in the sixteenth century, noted the relationship between this divine madness and sublime poetry. Drayton, referring to Christopher Marlowe, wrote:

> Had in him those brave translunary things
> That the first poets had, his raptures were,
> All air and fire, which made his verses clear,
> For that fine madness still he did retain,

6. Jamison, *Touched with Fire*, 2.
7. Cheney, *Manic*, 66–69.
8. Jamison, *Unquiet Mind*, 111.
9. Jamison, *Touched with Fire*, 51.
10. Jamison, *Touched with Fire*, 51.

Which rightly should possess a poet's brain.[11]

As noted, Jamison considers the "fine madness" of poets as a form of manic-depressive illness.[12] Hershman and Lieb agree with these sentiments: they write that "manic depression is almost indispensable to genius because of the advantages it can supply, and that if there have been geniuses free from manic-depression, they have been a minority."[13]

The early portraits of Jesus as mentally ill were based on the older medical models of mental disorder. The focus was on dysfunctional behavior. These perspectives drew pictures of backward patients, out-of-control raving madmen, constrained and exposed to hosing-down treatments. Indeed, the treatments used to be brutal: chains, bloodlettings, wet packs, asylums, ice picks through the earlobes.[14] But, in fact, as Jamison points out, most people with manic depression illness are without symptoms and are normal most of the time.[15] Manic depression is not like schizophrenia or Alzheimer's disease; it is not a dementing disease. People with manic depression are rational most of the time. It is true that in manic stages, reason may be lost, people may experience terrible fear, they may hallucinate or become psychotically manic or suicidally depressed, but the phases of depression or even manic stages are for limited periods of time.[16] Furthermore, patients suffering from manic depression often develop methods of self-control. Jamison has found that many well-known writers and poets and musicians suffered from mood disorders, either clinical depression or a form of manic depression. These include list of artists and writers hounded by these unavoidable shifts in mood.[17] In appendix B of her book *Touched by Fire*, Jamison lists writers and artists whom she suggests suffered from some form of manic depression.

These include:

Poets: Samuel Taylor Coleridge, T. S. Eliot, Friedrich Hölderlin, Robert Lowell, Sylvia Plath, Percy Shelley, and Lord Byron

11. Drayton, "Of Poets and Poesy," 108, lines 106–10.
12. Jamison, *Touched with Fire*, 2.
13. Hershman and Lieb, *Manic Depression and Creativity*, 11.
14. Jamison, *Unquiet Mind*, 103.
15. Jamison, *Touched with Fire*, 8, 96.
16. Jamison, *Touched with Fire*, 96.
17. Jamison, *Touched with Fire*, 267–70.

Writers: John Bunyan, Samuel Clemens, Joseph Conrad, Ernest Hemingway, Herman Hesse, Charles Lamb, and August Strindberg

Composers: Hector Berlioz, Robert Schumann, and George Frederic Handel

Artists: Vincent van Gogh, Paul Gaugin, Georgia O'Keeffe, and Dante Gabriel Rossetti

It is among these poets and artists that I place Jesus. I consider him as one of the greatest poets/prophets—but a poet likely endowed with the "fine madness," manic depression, as was Coleridge or Byron. It is this portrait, that of the poet clothed with the mood fluctuations of manic depression, that I think best describes the Gospels' picture of Jesus. We now turn to studies that support the claim that manic depression and creativity are related.

Andreason compared the thinking styles of writers, schizophrenics, and manic-depressives.[18] The thinking styles were similar between writers and manic-depressives but not between writers and schizophrenics. According to Andreason and Powers, "both writers and maniacs tend to sort into large groups, change dimensions while in the process of sorting, arbitrarily change starting points, or use vague, distantly related concepts as categorizing principles."[19] The creative cognition is far more similar to hypomanic processing than to the random associations of schizophrenia.[20]

Jamison points out that her book is focused on the idea that the mood swings of manic depression are consistent with those of the artistic temperament. These opposite ends of the bipolar spectrum and the fluctuations between them differ little from the common view of the artistic temperament. As Jamison points out, the mood fluctuations of manic depression do mirror the mood fluctuations of many well-known and famous artists. In her book, Jamison reviews the lives of many famous artists and finds there the very mood swings reflective of manic depression.[21] This does not mean that manic-depressive states cause creative thought. As Jamison puts it, innate creative thought catches fire as the artist moves from normal states to the hypomanic states. If the person is not inherently creative, the energy

18. Andreason, "Creativity and Mental Illness."

19. Jamison, *Touched with Fire*, 107.

20. Jamison, *Touched with Fire*, 108.

21. Jamison, *Touched with Fire*, 125–34.

that comes with the hypomanic or manic state cannot of itself create the talent that lies behind the creation of poetic beauty.

It is my hypothesis that Jesus was manic-depressive and was uniquely endowed with this "fine madness"; Jesus was extremely poetic and creative and, as Barnstone has said, one of the great world poets.[22] Talent resided in Jesus independently of hypomanic or manic ignition. But the energy of hypomania brought this talent to extraordinary levels. This does not mean that only artists endowed with a mood disorder are capable of greatness. Nor does it mean that manic depression alone is sufficient. "The manic drive in its controlled form and phase is of value only if joined to ability."[23] Artistic depth and sensitivity alone may not be sufficient; manic depression alone is not sufficient; but, combined, these two aspects of personality often produce greatness. In Jesus's case, his depth, joined with the energy and cognitive fire of the manic states, produced the beauty and grandiosity of his poetry as expressed in the Gospels, especially in John.

Jamison studied a group of distinguished British writers, poets, and artists.[24] A high percentage of the writers and artists (38%) had been treated for a mood disorder. A very high percent (89%) reported that they had experienced intense, highly creative episodes.[25] Further, 50% of the poets had been treated with drugs, psychotherapy, or hospitalization for a mood disorder; while in the general population, 1% experience manic-depressive episodes, and 5% experience depressive illness. Periods of mood elevation preceded creative periods. Writers reported many cognitive functions the same as or very similar to those of hypomania, e.g., increased energy, rapid speed of association, fluency of thoughts, rapid thinking, expansiveness of feelings and ideas, and increased awareness. Thus, this study indicated a high degree of overlap between intensely creative and hypomanic episodes with regard to the cognitive functions. Studies such as these establish a strong link between manic depression and affective disorders and artistic creativity.

There is a good deal of evidence that manic depression is an inherited disorder. Jamison cites a number of families, many of which are famous, wherein the illness was handed down from one generation to the next.[26]

22. Barnstone, *Poems of Jesus Christ*, i–xv.

23. Myerson and Boyle, "Incidence of Manic-Depressive Psychosis."

24. Jamison, *Touched with Fire*, 125–34.

25. Jamison, *Touched with Fire*, 77.

26. Jamison, *Touched with Fire*, ch. 6.

It has also been shown in several studies that creativity and bipolar disorder may be linked genetically. An important study by Dr. Ruth Richards addressed this issue. Richards and her coworkers found that normal close relatives of manic-depressive patients often showed higher degrees of creativity, as measured by Lifetime Creativity Scales, than normal unrelated control subjects. Richards hypothesized that there may be a compensatory advantage to genes associated with liability for bipolar disorder.[27] My portrait of Jesus is that of an extraordinarily gifted poet, blessed and cursed with the mood changes associated with manic depression. In this regard, it is interesting that he was sometimes considered a descendant of David, who, also as tradition has it, was considered a musician and poet and ostensibly composed many psalms. This would be consistent with the idea that a genetic link may underlie creativity and mood disorders. Indeed, Jesus is considered a great poet by Barnstone, himself a poet, and also by most biblical scholars.[28]

Before discussing Jesus as manic-depressive, it may be wise to review the features of manic depression as expressed in most texts. Manic depression, in fact, is comprised of a wide range of mental states. These phases vary widely, from cyclothymia, with significant but not dangerous thought processes, to the extremely disturbing moods of bipolar I, which may include suicidal depression or manic feelings of power and invincibility. The more extreme aspects of the disease consist of stages of depression with symptoms that may include hopelessness and existential despair or manic phases with elevated moods, rapid speech, and grandiose feelings of self-importance. The duration of depressive or manic stages ranges from two to four weeks to several months or even years.[29]

It is the hypomanic stage of manic depression that is most associated with creative thought processes, at least among those gifted with artistic talent. This is a stage of broad but meaningful, often transcendent, associations, abundant energy, and ebullient feelings. The expansiveness, the fluency, and the rapidity of thought associated with hypomania can result in highly productive periods. At this hypomanic stage, the individual may seek out and enjoy social contact. The person in a hypomanic state is ebullient and self-confident. The mood is often transcendent but almost always has an irritable undercoat. Nevertheless, the individual may enjoy social

27. Jamison, *Touched with Fire*, 81.

28. Barnstone, *Poems of Jesus Christ*, i–xv.

29. Jamison, *Unquiet Mind*, 114.

contact. As hypomania intensifies, mood and thought processes may have deleterious effects on families and acquaintances. After hypomania, the mood may become manic; the behavior at a certain level often becomes bizarre, raging, and violent.[30]

The dominant characteristic of manic-depressive illness is its cyclicity.[31] Manic depression lies on a spectrum, ranging from profound depression to extremes of mania. Most of the time, however, people are relatively normal. Moods may last a few days or, in some cases, over a year, but the mood eventually shifts. An important feature of manic depression is the daily fluctuation of moods within states of depression or mania. These mood variations occur both within cyclothymia, a mild form of manic depression, and within the more extreme levels of manic depression, bipolar I and II. Cyclothymia may be considered part of the bipolar spectrum. In cyclothymia, the alternating mood swings are less extreme than those of bipolar illness, ranging from mild depression to hypomania; like the more extreme forms of the illness, the alternating moods may last days, weeks, or months. The cycling may be continuous, but in some individuals, the cycling may abate for a time, and the person then experiences periods of normality.

It should be emphasized that the frequent and pronounced fluctuations of cyclothymia, and even the more pronounced shifts of mood and thinking in the more serious bipolar levels of manic depression, may occur even in the same day.[32] This symptomology presents a chameleon-like persona moving from euphoria to melancholia within short time periods. Lord Byron is a case in point. His is an excellent illustration of the cyclicity of manic depression. It was said that different people would portray Byron quite differently, and all on the basis of accurately recalled behavior. Yet, most often, he was normal. Some assume that one cannot be "mad" and normal, in control of reason, most of the time. Not so. Lucidity and normality are consistent with and indicative of the phasic nature of manic depression.[33]

30. Jamison, *Touched with Fire*, 27–28.

31. Jamison, *Touched with Fire*, 129–30.

32. Jamison, *Touched with Fire*, 151.

33. Jamison, *Touched with Fire*, ch. 5.

Manic Depression and Jesus

In this section, I describe the thoughts and images of manic depression. I refer to the poetry and writings of those gifted with the ability to put to paper their experiences while in various states of the manic depression spectrum. In so doing, we may determine whether Christ's behavior matches our sample of artists determined to be bipolar. I reference descriptions of the inner thoughts and feelings of those who have experienced the various moods of manic depression firsthand.

Charismatic Personality

Jesus was apparently a very charming, charismatic person. Marcus Borg notes that, "He attracted a following, including people who had left their previous lives behind. . . . There must have been something quite compelling about Him. . . . Followers experienced a presence around Him that was palpable and contagious."[34] Such a compelling personality seems to be a common characteristic of the hypomanic state of manic depression. In fact, Terri Cheney, who suffered from bipolar illness for years, lists charisma as one of the more important and pervasive features of a person in a hypomanic state. One of the attributes that Cheney observes about herself when in a hypomanic state is that people are drawn to her. She says several times in her book that her eyes were wells of empathy when manic. She was adept at seducing men, and even women were drawn to her charms when she was in an elated state. "I was 'perfect' when he saw me because I was perfectly hypomanic: three quarters of the way to mania, at that point where all things, but mostly the person you are with, seem utterly fascinating. I don't need candlelight then because I am naturally incandescent. If I smiled at you, you caught the glow."[35]

Lord Byron, a man of extreme and ungovernable shifts in emotion (considered manic-depressive by Jamison), provides an example of one who nevertheless demonstrated an ability to draw people to himself. Jamison notes how people were entranced by Byron. Jamison cites John Hobhouse's writing of Byron:

> His power of attaching those about him to his person was such as no one I ever knew possessed. No human being could approach

34. Borg, *Meeting Jesus*, 36.

35. Cheney, *Manic*, 141.

> him without being sensible of this magical influence. There was something commanding but not overawing in his manner. . . . He appeared exceedingly free, open and unreserved to everybody.[36]

It is easy to say that Jesus was charming or that he had a charismatic personality, but what does that mean? In the case of a poet or prophet, the charm resides, at least in part, in his words. I agree with Davies: Jesus was not a teacher.[37] He was a very charismatic person and a poet/prophet. He probably did not preach lengthy sermons. He probably did not spin lengthy parables, although he may have done so in his more normal moods. He was more likely to have walked with his disciples and talked of God and eternity, spinning a brilliant idiosyncratic quilt consisting of a variety of subjects, interpersonal, religious, social, and even political. It is easy to forget that Jesus did not *write* poetry; he communicated orally. And the format was likely more conversational than lectural. He conversed with his disciples, he likely preached at times, he taught but not so formally as often portrayed. How he may have talked, we cannot know. But he was a brilliant poet. His speech was apparently capable of drawing men and women to follow him and, in so doing, give up everything. Recall what the temple guards said to the chief priests and Pharisees after their unsuccessful attempt to arrest him: "No one ever talked like this man" (John 7:46). His speech may have been closely reflected by the grandeur of the Johannine rhetoric.[38]

Samuel Taylor Coleridge gives us a relatively modern illustration of how a man possessed of poetic talent might draw people with the beauty of his words. Spoken words, not written. As we have seen, Jamison considered Coleridge to have been manic-depressive. Coleridge's poetry had a mysterious, otherworldly aspect to it. It spoke simultaneously of both this world and another lying behind it. *The Rime of the Ancient Mariner* is illustrative of this point. Jesus's words, especially as recorded and presented in John, exhibit the same transcendent quality.

But perhaps more informative for us is William Hazlitt's description of Coleridge as he walked through the country talking to his friends. It is hard not to imagine Jesus walking with his disciples and talking to them in a similar fashion. "He could go on in the most delightful, explanatory way, over hill and dale, a summer's day, and convert a landscape into a didactic

36. Jamison, *Touched with Fire*, 166.
37. S. Davies, *Jesus the Healer*, 15.
38. C. Black, "Words That You Gave."

poem or a Pindaric ode. . . . He talked far above singing."[39] Or listen to Thomas Carlyle. His reminiscences of Coleridge picture a man whose talk was somewhat in the manner of Jesus's—quite elliptical and evasive yet transcendental:

> I have heard him talk for two stricken hours, his face radiant and moist. . . . He began anywhere: You put some question to him, made some suggestive observation, instead of answering this or decidedly setting out towards answer of it, . . . he would set out, into new courses, and even into new, and before long into all the universe, where it was uncertain what game you would catch, or whether any.[40]

Almost certainly, Coleridge is in a hypomanic state here. I suggest that Coleridge provides one of the better examples of how Jesus may have interacted with his disciples. And with all people.

Sublime Poetry

Jesus was a poet. As Borg states, "His verbal gifts were remarkable. His language was most often metaphorical, poetic, and imaginative."[41] That he was a poet is agreed upon by most scholars. Willis Barnstone, himself a poet, considers Jesus one of the great poets of all time.[42] He spoke in antithetical parallelism, as did the great prophets of Israel. He talked of the things of ancient Israel, simple everyday things, yet his speech carries an air of mystery and eternity.

The sublimity of Jesus's poetry, as expressed in John, is discussed in Black's article, "'The Words That You Gave to Me, I Have Given to Them': The Grandeur of the Johannine Rhetoric." The grandeur of Jesus's discourses in the Fourth Gospel stems from the feeling that "even when on earth [the Son of Man] is in heaven."[43] Black notes that the poetry of Jesus as recorded in John meets the characteristics of sublime speech outlined by Longinus and other great orators of the classical traditions. Black notes many characteristics of this kind of discourse and quotes from Roman and

39. Hazlitt, "On Going on Journey."

40. Jamison, *Touched with Fire*, 109.

41. Borg, *Meeting Jesus*, 30.

42. Barnstone, *Poems of Jesus Christ*, i–xv.

43. C. Black, "Words That You Gave," 229.

Greek writers regarding the characteristics of sublime speech. Part of this sublimity is the use of words that carry "heft, fullness and sonority." They should also convey a "purposeful obscurity."[44] In particular, he notes that chief among the marks of the sublime are "matters pertaining to divinity."[45] The words should move us at a transcendent level.

The English poets discussed by Jamison[46] travel in these sublime regions. As noted above, many, if not most, of the great English poets are said to speak and write "of translunary things."[47] As Jamison says, Coleridge, Blake, and others all display a cosmic sense in their poetry.[48] Jamison further suggests that expansiveness and mystical overtones are evident in much of the creative and hypomanic thought of a great many poets who, if I rightly interpret Jamison's 1989 study, wrote under some level of hypomania.[49] The production and use of unique and wide-ranging associations are typical of the upper range of hypomania in the gifted poet; the associations are broad but strikingly beautiful in their depth. The poetry of Coleridge is illustrative. Coleridge's poetry conveys mystical qualities. It is hard, if not impossible, to discern the mystical from the real in his poetry. Is the *Ancient Mariner* speaking of events on a sea of this world or another? As Yeats said of artists and writers, "We poets—we exchange civilities with the world beyond."[50]

Jesus's style attained the vastness and sublimity of many of the poets Jamison studied. Several examples of sublime discourse may be observed in Jesus's speech as portrayed in John.[51] As Kysar says, when Jesus speaks, "he sounds like one whose origin was in another realm."[52] His speech is elusive, ethereal, transcendent: "The water that I will give will become in them a spring of water gushing up to eternal life" (John 4:14). "I am the bread of life" (6:35). "I am the resurrection and the life" (11:25). He talks of being "glorified" (13:32). He says he is "going away" (14:28). He says that he "will find a place for you" and that in his Father's house, "there are

44. C. Black, "Words That You Gave," 227.
45. C. Black, "Words That You Gave," 223.
46. Jamison, *Touched with Fire*, ch. 4.
47. Drayton, "Of Poets and Poesy," 108, line 106.
48. Jamison, *Touched with Fire*, 109–10.
49. See Jamison, *Touched with Fire*, 78, 220.
50. Jamison, *Touched with Fire*, 104.
51. Jamison, *Touched with Fire*, 20–21.
52. Kysar, *John*, 19.

many mansions" (14:2). "You will seek Me and not find Me, and where I am you cannot come" (7:34). So it is with Jesus's use of "lifted up" (3:14, 8:28, and 12:32) to refer both to his ascension and crucifixion. These are striking examples of the expansiveness of his poetry.

Thus, the Johannine Jesus's style of speaking and his poetry in John is consistent with the cosmic reach of the poets discussed by Jamison. It is coincident with the sense of the mysterious, of another world lurking behind literal descriptions, that we find in Coleridge. Jesus's poetry also reminds us of the cosmic reach of Bryon: "In the wind's eye I have sailed, and sail; but for / The stars. . . . I have shunned the common shore / And leaving land far out of sight, would skim / The Ocean of Eternity."[53] This one characteristic, this cosmic reach, certainly does not by itself prove that Jesus was a manic-depressive but is certainly consistent with the sublime poetry of those possessed of a "fine madness." The sublimity of Jesus's poetry in John provides an additional feature consistent with the profile of the manic-depressive artists Jamison has studied.

But the fact that the Johannine Jesus's speech matches the criteria of sublimity discussed in Black and also the transcendence of the great poets does not mean that Jesus did in fact speak that way. In John 7:46, the temple officers report to the Pharisees that they had not been able to bring Jesus to them. Their somewhat unusual reason was that "never has anyone spoken like this."

Clifton Black led off his article "The Grandeur of Johannine Rhetoric" with these words and invites readers to ponder the following question: "To what extent is this assessment true?"[54] My hypothesis is, as I suspect is Black's, that Jesus spoke in the grand style reflected in the Gospel of John. Whatever talent Jesus had innately or when euthymic was vaulted to extraordinary levels when he was hypomanic and moving into the manic stage. However, we must ask: what is the evidence that Jesus did in fact say these things and speak in this style? At issue here is whether Jesus's words and deeds as transcribed in John are truly those of Jesus. Several strands of evidence point to the idea that the sublimity of speech attributed to Jesus in John does in fact go back to the historical Jesus. The most compelling evidence is that John was an eyewitness to the incidents he reports and writes of. As a devoted disciple, he was the one disciple entrusted to convey Jesus's

53. Byron, *Don Juan*, canto 10, sect. 4, quoted in Jamison, *Touched with Fire*, 151.

54. C. Black, "Words That You Gave."

message.[55] In addition, I think that John was able to accommodate to Jesus's speech in the manner suggested by the communication accommodation studies.[56] I shall take up these ideas in detail in chapter 8.

Communion/Identity with God

The third feature and one of the more common characteristics of the manic phase in a bipolar state is that of a sense of communion/identity with God. This is often placed in the category of "sin and religion" or "grandiosity" by the medical profession. The best description of this sense of communion with God was written by John Custance, a writer who was committed to various mental hospitals over a fifteen-year period for manic depression, bipolar I. He wrote about his experiences in a later book, *Wisdom, Madness and Folly*, published in 1952. He wrote of his experiences while in various states of manic depression. Some of the book was written while Custance was undergoing treatment in different hospitals. Custance describes his feelings: "It is actually a sense of communion, in the first place with God, and in the second place with all mankind, indeed with all creation."[57] This is, of course, similar to the mystics' sense of unity with God, reached to some degree by mystics of most cultures. Custance writes that in the manic phase he feels the "immediate presence of God. . . . I feel that I can talk to Him and He talks to me without the slightest difficulty."[58] And further on, "I feel so close to God, so inspired by His Spirit, that in a sense I am God. I see the future, plan the universe, save mankind: I am utterly and completely immortal . . . I reconcile Good and Evil and create light, darkness, worlds, universes."[59] Later, Custance writes, "In particular, in my sane periods, the sense of identity with God seems to me an appalling blasphemy. Yet it is absolutely overwhelming, however much I struggle against it, and endeavor to rationalize it on orthodox Christian lines as a vision vouchsafed by God."[60]

I suggest that Jesus experienced feelings similar to those of Custance during his manic/hypomanic periods. He likely experienced a compelling feeling that he was God but later, in a more normal stage, considered such

55. Bauckham, *Jesus and the Eyewitnesses*, 393–402.

56. Giles et al., "Accommodation Theory."

57. Custance, "Universe of Bliss," 46.

58. Custance, "Universe of Bliss," 47.

59. Custance, "Universe of Bliss," 53.

60. Custance, "Universe of Bliss," 54.

thoughts as blasphemous. Or possibly when in a mild hypomanic phase, he reverted to a role as God's representative come from heaven, speaking only what the Father commanded.

Jesus's "I am" sayings present this very picture. At times, Jesus utters statements that show the surprising assertion that he and God are one. These are the well-known absolute "I am" statements ("I am" sayings without a predicate). Perhaps the best example of the absolute "I am" sayings is John 8:58: "Before Abraham was, I am." Bauckham considers such sayings as expressions of a complete unity with God.[61] At these times, Jesus felt he was God. At other times, Jesus, perhaps in a more rational, hypomanic state, asserts that he is God's representative on earth. These assertions are the "I am" with predicate-statements, e.g., "I am the good shepherd" (John 10:11). Thus, we see that Jesus's sayings mirror to a surprising extent the complex relationship with God expressed so well by John Custance. While in a manic state, Jesus identifies with God; at other times, he considers such feelings as blasphemous and considers himself as God's emissary who brings salvation to the world.

Messianic Script

Let's review the apocalyptic script of the common tradition in Israel as it existed in Jesus's day. I take this script primarily from Allison.[62] In the beginning, God created a good world, but demonic spirits brought evil to it. Nevertheless, a day is coming when God will intervene and repair this broken world. He will restore scattered Israel. However, before then, the world will undergo a great tribulation, when the battle between good and evil intensifies. God will send one or more messianic figures at that time. This messianic figure will judge the world, reward the just, and punish the unjust.[63] The Apocalypse of Enoch adds that the supernatural Son of Man described in Daniel is the Messiah who will return to earth, after receiving the kingdom from the Ancient of Days. The earth will be transformed into a resplendent state of existence. Sickness and death will be abolished. It is likely that Jesus knew of these Scriptures. The question is: did Jesus think that he was the Son of Man described in Daniel?

61. Bauckham, *Testimony of Beloved Disciple*, 247.

62. Allison, *Constructing Jesus*, 32–33.

63. Allison, *Constructing Jesus*, 32; Schweitzer, *Psychiatric Study of Jesus*, 48.

Biblical scholars are divided on this issue.[64] Schweitzer maintained that Jesus did think of himself as the Son of Man and Messiah, although, as Schweitzer maintains, he did not declare himself so until he started on the road to Jerusalem. He was convinced that his death is an atonement for sin. He thought he would receive the kingdom after his death and return as the supernatural Messiah at that time.[65] As Allison says, "When He looked into the future He saw thrones, including one for Himself."[66]

So then, at least according to the more conservative biblical scholars, Jesus did think of himself as Daniel's Son of Man. Liberal scholars, some from the Jesus Seminar—e.g., Borg, Patterson—and many others insist that the coming Son of Man sayings are secondary.[67] However, that Jesus considered himself Israel's Messiah is feasible and even likely if we grant that he suffered from manic depression. Many features of what may be called a messianic script occur in the manic phase of bipolar disorder. The idea that one is an agent of God and sent to carry out or at least play a major role in bringing about God's divine purposes is not uncommon.

Custance writes that during one of his manic phases, he experienced the existence of a great pattern to worldly events, a pattern of divine purpose, and that "I had something to do with that purpose; it seemed that some sort of revelation was being made to me, though at that time I had no clear idea about what it was."[68] He was able "to see the future, plan the Universe, save mankind."[69] These statements are clearly messianic in character: Custance here feels that he has something to do with a great divine purpose and that he is able to save mankind as part of that purpose.

Anton Boison was chaplain in a mental hospital and observed this messianic scripting in many patients. While there, he studied the thought processes of the mentally ill patients, most of whom had been diagnosed with dementia praecox.[70] At that time, bipolar disorders and schizophrenic disorders were often mixed into the same broad category, dementia praecox; however, many of the patients described by Boison demonstrated mood swings indicative of manic depression. Attending to the inner world

64. R. Miller, *Apocalyptic Jesus*, 31–82.
65. Schweitzer, *Psychiatric Study of Jesus*, 52.
66. Allison, *Constructing Jesus*, 303.
67. R. Miller, *Apocalyptic Jesus*, 31–82.
68. Custance, "Universe of Bliss," 50.
69. Custance, "Universe of Bliss," 53.
70. Boison, *Exploration of Inner World*, 15–57.

of the mentally ill was a rarity in those days. But being a chaplain, Boison attended to the religious thoughts of his patients. Boison noted that many of his patients manifested a messianic consciousness not dissimilar from that of Jesus. Boison noted that these patients maintained that they were able to directly communicate with God. They displayed a sense of peril and imminent world catastrophe. They reported that they were an agent of God sent to save the world or to play an important role in the salvation of the world. They had been charged by God with a mission. These all were recurrent thoughts among these patients. Boison noted that not only Jesus but also several of the great prophets of Israel demonstrated these characteristics.

In more modern times, certain great men of religious genius—e.g., George Fox, John Bunyan, Emmanuel Swedenborg—have each demonstrated a messianic script. Fox proclaimed that the day of the Lord was on the horizon and that he had been chosen to preach its imminent arrival. John Bunyan experienced similar ideas. As did Fox, Bunyan experienced alternating moods of depression and manic elation. Swedenborg considered himself chosen by the Lord to reveal the secrets of the spiritual world. He preached the imminent second coming of Christ.[71] Recently, Goodwin and Jamison have explored the effect of mood disorders in the lives of Martin Luther, Swedenborg, and Fox.[72]

The idea that one has been appointed by God to carry out a mission on earth still reverberates among patients today. Note that the messianic script appears in patients of lesser fame than men like John Bunyan. Here is an example taken from Barlow and Durand. The patient is Mary. She was diagnosed as manic-depressive, bipolar I.

> I'm incognito for the Lord God Almighty. I'm working for Him. I have been for years. I'm a spy. My mission is to fight for the American way . . . the Statue of Liberty. . . . I can bring up the wind, I can bring the rain, I can bring the sunshine, I can do lots of things.[73]

Here we get a sense of mission, secrecy, and power, all of which were paralleled in the writings of John Custance. And reported of his patients by Boison.

71. Boison, *Exploration of Inner World*, 58–82.

72. Goodwin and Jamison, *Manic-Depressive Illness*, 360–64.

73. Barlow and Durand, *Abnormal Psychology*, 230.

Reconciliation

William James talks of a special type of consciousness, mystical or cosmic consciousness, from which our rational consciousness is separated by the "flimsiest of screens."[74] For James, the keynote of this type of consciousness is the reconciliation of opposites. In this type of consciousness, the opposites of the world are unified.[75] James stresses the abundance of self-contradictory phrases in mystical literature, e.g., "whispering silence" or "dazzling obscurity."[76] Cosmic consciousness also provides the reconciliation of the future and present concepts of time. Eternity is now—"the doctrine, for example, that eternity is timeless, that our immortality if we live in the eternal, is not so much future as already now and here."[77]

These mystic experiences parallel those found in manic phases of manic depression disorder. Custance, who suffered numerous manic episodes, writes of his tendency to combine opposing concepts while in such states. Here is Custance as he recalls one of his more vivid experiences while in a manic state: "The Eternal Feminine draws us forever on, but at the last, and beyond Time and Space, the opposites are reconciled, the Eternal Masculine and Feminine are united and there is peace."[78] Later, Custance speaks of identifying with and reconciling good and evil. "All nature and life, all spirits, are cooperating and connected with me; all things are possible. I am in a sense identical with all spirits, from God to Satan. I reconcile Good and Evil and create light, darkness, worlds, universes."[79] Jamison notes: "The ability to reconcile such opposite states, whether they are of mood thought or vitality, is a critical part of any creative act."[80] She observes that "the explicit use of intense and opposite mood states was particularly pronounced in the Romantic poets and composers." Jamison relates this to the ever-changing moods of the manic-depressive: "The undulating, rhythmic and transitional moods so characteristic of manic-depressive illness and its temperaments can also blend, or harness seemingly contradictory moods,

74. James, *Varieties of Religious Experience*, 217.
75. James, *Varieties of Religious Experience*, 210.
76. James, *Varieties of Religious Experience*, 229.
77. James, *Varieties of Religious Experience*, 229.
78. Custance, "Universe of Bliss," 50.
79. Custance, "Universe of Bliss," 53.
80. Jamison, *Touched with Fire*, 128.

observations, and perceptions."[81] Furthermore, many of the religious figures that James refers to as examples of attaining mystical thought have been assessed in terms of manic depression, e.g., George Fox, Emmanuel Swedenborg, Martin Luther.[82]

Reconciliation in the Gospel of John

Kysar notes that John seems fond of paradox.[83] He cites many of the paradoxical or contradictory statements written throughout the Gospel. Perhaps the most intriguing paradox is contained in the prologue to John. Here it is written that "the word was with God and was God" (John 1:1). How can the word, i.e., Jesus, be both? Here Jesus's individuality is expressed as "with God" or separate from God; but then his identity with God is expressed as "was God." Kysar thinks, as do many biblical scholars, that this is a way of expressing a kind of Johannine theology.[84] I suggest, however, that this portrays Jesus, confiding his feelings to John. Jesus, in a manic phase, experienced intense feelings that he was God, but then, as did Custance, he realized that this was blasphemy.[85]

Kysar wrestles with this evident contradiction in John, that is to say, that one can identify with God and yet maintain a suitable distance from him. He cites passages in John that indicate that Jesus felt both ways. Kysar cites passages that indicate Jesus is one with the Father: John 10:30, 38; 17:1, 22; that their works are one (5:19); and then those that indicate a separate identity, e.g., 3:35, to the effect that the Father loves the Son, and has given "all things" to him.[86] According to Kysar, John is "struggling to define the relationship of the founder of his faith to God." Note that Kysar is attributing these sayings to John as interpretations of Jesus's relationship to God. However, I suggest that this is not John's theology; this is Jesus talking, likely in a hypomanic and/or manic state. John is trying to write down as best he can remembrances of his talks with Jesus and as best he can what Jesus actually said.

81. Jamison, *Touched with Fire*, 127.
82. Jamison, *Touched with Fire*, 299.
83. Kysar, *John*, 55.
84. Kysar, *John*, 43.
85. Custance, "Universe of Bliss," 53.
86. Kysar, *John*, 54–55.

Perhaps the more interesting issue in John concerns Johannine eschatology. The Gospel of John appears to express both a futuristic and a realized eschatology.[87] The futuristic *verses* comprise both those concerning judgment and resurrection. The verses that clearly indicate that judgment will occur on the last day are John 12:48 and 6:39–40, 54; both sections indicate that the resurrection will occur on the last day.

Some verses indicating a present eschatology follow. In John, Jesus talks with Martha, who says, "I know that he will rise again in the resurrection at the last day" (11:24). Jesus responds, "I am the resurrection and the life. He who believes in Me, though he may die, he shall live" (John 11:25). To have faith in Christ is to have eternal life (5:24; 11:25–26). In one astonishing verse, both the realized and the futuristic sayings are placed together: "Most assuredly I say to you, the hour is coming, and now is when the dead shall hear the voice of the Son of God and those who hear will live" (John 5:25). This is high poetry, likely hypomanic, and not unlike that of the great Romantic poets.

I think in John we have the author's reverent attempts to recall the exact words of Jesus. I suggest that CAT theory[88] and its studies, along with Rubin's studies on the accommodation of nonexperts to ballad structure,[89] provide empirical evidence that students may imitate the language of a mentor and be successful at doing so.

Universal Benevolence: Sense of Communion with Fellow Human Beings

As people move through hypomania to manic states, they often experience a heightened sense of well-being. "As it progresses this feeling of well-being is often accompanied by a sense of benevolence and communion with nature. . . . These feelings are analogous to the beautific experiences of saints and other great religious leaders. This feeling of communion with nature brings a feeling of empathy with all creatures."[90] This consciousness of empathy may be extremely compelling. Theodore Roethke provides a description: "Suddenly I knew how to enter the life of everything around me. I

87. Kysar, *John*, 119.

88. Giles et al., "Accommodation Theory."

89. Rubin, *Memory in Oral Traditions*, 290–93.

90. Goodwin and Jamison, *Manic-Depressive Illness*, 169–73.

knew how it felt to be a tree, a blade of grass, even a rabbit. . . . One day I was passing a diner, and all of a sudden I knew what it felt like to be a lion."[91]

This extreme empathy has been noted by many psychiatrists as a feature of manic-depressive patients. This feeling has practical effects. As Custance says, recalling his thoughts during manic periods:

> I have no objection to being more or less herded together . . . with men of all classes and conditions. Class barriers cease to have any existence or meaning. I seem to be filled with a sense of universal benevolence and constantly bear in mind the text Love your enemies. I take pleasure in actual physical contact with my fellows.[92]

Custance here refers to the behavior of St. Francis towards lepers and the fact that he did not refrain from kissing their sores.

The feeling of love and compassion discussed by Custance coincides with Jesus's focus on love and compassion as portrayed in the Gospels. According to Marcus Borg, Jesus practiced politics of compassion and attacked the purity system of ancient Israel, a system of sharp social and economic boundaries. Jesus touched lepers; he frequently ate with "outcasts" and "reclined at table with tax collectors and sinners." His followers "included women, untouchables, the poor, the maimed and the marginalized," without regard for rank. "He preached love for all persons."[93]

What moved Jesus? Was he moved to compassion by his knowledge of Scripture? He does admonish us to be merciful as God is merciful (Luke 6:36). But Borg suggests that the "spirit" was the primary force. Life in the spirit is an internal transformation whose end state is compassion.[94] Borg's emphasis on psychological factors, i.e., the spirit, is in the correct direction but needs scientific definition. In my view, it was the transformation into hypomanic/manic stages of manic depression, which was voiced by Jesus (and possibly many other Jewish prophets through the ages) as the process of being caught up in the spirit, that generated his compassionate behavior.

91. Jamison, *Touched with Fire*, 28.

92. Custance, "Universe of Bliss," 47.

93. Borg, *Meeting Jesus*, 50–61.

94. Borg, *Meeting Jesus*, 61.

Kingdom of God

According to apocalyptic literature, the once-good world is now a broken world filled with evil spirits. God will intervene in the future, but before that, the world will undergo a great tribulation. God will at some future point send a messiah who will repair this world and also impose judgment on both the living and the dead. A new world will ensue; the earth will be transformed into a supernatural state, a very "splendid" state.[95]

A common feature of hypomania/mania consists of heightened sensitivity to sensory impressions. This is called *photism*. However, these scientific descriptions do not convey the intense beauty conveyed by these sensations. Custance wrote that for several months he passed through experiences that are virtually indescribable. As he puts it, he was "transported into the Kingdom of Heaven. . . . The ordinary beauties of nature, particularly, I remember, the skies at sunrise and sunset, took on a transcendent liveliness beyond belief. . . . Every morning, quite contrary to my normal sluggish habits, I jumped up to look at them, and when possible to drink in, in a sort of ecstasy, the freshness of the morning air."[96] In this state of elation, Custance feels at peace and utterly and completely forgiven. Custance's observation that he feels at peace and forgiven provides evidence that, in this state, people may feel not only that nature is beautiful but that they have entered into another world, a supernatural world.

Another example of manic photism was experienced by Terri Cheney while on safari in Africa. Cheney went out one day with her group but could hardly contain herself. She kept standing up in the jeep and making "sweeping pronouncements" like "surely this is how God meant the world to be" or "it is just so hopelessly beautiful." She cried throughout the trip.[97]

It is not hard to imagine Jesus, like Cheney or Custance, imagining that this earth is God's country but, in his way of thinking, that this is the "kingdom of God." The intense beauty of the earth at these times would surely have referenced Scripture for Jesus. He may well have taken the term *kingdom of God* from Dan 7, where the Son of Man is invested with a kingdom. In particular, the ecstatic feelings of Jesus so well described by

95. Schweitzer, *Psychiatric Study of Jesus*, 48.

96. Custance, "Universe of Bliss," 51.

97. Cheney, *Manic*,108.

Custance and Cheney would likely have retrieved the biblical scripts referring to the apocalyptic kingdom, the world to come, a new heaven and new earth (Rev. 21:1). The fact that manic patients often experience the extreme beauty of nature suggests that Jesus too, in a manic phase, experienced this photism, an implication that points to the definition of the kingdom of God in Jesus's mind as a place, rather than only as the reign of God in the heart.[98]

Risky Behavior/Courting Death

It is well known that patients suffering from bipolar I may engage in risky behavior. Expansive moods and grandiosity may result in reckless driving, spending sprees, poor business spending, and investing or even giving away money.[99] Persons with manic-depressive symptoms may court death and actually commit suicide as a way out of the constant fluctuation between extreme moods, oscillating between mania and depression, and especially as an escape from the existential despair attendant on black depressive states. Cheney writes: "When you are seriously depressed suicidal ideation can be the only thing that keeps you alive. Just knowing there's an out—even if its bloody, even if its permanent—makes the pain almost bearable for one more day."[100] Of course, with manic-depressive persons, idealizing suicide often results in actually committing suicide. The suicide rate for manic-depressives is astonishingly large. Before the availability of drugs to treat manic depression, one in five suffering from the disorder committed suicide.[101]

In some cases, putting oneself in danger and thus increasing the likelihood of death is a way of coping with depression. Jamison writes that Byron "wrote and talked about suicide and actively engaged in a lifestyle likely to bring about an early death. . . . To a degree he saw his involvement with the Greek independence cause as a probable road to death, and it is likely that had he not died in Greece he would have killed himself in another way."[102] Ernest Hemingway's lifestyle and involvement in the Spanish Civil War presents a similar pattern. Hemingway is considered manic-depressive by Jamison. He was haunted by the extreme moods, mercurial rages, and

98. Allison, *Constructing Jesus*, 176.

99. APA, *Diagnostic and Statistical Manual*, 128.

100. Cheney, *Manic*, 1.

101. Jamison, *Touched with Fire*, 16.

102. Jamison, *Touched with Fire*, 153.

morbid thoughts attendant on depression throughout much of his life. Finally, he did commit suicide.[103]

This pattern again presents itself in Jesus's final days, but with important differences. Jesus's last journey to Jerusalem for Passover was likely a suicidal act.[104] True, but what is the basic motive here for Jesus? I think it is likely that Jesus suffered from manic episodes while in Galilee (Mark 3:21–22).

It was during these episodes that he may have wondered about his relationship with God. Oscillating between identification and agency. Taking on the mantle of the Son of Man as expressed in Daniel. Or God per se as he uttered the absolute "I ams" or identified with the figure of the good shepherd in Zech 13. His moods would have shifted between depression, hypomania, and mania, and his persona with them. At a certain point, he decided to go to Jerusalem. This was perhaps to bring things to a head and to put an end to the constant torture, shifting identities, and chameleon-like personas of manic depression. That he decided to go to Jerusalem, fully aware of the danger he was exposing himself to, is clear. He purposely staged his entry as a king of the Davidic line, an act that would surely have presented a problem for the Romans and practically insure his crucifixion. Jesus probably felt the tortures of the constant shifting of manic-depressive moods; he did say that whoever does not hate his own life cannot follow him (Luke 14:26). Jesus was able to transmute his pain into the sanctifying ideas laid out in Jewish Scripture. He would die but return as king.

Social Engagement or Social Isolation

In manic depression, an individual's social behavior is often unpredictable but generally cyclic and may reflect the change of moods, at times seeking social contact and other times avoiding it, seeking solitude and seclusion. It is in the depressive states that we find definitive withdrawal characteristics.

Persons suffering from manic-depressive illness are generally very sensitive to social currents, but it is not uncommon for them to mask the intensity of their feelings. One of the more interesting things I found in reading Terri Cheney is how often she would choose solitude over social interaction. She would hide from people, hide her "ups and downs."[105] She

103. Jamison, *Touched with Fire*, 228–30.

104. Grant, *Saint Peter*, 82.

105. Cheney, *Manic*, 141, 161, 180.

would literally hide under her desk in her office to avoid her colleagues when feeling the onset of the more intense mood states.[106] It would seem that people who are manic-depressive often try to cover their more extreme states.

Often, individuals suffering from manic depression try to distance themselves from others or mask the symptoms, particularly when experiencing the more profound forms of depression. As Jamison puts it, depression is hard on relationships. It embodies not only bleak despair but anger and withdrawal.[107] In deep depression, the individual no longer derives pleasure from others and shrinks from their company.

A person in hypomanic states generally seeks social engagement. However, there are times when even a hypomanic person may not be able to endure social situations. At that point, they remove themselves from what for them has become an intolerable social situation. Manic-depressive moods are extremely volatile; the individual is very sensitive to individual and group emotions and tone. A person moving into hypomania or the milder stages of mania thinks quickly, more so than most around him. This enhanced level of cognitive processing can impose on an individual the need to hold their tongue as they suffer from an increased desire to talk. Their thoughts and associations come fast, and the thoughts are expansive and wide ranging. Cheney noted than she knew ahead of time what others will say. This situation may lead the hypomanic individual to lose patience and opt out of a social gathering. In the following excerpt, Cheney describes her behavior while attending a writer's workshop at Esalen Institute on the California coast.[108] Cheney was becoming manic shortly before the workshop began. She writes that she could not stand the opening session. Her thinking was becoming faster, and as her thought processes speeded up, she began to perceive people as talking slowly. It became hard to pay attention to them. She found it hard not to talk, although she tried not to. She got through the first day and most of the next day. But then she had to get away. Towards evening, she ran to the edge of the cliffs and howled to the moon. She "howled like a moon sick dog until the sky finally turned black."[109] She drove to Carmel, where she went shopping and bought, among other things, a large number of kites. Later, she drove back to Esalen in the rain,

106. Cheney, *Manic*, 161.

107. Jamison, *Touched with Fire*, 20–26.

108. Cheney, *Manic*, 145.

109. Cheney, *Manic*, 146.

with the sun roof retracted and some of the kites open but tied in the car. When she arrived, she went back to her room to wait out the storm.[110] This pattern of enjoying and even dominating social intercourse, then escaping the social situation and withdrawing from social intercourse, is consistent with the phasic character of bipolar disorder—and also with the behavior of Jesus.

It is normal to want to escape from some social situations. But the manic behavior is laced with an emotional intensity not found in a normal person. Another example of the tendency to seek isolation was recorded by Cheney. Cheney was spending some time with her boyfriend, Rick. She was having dinner with Rick, but tensions between them were growing. She felt herself becoming more and more manic; her mind was running fast and she was planning her exit. She convinced Rick that she wanted to go for a walk. She walked down to an ocean beach just outside La Jolla, stepped into the freezing water, and took off all her clothes. The tide was coming in. After a while, the water was up to her chin. She stayed in the ocean all night. She looked up and "the stars came loose from their moorings and started chasing one another across the sky. For a brief moment the entire sky was afire." Sometime later she realized that she was in danger. Enormous waves hit her, but she made it back to the beach and climbed to safety. She returned to her room.[111]

It has been noted that Jesus's behavior demonstrated a "disordered running to and fro" consisting of periods of public activity alternating with periods when he "avoids the people and tries to withdraw into the solitudes."[112] Schweitzer wrote that this behavior "is so puzzling" that one might consider it to be indicative of emotional instability. Jesus's first entry into Capernaum (Mark 1:21–39) provides an example. Jesus had been preaching in the synagogue. Great crowds had gathered to hear him speak. When finished, he left, and no one could find him. His disciples finally found him in the morning on the outskirts of town, but nothing could persuade him to return. Schweitzer notes that several psychiatrists considered this an example of emotional instability.[113] Schweitzer, admitting that this behavior is puzzling, nevertheless argues that this episode simply shows that Jesus was tired and wanted to rest. However, it seems that the constant

110. Cheney, *Manic*, 146–51.

111. Cheney, *Manic*, 95–98.

112. Schweitzer *Psychiatric Study of Jesus*, 68.

113. Schweitzer *Psychiatric Study of Jesus*, 68.

alternation between avoiding social contact and seeking it, coupled with a somewhat bizarre or "disordered" aspect to the behavior, does indicate a degree of emotional instability. It is certainly consistent with the emotional instability and constant changes of mood in manic depression.

Secrecy

Jamison points out that one of the more dramatic and clinical features of acute mania or the mixed state of manic depression is paranoia. "Bizarre, driven, paranoid, and impulsive patterns of behavior are common."[114] Paranoid personalities are given to suspiciousness and demonstrate a mistrust of others. Their relationships are fraught with difficulty. Innocent remarks may be interpreted as attacks. Paranoid personalities are unable to confide in others.[115]

We have already noted that persons suffering from manic depression demonstrate an almost bizarre degree of secrecy. Terri Cheney wrote that for a number of years after graduating from college, she "lived in terror of being found out."[116] She was terrified that people would discover that she was manic-depressive, that she was not normal, that she was subject to extreme emotions. She "couldn't stand scrutiny." She writes that she "never knew when depression would come to call." And that she "hated every moment of this existence."[117] No one saw her during her depressive periods.[118] It was not just depression that Cheney tried hide. She constantly worried that people would notice other aspects of her abnormal behavior. As mentioned, while on safari in Africa, she became entranced with the beauty of the land and fell into manic photism while on an excursion through the country. She cried "too much beauty and started to sob." She writes: "Had I crossed the invisible line that separates me from 'normal people'?"[119]

Kay Jamison also writes of her thought processes during the extreme moods of manic depression. She, like Cheney, tried to hide her more extreme emotions. She writes that she made great effort to hide her despair while in black depressive states. She made an enormous effort not to be

114. Jamison, *Touched with Fire*, 31.

115. Barlow and Durand, *Abnormal Psychology*, 448.

116. Cheney, *Manic*, 180.

117. Cheney, *Manic*, 24–29.

118. Cheney, *Manic*, 142.

119. Cheney, *Manic*, 108.

noticed. During one especially lengthy period of a very black depression, she avoided people, because she did not want to afflict them with her despair and suffering. She became afraid to leave her office, not wanting to inflict her bleak and dreary outlook on others.[120]

This all brings to mind the observation made by Stuhlmacher that "there was a certain veiledness or indirectness to Jesus' self-expression in his words, deeds, and relationships."[121] A number of verses in Mark express a secrecy theme: that observers should keep Jesus's activity or identity secret. This so-called messianic secret, far from a post-Easter invention,[122] is likely based on Jesus's tendency to hide his identity due to the paranoid tendencies common in manic depression patients. It is well known that manic-depressives display features of paranoia in mixed or manic states.[123] I suggest that Jesus is indirect or elliptical primarily in order to hide his grandiose thoughts. Jesus's intelligence and poetic talents, enhanced by hypomanic energy, gave him the ability to cover and elide the thoughts that he is God incarnate. Jesus appears more forthcoming in John. Both types of "I am" phrases, those with a predicate and without a predicate (the absolute "I ams") are recorded in John. I argue, however, that the oral tradition underlying the Synoptics worked to omit sayings of high Christology, whereas John, as first-order eyewitness testimony, reflects sayings much more likely to have been said by Jesus. I take up these arguments in much greater detail in chapters 8 and 9.

Hallucinations

In the psychotic phase of mania or depression, people are subject to vivid hallucinations.[124] During a manic phase, Custance experienced one such hallucination:

> The great male and female organs hung there in midair. They seemed infinitely far away from me and infinitely near at the same time. I can see them now; pulsing rhythmically in a circular

120. Jamison, *Unquiet Mind*, 24–29.

121. Stuhlmacher, as quoted in Witherington, *Christology of Jesus*, 265.

122. Wrede, *Messianic Secret*.

123. Jamison, *Touched with Fire*, 31.

124. Jamison, *Touched with Fire*, 29.

> clockwise motion. . . . I was not sexually excited: from the first the experience seemed to me to be holy.[125]

Hallucinations occurring during manic episodes may be beautiful, vivid, and intense. Jamison wrote of a hallucinatory experience she incurred during a manic stage, "I found myself in that glorious illusion of high summer days, I found myself gliding, flying, now and again lurching through cloud banks and ethers, past stars, and across fields of ice crystals."[126]

During one of Custance's bouts with depression however, the hallucinatory experiences were not so pleasant: Custance wrote of seeing devils in his pillow, in the bushes, and trees outside of the hospital. He recalled having sold his soul to the devil. He experienced intense fear and was sure demons would come to drag him into hell. Hallucinations occur primarily at deeper levels of depression or the more elevated moods of mania. It should be emphasized these hallucinatory periods do not define manic depression. A majority of the time, manic-depressives are able to readily negotiate social situations even while hypomanic. Most manic-depressives are normal most of the time, and most never become psychotic.[127] Given these considerations, it would not be unusual for Jesus to have had hallucinations during his desert trials or to have had hallucinations at his baptism but to have interacted with people in apparently normal ways—although those suffering from manic depression often put forth a great deal of effort to appear normal.

Depression

Kay Jamison at one point, talks of a "long and lacerating, black suicidal depression":[128]

> From the time I woke up in the morning to the time I went to bed at night, I was unbearably miserable and seemingly incapable of any kind of joy or enthusiasm. Everything—every thought, word, movement—was an effort. Everything that once was sparkling now was flat . . . If I can't feel, if I can't move, if I can't think, if I can't care, then what conceivable point is there in living?

125. Jamison, *Touched with Fire*, 50.
126. Jamison, *Unquiet Mind*, 90.
127. Jamison, *Touched with Fire*, 96, 154.
128. Jamison, *Unquiet Mind*, 110–11.

> The morbidity of my mind was astonishing. Death and its kin were constant companions. It was Death everywhere, and I saw winding sheets and toe tags and body bags in my mind's eye. Everything was a reminder that everything ended at the charnel house. . . . And always everything was an effort. Washing my hair took hours to do, and it drained me afterwards.[129]

Jamison did go to work during this time. But, she was afraid to leave her office. She went days without sleep. At times, lethargy gave over to violent rage. One time, in a rage, she pulled a lamp off of the wall. A friend who was with her at the time could not contain her. She writes: "My body is full of destruction and wild energy gone amok."[130]

Terri Cheney also provides a striking description of clinical depression. Cheney felt her mood begin to plummet while on safari in Africa. She wrote that "when the depression finally struck again, I not only believed that I had a right to suffer, I felt I owned the patent on it." She asked God why things happened as they did. Why did the plague hit this Masai village? Why did her boyfriend have to die? She wrote that she fully expected something cataclysmic to occur.[131] Cheney writes that during these states of depression, she "hated every moment of this existence."[132]

A common feature of the more extreme levels of depression is a preoccupation with sin and religion.[133] Custance writes of the feelings of intense guilt and despair that he experienced during depression. While in the hospital, Custance described his last attack of depression. He notes that he had suffered two episodes of depression before. In his two prior episodes of depression, "he was utterly miserable, but his miseries were of the more human variety." His third bout of depression, which came while in the hospital, was cast in the framework of Christian hell. He felt as if God had deserted him. The keynote was an "overpowering sense of fear." He was convinced that he had committed the "unforgivable sin." He had sold his soul to Satan. He lived in constant fear of being dragged alive into everlasting hell. He describes what he called the "Horrific Vision." He saw devils everywhere. When he went outside of the hospital, he saw devils in the trees and bushes. The material world seemed less and less real as time went

129. Jamison, *Unquiet Mind*, 110–11.

130. Jamison, *Unquiet Mind*, 120.

131. Cheney, *Manic*, 112–13.

132. Cheney, *Manic*, 24.

133. Jamison, *Touched with Fire*, 22.

on. "Moving cracks and fissures" appeared in the walls and floors. Fear was constant. At one point, he jumped out of the hospital window, with the idea of killing himself. He was sure that he had been doomed to hell for eternity.[134] Although couched in Christian terms, it is a good illustration of psychotic episodes of bipolar depression.

Depression of the kind experienced by Cheney and Custance would likely have connected Jesus with Isa 53. According to Isa 53, the suffering servant was "a man of sorrows." He bore our griefs and sorrows as well as our sins. The intensity of depressive experiences as found in manic depression, i.e., grief, sorrow, and guilt, would almost certainly have brought to Jesus's mind Isa 53. Emotion is itself a powerful retrieval cue.[135] Within this framework, Jesus could very well have thought that he was the suffering servant of Isa 53. Furthermore, he could well have thought that his intense guilt, the guilt of manic depression, such as experienced by Custance, was the result of taking on the sins of many.

Mixed States

Those suffering from manic depression may become irritable and angry to the point of losing control at any point on the bipolar spectrum, in mania or depression or points between. As Jamison writes, "Both my depressions and manias had violent sides to them. She describes her more violent episodes as "being wildly out of control, physically assaultive, screaming insanely at the top of one's lungs, running frenetically with no purpose or limit, or impulsively trying to leap from cars."[136]

The most dangerous phase of manic depression is the so-called "mixed state," wherein manic energy is mixed with depression and despair. It is here that one's anger most frequently results in destruction and hostile, violent behavior. Jamison describes such experiences as black mania or mixed states. These contain the energy of mania but with a mood of despair.[137]

One of the best descriptions of mixed state is given by Cheney: "In a mixed state you have all the relentless agitated drive of mania, but none of its euphoria. Instead, you feel depression's misery and self-loathing. It's the most dangerous condition possible the one in which most suicides occur.

134. Custance, "Universe of Bliss," 54.

135. Bower, "Mood and Memory."

136. Jamison, *Unquiet Mind*, 120.

137. Jamison, *Touched with Fire*, 121.

No longer protected by depression's inertia, you now have the ability to act on your despair."[138] Note that the mixed state is not a mixture of depression and elation, but rather a mixture of depression and manic energy. As Jamison puts it, these states are "associated with the damaging and killing sides of manic-depression illness."[139]

Sometimes, the mixed state will slowly creep up and crescendo into violence. Jamison writes that her white manias were becoming more and more mixed with agitated depression and that her depression was getting worse and more suicidal.[140] At other times, the onset is sudden and even physically assaultive.

Thus, there are two types of black depression. A passive one: here the individual experiences ennui, isolation, lethargy, and lack of feeling. Here, as Hector Berlioz puts it, "one's only wish is for silence, and solitude and the oblivion of sleep."[141] There is also an active form of black or extreme depression. This arises in a mixed state, which occurs during the times when one's moods are shifting, wherein mania and depression coexist. The feelings are active, tumultuous, and very painful. This is where most suicides occur. The more passive type of depression does not provide sufficient energy to act on the despair, but the more active type provides energy for action, often violent action. It is not unusual for the onset of an active depressive state to occur suddenly.[142] Berlioz described one of his attacks: "The fit fell upon me with appalling force. I suffered agonies and lay groaning on the ground. Stretching out abandoned arms, convulsively tearing out handfuls of grass. And wide-eyed innocent daisies struggling against a crushing sense of absence, against a mortal isolation."[143]

Of the mixed state, Jamison writes that she had entered a fearful state of depression: "But—and it was a crucial but—I could still move. Not only could I move, I had to move. I was full of restless undissipated energy, that had no place to go, making me want to strike out, preferably something that would crash and tinkle into a thousand satisfying tiny pieces."[144] Cheney recalls: "I thought of our hotel room with the wrap around picture window

138. Cheney, *Manic*, 184.

139. Jamison, *Touched with Fire*, 36.

140. Jamison, *Unquiet Mind*, 103.

141. Jamison, *Touched with Fire*, 19.

142. Jamison, *Touched with Fire*, 19.

143. Jamison, *Touched with Fire*, 19.

144. Jamison, *Unquiet Mind*, 103.

view, and suddenly it made sense: no wonder I couldn't enjoy the massages. The entire time I'd been fantasizing about how it would feel to take my fist and smash all that glass, smash it over and over again until nothing remained but a heap of shards."[145]

This violence is often accompanied or preceded by extremely negative emotions, emotions of anger and hatred. Cheney asks: "When did I become so full of hate? . . . I hated the world, hated myself, and dying sounded just fine to me: all classical signs of depression. . . . When did I become so full of hate. When did it all become so hateful?"[146]

Surely, Jesus experienced these intense emotions. The following episodes are informative in this regard. At one time when preaching to a large group of people, Jesus said, "If anyone comes to Me and does not hate his father and mother, wife and children, brothers and sisters, yes, and his own life also, he cannot be My disciple" (Luke 14:26). Here the fact that Jesus includes hatred for his own life provides evidence that this feeling of hatred for his family is predicated on the self-loathing found in the depressive or mixed state of the bipolar spectrum.

Mark 3:19b–21 tells a story that shows that there were times when Jesus may have displayed extreme manic behavior, perhaps while in a mixed state, such that Jesus's own family tried to restrain him. He was preaching and healing in Capernaum in Galilee; great crowds followed him. He and his disciples barely had time to eat. His mother and brother sought to restrain him. His own people tried to take hold of him and cried, "He is out of his mind." They tried to lay hold of him, restrain him. This verse is generally ignored by Christian scholars but acknowledged by Jewish scholars.[147] It is, interestingly, difficult to categorize it as secondary, i.e., added by the early church, as it is an argument against interest; that is, it argues against the idea that Jesus was emotionally stable. Mark 3:22 adds to the picture of Jesus as experiencing episodes of dark or black manic rage, particularly since this verse is recorded in the context of Mark 3:21. Mark 3:22 reads: "And the scribes who came down from Jerusalem said, 'He has Beelzebub,' and, 'By the ruler of the demons He casts out demons.'"

Three other verses, the so-called "hard" sayings of Jesus, present a Jesus who was estranged from his family and indeed admonished others to leave their own families. Once when Jesus was teaching, he was surrounded

145. Cheney, *Manic*, 184–85.

146. Cheney, *Manic*, 184.

147. J. Miller, *Jesus at Thirty*, 13.

by a multitude of people. One of the group said to him, "Look, your mother and your brothers are outside seeking you." He told the group that whoever does the will of God is his brother and sister (Mark 3:31–35). When a young man wanted to bury his father before traveling with Jesus, Jesus told him to "let the dead bury their own dead, but you go and preach the kingdom of God" (Luke 9:59–60). And, on another occasion when someone told Jesus that he wanted to follow him but needed first to say goodbye to his family, Jesus said, "No one, having put his hand to the plow, and looking back, is fit for the kingdom of God" (Luke 9:62). These episodes are consistent with the bouts of anger and generalized hatred often found in the mixed phase of manic depression.

Miller cites these verses as indicative of Jesus's estrangement from his family.[148] Then, following Erickson, he postulates that Jesus's estrangement may have resulted in a new generative phase of his life, but such analytic psychology is too abstract and misses the underlying feeling and motives indicated by such verses. Other psychoanalytic perspectives on Jesus's life may well contain a good deal of truth. For example, the view that Jesus's troubles with this family stem from unresolved Oedipal issues may well provide a valid psychoanalytic framework for these aspects of Jesus's behavior. But they throw little light on whether the Gospels accurately reflect the deeds and sayings of the historical Jesus.

We should not overlook two other well-known scenarios that cast a substantial degree of doubt on Jesus's emotional stability. These verses are consistent with black depressive episodes: rage, anger, fear, or hatred.

Temple Rage. One such episode describes Jesus's anger at the merchants who occupied booths in the temple grounds. This story is outlined in John 2:14–16. These verses record Jesus, in what was likely a violent rage, taking a whip to the money changers and those who sold sacrificial animals in the temple and driving them out of the temple grounds. "He upset the tables, poured out the changer's money and drove out the animals" At this point, John notes that some of Jesus's disciples recalled words from Ps. 69: "Zeal for your house has eaten me up." This is a very telling reference by John. In this psalm, David pleads to God to save him. He cries, "For the waters have come up to my neck, I sink in deep mire" (Ps 69:2a–c) . . . . "I am in trouble" (17b). "Shame has covered my face, I have become a stranger to my brothers, and an alien to my mother's children" (7b–8) . . . . "But I am poor and sorrowful" (29). We might think that John here is recalling

148. J. Miller, *Jesus at Thirty*, 81–86.

a single verse concerning Jesus's righteous zeal at the time of his temple outburst (Ps 69:9a). But to one who is well versed in Scripture, a reference to a particular verse likely retrieves the entire emotion-laden narrative or "memory-feeling"[149] underlying the psalm that contains it; and therefore, it provides a look through John's eyes into Jesus's state of mind, not only at the time of the temple episode but at various and many other times during his life. Note also that the psalm describes the singer's alienation from his family. Thus, it is even more likely that John thought of the psalm in part as a portrait of Jesus's estrangement from his family; indeed, that it was probably an underlying script of Jesus's life, at least since the manic depression had taken hold. It is quite reasonable to posit that John thought that the feeling tone of Ps 69 reflected the desperation of Jesus in his latter days in Jerusalem.

Cursing the Fig Tree. Two verses portray Jesus cursing a fig tree: Mark 11:12 and 13. Coming into Jerusalem from Bethany, Jesus was hungry and noticed a fig tree nearby but found that it had no figs growing on it. At that, he cursed the tree and pronounced that it should never bear figs again. This is clearly an irrational burst of anger, common in bipolar states.[150] Albert Schweitzer suggests that the deed is rational in the broad context of apocalyptic literature. In the supernatural world of the future, all of nature would become wondrously fertile. But Jesus cursed this tree for all eternity because it had deceived the future Messiah in his earthly state. Schweitzer's defense is based on the idea that Jesus's curse was rational when viewed from the standpoint of Jewish apocalyptic literature; however, even so, this defense attests primarily to Jesus's grandiose view of himself. Thus, Schweitzer's actual defense provides more evidence that Jesus was suffering from the delusions of grandeur so common in manic-depressive disorders. Still, Schweitzer's view that some acts of Jesus's that appear irrational to us would not have appeared odd when considered from the viewpoint of Jewish culture has merit. Jewish culture did foresee a future time when a messiah would appear and that he would come from the house of David. The new world would bring about a reversal of values, when the meek and poor would be elevated to the highest positions. If Jesus was poor and thought he was of the Davidic line, his grandiosity does take on a degree of rationality in the Jewish culture. Nevertheless, when all is said, Jesus's personal acceptance of

149. Conway, "Memory and the Self."

150. Schweitzer, *Psychiatric Study of Jesus*, 71.

the messianic role carries with it a level of grandiosity that is commensurate with manic depression.

One wonders if the depths and beauty of the verses collected in the Sermon on the Mount linking emotions with actions, e.g., hatred and murder, were born of the ethical insights of this extraordinary gifted man while experiencing universal love during manic states and also hatred and its correlative violent fantasies during a black depression. This sermon, or the concepts underlying it, could not have been generated by a scholar perusing the Old Testament for verses of Scripture hinting at or implying but never saying that you should "love your enemies." These ideas were born of intense feelings and empathy generated in manic-depressive states. Jamison expresses this idea in her epilogue: "This communion with all creatures . . . How it must be to be old, to be sick to be dying, the cyclical occurrence and very intensity of the extreme moods in manic depression seem to generate understanding."[151] This deep empathy gave Jesus his healing power. And it drew people to him then and down through the ages.

151. Jamison, *Touched with Fire*, 217–19.

8

Jesus's Manic Depression

The Primacy of John

Oral tradition is often portrayed as emanating from the source (Jesus) in the shape of a V, consisting of the Johannine and Synoptic traditions separating early on and diverging to form the differences seen between the Synoptic Gospels and the Fourth Gospel.[1] Generally, these differences are thought to be due in part to geographic location but more commonly due to the differing needs and interests of particular communities.[2] In my view, the traditions likely solidified before communities formed around them. First came the conversations between the disciples, conversations occurring both during Jesus's life and after his death. Collective memory solidified early as a function of these conversations.[3]

Jesus did not talk or behave differently as a function of geographic location or audience. It seems likely that the manic episodes of Christ occurred in both Galilee and Jerusalem. Jesus's speech was likely of a highly poetic quality at times, particularly when he was in a hypomanic or manic state, likely more literary and hypotactic when in more normal or even lighter hypomanic states. The split in the tradition occurred because dominant, strong personalities, particularly Peter and the Beloved Disciple, observed and processed Jesus differently. Cuc et al. found that the collective

1. Kysar, "John's Anti-Jewish Polemic."
2. Kysar, "John's Anti-Jewish Polemic."
3. Hirst et al., "Of Sins and Virtues."

memory flowing from conversation is primarily reflective of the memory of those individuals who dominate the conversations.[4] Thus, it is even predictable that two separate streams of tradition would emanate from the source, namely the Petrine and the Johannine traditions. Cullmann points out that the Johannine and the Galilean groups were present in Jerusalem after Jesus's death;[5] conversation within these groups would have been based on the leadership within each group. In this chapter, I am primarily interested in the thinking of the Johannine group and John's Gospel.

I view the Gospel of John as the primary source for assessing the life of Jesus. I say this primarily because of the manic depression hypothesis, which throws John into the bright light of the center stage. The manic depression hypothesis illumines the words and deeds of Jesus. Jesus did imagine that he was God and said so. He likely asserted that he was sent from God but just as often said he was God. This assertion of divinity is not uncommon among manic-depressive patients. Thus, under the hypothesis that Jesus suffered from manic depression, the Gospel of John becomes highly credible. John is attempting to accurately recall and report Jesus's statements. He is not writing an interpretive novel about Jesus. He alone unabashedly maintains that Jesus is fully God.[6] He plainly reports Jesus's "I am" statements, including those without a predicate, e.g., the famous "before Abraham was, I am" (John 8:59) assertion. These clearly show that Jesus did in fact think of himself as identical with God. Custance, who suffered from bipolar I disorder, recalls a feeling of identity with God (but when in a hypomanic or even a euthymic state dismisses this as blasphemy). Custance feels this identity with God even in a secular culture. But Jesus's feelings concerning his relationship with God were probably more complex and frightening than those of Custance. Given Jesus's Jewish culture, this feeling of identity probably bore an intensity not conceivable today. Jesus felt he was God incarnate, best expressed by the "I am" sayings recorded in John. However, identification with God would have constituted a terrifying blasphemy. These disparate feelings, the sense of identity with God and its attendant guilt, would have produced a severe crisis of identity in Jesus and compelled him to seek scriptural solutions.

4. Cuc et al., "On the Formation."

5. Cullmann, *Johannine Circle*, 55–56.

6. Komoszewski, *Reinventing Jesus*, 174.

EYEWITNESS EVIDENCE

One of the most efficacious methods of distinguishing between experience-based and non-experience-based testimony is statement validity analysis (SVA).[7] As part of SVA, Steller presented a compilation of verbal content criteria that a large number of studies had indicated would be useful to distinguish fabrication from truthful statements. This list, called criteria-based content analysis (CBCA), forms the core of SVA. Since 1989, a host of studies have confirmed the utility of using CBCA.[8] Indeed, SVA and CBCA assessments are admissible as evidence in several North American courts and in some European countries, e.g., Sweden, Germany, and the Netherlands. Some researchers have argued that the validity of SVA and CBCA has been conclusively demonstrated and pressed its wider use in American courts;[9] others have expressed doubt.[10] In Vrij's opinion, the approach is 70% accurate overall; but that figure is too low for consideration in criminal cases. Vrij reviewed thirty-seven studies that used CBCA to distinguish truthful statements from fabrications.[11] Two types of studies were included in the review, field studies and laboratory studies. In the field studies, actual witness' statements were analyzed. Criteria such as confession, DNA evidence, polygraph results, and conviction were used to determine the accuracy of the statements. In the laboratory experiments, subjects were told to lie or tell the truth about observed events. The crimes studied by Vrij were child sexual abuse crimes. The witnesses were both children and adults. The statements in the study were from victims, witnesses, and suspects. Although the early work in this area involved cases of child sexual abuse, the CBCA has been extended to other crimes.[12] Volbert and Steller suggest that caution is called for in applying these criteria, especially since witness reports may be based on false memories, which they assert may be rather detailed and contain some vivid imagery. Therefore, one should assess the degree to which the statements were made under suggestive circumstances. Also, personal and situational variables should be taken into account in analyzing individual cases. Seventy-percent accuracy rates have been reported over a

7. Steller and Köhnken, "Critera-Based Statement Analysis."

8. Volbert and Steller, "Is This Testimony Truthful," 210.

9. Zaparniuk et al., "Assessing the Credibility."

10. Brigham, "What Is Forensic Psychology"; G. Davies, "Statement Validity Analysis."

11. Vrij, "Critera-Based Content Analysis."

12. Porter et al., "Nature."

large number of laboratory studies made on the basis of content analysis alone.[13] Vrij argues that while an error rate of 30% would not be admissible in criminal trials to show that the defendant was guilty beyond a reasonable doubt, still, it does meet a less stringent criterion that the report is more likely than not experience based and therefore is useful for police work.[14] In addition, a validity rate of 70% makes the CBCA valuable as a tool for examining witnesses to historical events. In fact, the research shows that reports that meet the CBCA criteria have a 70% likelihood of being able to differentiate between experience-based and non-experience-based statements. In this approach, witnesses' statements are assessed for the presence of nineteen criteria.[15] The most important criteria for our purposes are as follows: quantity of details, contextual embedding, descriptions of interactions, and reproduction of conversations. Contextual embedding is by far the most important of the listed criteria. Merely satisfying a SVA checklist is not sufficient. The criteria need to be embedded in specific episodes and located in realistic time and place frames.

What does the experimental literature, other than the SVA literature, say concerning autobiographical memory and memory for detail? A large number of experiments indicate that memory for real events contains more imagery than those for imagined events. Johnson et al. found that recollections of real events contained higher ratings on visual detail than recollections of imagined events.[16] Most interesting was the finding that memory for real events contained higher ratings for spatial locations and relative positions of objects than did the memory of imagined events. In addition, Schooler et al. found that false memories (suggested by post-event information) for objects contained fewer "sensory details" than memories for actual objects that had in fact been presented.[17]

Many scholars, mostly outside of the field of cognitive psychology, suggest that the presence of irrelevant imagery is related to accuracy. A word about this theory needs to be addressed, as various theologians across the range of liberal to conservative have expressed this idea. Mark's text regarding the feeding of the five thousand, that the grass was green (Mark 6:39) is often cited as evidence of eyewitness presence. This idea is probably

13. Vrij, "Critera-Based Content Analysis."

14. Vrij, "Critera-Based Content Analysis," 34.

15. These criteria are listed in their entirety in Vrij, "Critera-Based Content Analysis."

16. Johnson et al., "Phenomenal Characteristics of Memories."

17. Schooler et al., "Qualities of the Unreal."

based on the copy theory of memory—that copies of experiences are imprinted on the brain regardless of attentive processes and later may emerge when recollecting an event. Such a theory formed the basis for flashbulb memory. However, there is little evidence to support this view.[18] Also note that in CBCA analysis, inclusion of superfluous statements is not a significant criterion.[19] In fact, as we saw earlier, experimental evidence indicates that very quickly, within seconds, and probably milliseconds, attentive and reconstructive processes take over during the early stages of information processing,[20] removing irrelevant information. A famous study by Brown and Kulik in 1977,[21] wherein subjects were asked after two years for details of their experiences when they first heard that John Kennedy had been killed, is often used to substantiate copy theory. Subjects reported "utterly idiosyncratic" and in a sense, accidental content. This was considered evidence at least early on that the subjects had printed a copy of their experiences pertaining to when Kennedy was killed and retained this copy for over a year. However, later studies of flashbulb memory have cast doubt on this interpretation.[22]

It is not the occasional irrelevant imagery that counts, even if we could decide what is relevant for a particular witness. It is the pervasive continuous use of imagery interwoven into the testimony that counts. It is part of the truth for John. It is picked up by the schema in construction because it is important. This is why detail is preserved in the PEMs.[23] This is why, in the discussion by Pillemer, a young college student's memory was so graphic. The detail is woven into the narrative and the emotion.

John Robinson, in *The Priority of John*, has made a strong case that John among the four Gospels is the first among equals in terms of portraying and reflecting the historical Christ.[24] This approach is decidedly contrary to the mainstream thought concerning John. Most scholars have taken the position that the Synoptic Gospels are better suited to draw a picture of the real Jesus. It is often thought that John is too theological and

18. Baddeley, "Reflections on Autobiographical Memory"; Brewer, "What Is Recollective Memory."

19. Vrij, "Critera-Based Content Analysis," 5.

20. Radvansky and Ashcraft, *Cognition*, ch. 4.

21. Brown and Kulik, "Flashbulb Memories."

22. Baddeley, "Reflections on Autobiographical Memory," 73–74.

23. Pillemer, *Momentous Events, Vivid Memories*, 3.

24. Robinson, *Priority of John*, 1–35.

that the Gospel presents a rather fictionalized Jesus. Maurice Casey is particularly scathing in his assessment of John. He considers the Gospel nothing more than a diatribe of the Johannine community against the Jewish leaders in Jerusalem and simply untrue.[25]

Thus, it was surprising to me that the evidence from the eyewitness literature should be more supportive of the arguments of Robinson than the opinion of perhaps a majority of theologians. John provides a precise chronological picture of events. The geographical and topological detail is striking. John takes care to delineate precisely the relative positions and elevations of places and regions; for instance, Bethany is described as two miles from Jerusalem. In contrast, the Synoptics' chronology of Jesus's ministry is sketchy at best; its topological presentation is extremely vague. The Synoptics do not include several of Jesus's visits to Jerusalem. John also portrays the movements of people with some precision in numerous scenes; for instance, the portrayal of Pilate's movements in and out of the praetorium when interrogating Jesus and talking to the crowd is realistic. When narrating the story of the woman of Sychar, John even attempts to describe how a wearied Jesus sat at the well. John describes Bethsaida, the Pool of Siloam, and the Stone Pavement where Pilate sat in judgment of Jesus. Also, Jewish trial proceedings are detailed and have been corroborated as conforming to Jewish legal proceedings.[26]

The Johannine scenes generally contain movement and two or more locations. This in turn furnishes a spatial basis for retention of conversation per the well-known and ancient mnemonic rule that verbal discourse is better retained when cast in a spatial format. This is the mnemonic device called the *method of loci*.[27] Concepts, conversations, or activities may be more readily recalled when they have occurred in different locations and the information is accessed and retrieved by place.

Listen to William Sanday regarding the graphic detail with which John has written the scenes in the Fourth Gospel concerning Jesus's ministry in the south.

> The historical value of the Fourth Gospel comes out strongly in this period. Rarely has any situation been described with the *extraordinary vividness* and truth to fact as chapter 7 (see esp. vv. 11–15, 25–27, 31, 32, 40–52). Not less graphic are the details of

25. Casey, *Is John's Gospel True*, 218–29.
26. Robinson, *Priority of John*, 270.
27. Radvansky and Ashcraft, *Cognition*, 175.

> chapter 9; and there is a *marked precision* in the statements of John 10:22f., 40f., 11:45–57.[28]

Much of John's exposition of geographic and topographical detail in John has been confirmed by archeological data. The pools of Bethesda and Siloam have been excavated; the Stone Pavement has been discovered, although its site has been contested.[29] The testimony is very detailed, much more so than in Mark. Generally, this kind of precision indicates that a witness has been present at the scene. This is true even if the detail is not corroborated—as long as the testimony has not been discredited. As we have seen, in the case of John's Gospel, major parts of the geographic and testimony have been corroborated through archeological work.

Where does that leave us with regard to John and the experimental data? The Gospel is rich in each of the major SVA criteria; the Gospel is very detailed. Conversations and interactions between persons are portrayed, and the detail is embedded in time and place. It isn't the quantity of detail, the conversation itself, or the social interaction that attests to eyewitness reporting, but the fact that these criteria are placed within specific episodic scenes. This argues in support of eyewitness presence. In brief, the data from experimental psychology is consistent with and supportive of the conclusion that John—that is, the author of John—was indeed an eyewitness to the events recorded in his Gospel. These events were extremely important and life changing for a young man. They would have been recalled in some detail, but a major caveat must be expressed here. Very likely, John was an eyewitness to these events and did recall them in some detail. However, this does not mean that all of the detail is accurate. John Dean's testimony to Congress offers a case in point. His testimony was very precise and detailed (although mostly conversational) but was subject to reconstructive processes.[30]

John was probably an eyewitness; nevertheless, his material could have developed in stages out of unwritten preaching material, composed for various apologetic, catechetical, and liturgical purposes, and have gone through different editions and redactions; but all that is still compatible with first-order witness perception.[31] SVA analyses and experimental literature indicate that the Gospel of John is reflective of first-order eyewitness

28. William Sanday, as quoted in Hunter, *According to John*, 60.

29. Robinson, *Priority of John*, 53–59.

30. Neisser, "John Dean's Memory," 114.

31. Robinson, *Priority of John*, 21.

testimony. First-order eyewitnesses generally produce testimony much closer to the original language, style, and actions of people involved in any given scene than information obtained from countless retellings. Of course, eyewitnesses may distort information, but communication accommodation theory (CAT) may mitigate this problem.

Communication Accommodation Theory (CAT)

I have already pointed out that the author of the Gospel of John is most likely an eyewitness to the events in Jesus's life and that this increases the credibility of the content information put forth in John. I consider the Beloved Disciple to be the author of the Gospel of John.[32] The Beloved Disciple claimed a place of special intimacy with Jesus and, as such, was the one entrusted to convey the truth of Jesus after his death.[33] The Beloved Disciple was credited with spiritual insight into Jesus. He was the One "entrusted to keep His teaching alive."[34]

In view of this special intimacy with Jesus, the Beloved Disciple would have been especially prone to copy and incorporate the style of the speaking and thinking processes of his teacher, Jesus. This intimacy between teacher and disciple allows us to apply the findings of communication accommodation theory[35] to the relationship. The intimacy of the relationship between the Beloved Disciple and Jesus makes it somewhat difficult to find parallel relationships in the modern world for which we have CAT data. However, one group of studies presents itself: that of assessing communication accommodation between client and psychotherapist.[36] Lennard writes that "during therapy there is a growing similarity in verbal behavior between therapist and patient."[37] This is evident in various categories of expression used to describe the thoughts, feelings, and actions of clients in therapy. In one study, Meara et al.[38] studied the communicative accommodation of one client, Gloria, to three different types of therapy: client-centered, gestalt, and rational-emotive therapy. The sessions were compared for different

32. Bauckham, *Jesus and the Eyewitnesses*, 384.
33. Bauckham, *Jesus and* the *Eyewitnesses*, 393–96.
34. Bauckham, *Jesus and the Eyewtinesses*, 401.
35. Giles et al., "Accommodation Theory."
36. Lennard, "Some Aspects," 2:225.
37. Lennard, "Some Aspects," 2:225.
38. Meara et al., "Comparison of Stylistic Complexity."

categories of stylistic complexity: 1) the number of sentences, 2) average sentence length, 3) average block length, 4) average clause depth. It was found that the patient's stylistic pattern and complexity varied with the speech forms of the therapist. In a study by Ferrara, accommodation was observed at two levels: the syntactic and discourse level.[39] Syntactic accommodation was found in terms of various syntactic features but, most interestingly, also in terms of speech concertizing: extending another's thought in a syntactically and semantically similar manner. Accommodation at the discourse level is illustrated by the concept called "echoing." Here the therapist makes an interpretation and the client responds with an exact match, accommodating the therapist, matching his syntactic, semantic, and prosodic manner. This process is illustrated by the following exchange:

> T: You don't want to be one of his kids.
> C: I don't want to be one of his kids.[40]

According to Ferrara, "these echoings represent very important moments in therapy when the therapist has made an insightful interpretation of the client's experience that is so accurate that the client adopts the statement wholesale, accommodating speech to an exact match of the interlocutors semantic, syntactic, and prosodic features."[41] It perhaps goes without saying that the client adopts these speech forms over the long term, while engaged in therapy, certainly, but also after the termination of therapy, post-therapy, as central insights into their own and others' behavior.

If we follow the client-therapist model, it is quite possible, even likely, that John preserved Jesus's speech both at a syntactic and semantic level—that is to say, preserved not only the substance but the rhythm and style of Jesus's speech patterns. This in turn would suggest that Jesus did in fact talk of his preexistence with God and in particular utter the "I am" statements reported in John (and those reported in the Synoptics). It has been shown that the major concepts and key phrases of particular psychotherapeutic methods are retained by patients. This suggests that the classic "I am" assertions would have been retained by at least a number of Jesus's disciples. The "I am" phrases would have been particularly significant and would have been deeply processed in John's mind as statements central to Jesus's

39. Ferrara, "Accommodation in Therapy."

40. Ferrara, "Accommodation in Therapy," 214.

41. Ferrara, "Accommodation in Therapy," 214.

identity. CAT would also give credence to other sayings or concepts of Jesus reported by John, e.g., that he must die and would return.

Finally, I argue that it was primarily John that accommodated so deeply and extensively to Jesus's speech; this was not the case with Peter. The Beloved Disciple was considered a perceptive witness, as opposed to one chosen for active service.[42] He was considered by Jesus to have spiritual insight into the meaning of events. A special disciple entrusted to keeping the master's teaching alive was common in the ancient world.[43] All this makes the Beloved Disciple the primary candidate for accommodation. However, the New Testament assigns a different role to Peter. Peter was assigned the role of shepherding the church, the role of administering the affairs of the church. But the one whom Jesus loved, who would perpetuate the spiritual truths of Christ, was the Beloved Disciple.[44] Peter was able to organize the church but did not understand Jesus. Pollard has argued that the Synoptics reflect Peter's and the disciples' "dim understanding of Jesus." Speaking of the concept of the messiah, Pollard notes that "there was a vast difference between what Peter understood by the title and the meaning it had for Jesus Himself." John however, "sees the personality of Jesus as it really was."[45] Accommodation is a function of the individual characteristics of those involved in relationships. It has been shown that the intimacy of a relationship is a major factor in predicting successful accommodation.[46] The fact that Peter did not enjoy the special intimacy with Jesus that the beloved disciple did would predict a lesser degree of accommodation on the part of Peter than that of John.

Biblical Scholarship

The idea that the Johannine tradition closely reflects the words of Jesus is not without support in the biblical literature. Matthew Black, writing of the form and language of Jesus's teachings in John's Gospel, comments:

> An inspired targumizing of the Aramaic sayings tradition, early committed to a Greek form, is the most likely explanation of the

42. Bauckham, *Jesus and the Eyewitnesses*, 395.
43. Bauckham, *Jesus and the Eyewitnesses*, 401.
44. Bauckham, *Jesus and the Eyewitnesses*, 395–402.
45. T. E. Pollard, as quoted in Robinson, *Priority of John*, 362.
46. Giles et al., "Accommodation Theory," 43.

> Johannine speeches. . . . The Rabbinical character of the Johannine discourses and their predominantly poetic form do not discourage the belief that much more of the *ipsissima verba* may have been preserved in the Fourth Gospel—with John as the inspired "author"—than we have dared believe possible for many years.[47]

C. H. Dodd approaches the dating of the Johannine discourses from a different angle.[48] In the farewell discourses of Jesus with his disciples, Jesus talks much of his imminent taking leave from them but adds that he will see them again in the future (John 13:31—14:31). According to Dodd, the regulatory theme of these discourses was the theme of departure and return. The theme was stated in broad general terms. Jesus said they would see him again in a little while but was not specific. John 13 and 14 refer to Jesus's departure and return; later, Jesus spoke in visual terms, e.g., John 16:16: "A little while, and you will not see Me; and again a little while, and you will see Me."

Dodd notes that the Synoptics contained similar predictions embracing the theme of Jesus's leave-taking and return. These consist of the passion predictions and the coming Son of Man predictions (e.g., Mark 8:38; Matt 25:31; Luke 9:26). These predictions contain apocalyptic imagery and often refer to Christ's coming in glory with attending angels. Dodd suggests that Johannine language concerning Jesus's theme of departure and return is older than that of the Synoptics. In essence, he maintains that John's predictive verses of departure and return are older because they are of an ambiguous nature and simpler and less detailed. Dodd maintains that the broad ambiguous language of John "invited attempts to give them (the Johannine predictions) a more specific meaning."[49] However, it is not simply the amount of detail in the Synoptic parallels but the content of the elaborations that provides evidence of later provenance. These Synoptic elaborations incorporate Old Testament Scripture; e.g., the verses that speak of the Son of Man coming in clouds of glory with his holy angels (e.g., Mark 8:38) reminds us of the imagery of Dan 7:13. This incorporation of meta-memorial material is a common occurrence as information is transmitted over time from one person or community to another. Successive

47. M. Black, *Aramaic Approach*, 257–58.

48. Dodd, *Historical Tradition*, 413–20.

49. Dodd, *Historical Tradition*, 420.

retellings and especially successive conversations have been shown to cause the incorporation of cultural stereotypes into the transmission process.[50]

I might emphasize that Dodd is quite explicit in affirming that the Johannine language runs close to that of Jesus. He is not merely saying that the Johannine language is more ancient than that of the Synoptics:

> I suggest that John is here reaching back to a very early form of tradition indeed, and making it the point of departure for his profound theological interpretation; that the oracular sayings which he reports have good claim to represent authentically, in substance if not verbally, what Jesus actually said to his disciples—a better claim than the more elaborate and detailed predictions which the Synoptics offer.[51]

Robinson insists that John stands even closer to the source than Dodd suggested.[52] According to Robinson, Dodd always refers to an independent tradition predating the Synoptics, including Q, a tradition that reaches back to the source. Dodd denies John's literary dependence on the Synoptic Gospels but believes that he relied on another tradition to which he (John) stood in an external and secondhand relation.[53] Robinson, however, says there is no evidence that John stood outside this tradition and further that John "gives no impression of being dependent on a tradition emanating from source to which he stood in a second-hand relation."[54] Robinson says, more positively, that he agrees with P. H. Menoud that it is as if John is saying to us: "La tradition, c'est moi!"[55] Here Robinson is referring to the entire Johannine tradition, not merely the eschatological verses. For Robinson, as we shall see, this includes the "I am" statements, both the absolute ones and those with a predicate.

Hunter makes a similar argument for what he calls the three *hypsoun* sayings, John 3:14, 8:28, and 12:32:[56]

> "Just as Moses lifted up the serpent in the wilderness, so the Son of Man must be lifted up." (John 3:14)

50. Bartlett, *Remembering*, 84–94; Lyons and Kashima, "How Are Stereotypes Maintained"; Kashima, "Maintaining Cultural Stereotypes."

51. Dodd, *Historical Tradition*, 420.

52. Robinson, *Priority of John*, 12–18.

53. Robinson, *Priority of John*, 13.

54. Robinson, *Priority of John*, 13.

55. Robinson, *Priority of John*, 14.

56. Hunter, *According to John*, 92.

> "When you have lifted up the Son of Man, then you will know that I am He." (John 8:28)
>
> "And I, when I am lifted up from the earth, will draw all men to Myself." (John 12:32)

Hunter notes that three Johannine verses all state that the Son of Man, Jesus, must be "lifted up." Hunter argues that these sayings run very close to the source in that it is in Aramaic (not Greek) that the double entendre *crucify* and *raise up* first emerges.[57]

These verses correspond to the three Synoptic predictions of the passion (Mark 8:31, 9:31, and 10:32ff). Hunter contends that since they are less detailed than the Synoptic verses, they are "conceivably more ancient than they."[58]

I agree in part. However, it is not merely that they are less detailed. The Synoptic verses indicate that the Son of Man must suffer,and be raised up on the third day. One states that the Son of Man will be mocked, scourged, and spit upon (Mark 10:34); another that he will be betrayed (Mark 9:31); and finally, that he will be "rejected by the elders and chief priests and scribes" (Mark 8:31). Clearly, these verses have incorporated historical events, events that likely did occur before the predictions. Bartlett has shown that historical events that are not part of the original story can and likely will be incorporated into the story as it is transmitted through a community and retold many times.[59]

In conclusion, it appears that statement validity analysis and communication accommodation theory provide empirical support for the concept that the author of John is an eyewitness to events in Jesus's life and that he attempts to report Jesus's actual words, phrases, and actions. These findings from cognitive and social psychology are in accord with the suggestion reached by a number of biblical scholars that the Johannine sayings run back to early tradition. However, we should not lose sight of the fact that it is the hypothesis of manic-depressive illness that best explains the high christological assertions of Jesus. This hypothesis fits my assertion that it is the historical Jesus who is responsible for the sayings of the Johannine Christ. Manic-depressive patients often report intimacy and identity with

57. Hunter, *According to John*, 92.

58. Hunter, *According to John*, 92.

59. Bartlett, *Remembering*, 84–89.

God and, in addition, report behavioral features that fit other facets of Jesus's behavior.

Historical Issues Arising from John

I have provided evidence primarily from cognitive psychology that the sayings of Jesus in John were not fictional constructions of the evangelist but, rather, may well run close to the actual words of Jesus. Still, even assuming that these are Jesus's words, several major substantive issues plague the Gospel of John.

Christology

The first issue concerns the question of Jesus's identity and more specifically the nature of his divinity. Even accepting that Jesus's sayings and discourses were credibly reported by John, there are different perspectives concerning the divine status of Jesus as expressed in those verses. Perhaps the most important group of sayings in this regard are the "I am" verses of John. Still, even here, disagreement abounds. Many scholars take the view that the "I am" statements are indicative that Jesus is a kind of agent or representative of God. For instance, Kysar thinks that these assertions imply that Jesus is the "functional equivalent" of God on earth.[60] Robinson has a similar perspective. He suggests that the "I am" statements refer to the "I" of Western mysticism, indicative of a oneness with God but not an identity with God:

> Jesus is a man who incarnates in everything he is and does the Logos who is God. The "I" of Jesus speaks God, acts God. He utters the things of God, he does the works of God . . . . He speaks and acts with the "I" that is one with God utterly identified yet not identical, his representative, not his replacement.[61]

Robinson does not think that John portrays Jesus as a divine person equal to God. The Jesus of John is not God; nor is the Jesus of John a preexistent person. For Robinson, the Word is the self-revelation of God. The Word became a person in Jesus. Robinson takes pains to emphasize that the Johannine Jesus was not a preexistent person. As Robinson says, "Just because the

60. Kysar, *John*, 60.

61. Robinson, *Priority of John*, 393.

'Logos' came into existence or expression as a person does not mean that it was a person before."[62]

One of the more provocative and interesting interpretations of the Christology expressed in John is that of James Dunn. For Dunn, the Johannine Jesus was a divine person existent before the world was made.

> Now at last we have the thought of Jesus as Son of God not merely from his resurrection or from the beginning of his ministry or from the beginning of his life but from eternity, and of the Logos-Son no longer as the impersonal, even if personified, utterance of God but as the Son of God conscious of his existence with the Father before the world was made. Here indeed in a clear and emphatic way we have a conception of personal pre-existence.[63]

According to Dunn, in asserting the heavenly origin of Jesus from the beginning of time, John's emphasis on the preexistence of Jesus is a concept far beyond the agent or *shaliach* model. For Dunn, Jesus is presented in John as the Messiah, the Son of God and the Son of Man combined. These titles all stem from the identification of Jesus with the incarnate Wisdom/Logos. According to Dunn, for John, the confession that Jesus is the Messiah is to confess "that He is God in His self-revelation." Dunn thinks that John's view of Christ should be interpreted through the prologue, which identifies Jesus as the incarnate Logos, the Logos/Son. Although Dunn asserts that John's Jesus was preexistent and a person, still he is not identifying him with God in his entirety.[64]

Richard Bauckham takes still a different stance. He maintains that the absolute "I am" statements of Jesus are indicative of a complete, unconditional identification with God. Bauckham makes it clear that Jesus did not use the absolute "I am" statements as an agent of God, but rather that they reflected his self-perception, a perception of identity with God. To quote Bauckham:

> The "I am he" declarations are among the most emphatically monotheistic assertions of the Hebrew Bible and if Jesus in the Fourth Gospel repeats them, he is unambiguously identifying himself as the one and only God, YHWH, The God of Israel. It

62. Robinson, *Priority of John*, 380.

63. Dunn, *Christology in the Making*, 258.

64. Dunn, "Let John Be John," 315.

> does not do justice to these sayings to see them, as some scholars do, merely as an expression of an agent or emissary.[65]

Later, Bauckham notes:

> There is no doubt that it is an important aspect of the understanding of Jesus in John that in this sense he does act as God's emissary. . . . As God's agent he has full powers to act for God. . . . But when these ideas are put in their wider context of the Fourth Gospel including the absolute "I am" statements it is clear that it is not sufficient to suppose that God sends *someone else* to act as his agent in salvation.[66]

Most provocative is this disparity between the interpretations of Robinson and Bauckham regarding the person of Jesus as portrayed in John. The obvious question is: what did Jesus himself think? Did Jesus consider himself as an agent of God or as God? I ask this because the bulk of scholarship today views the Gospel of John as the theological construction of its author. Here the literature on manic depression helps. Custance's exposition of his manic thoughts are immensely valuable. Custance insists that he felt as if he were God, but then in a relatively mild hypomanic state he considers such thought analysis blasphemy.[67] Could it not have been the same with Jesus? Could not the seeming contradictions in John regarding the relationship of Jesus to God, i.e., regarding the level of Christ's divine nature, have originated with Jesus? A manic-depressive Jesus.

John's Jesus clearly uttered "I am" statements, both those with a predicate and the absolute statements. But he also uttered many other types of statements. He talked in several contexts other than those during which he uttered the absolute "I am" statements, as if he were God incarnate. However, in many other instances, he spoke as God's agent. For instance, in John 10:30, he asserts he is "one with the Father." But, as Robertson notes, he also uttered many statements indicating that he was only an agent of God. Robertson lists a number of these. A good example is John 8:28: "I can do nothing on my own authority, but in all that I say I have been taught by my Father."[68]

65. Bauckham, *Testimony of Beloved Disciple*, 247.

66. Bauckham, *Testimony of Beloved Disciple*, 247–48.

67. Custance, "Universe of Bliss," 54.

68. Robinson, *Priority of John*, 369

In the manic state, Jesus likely felt that he was God. But it seems reasonable that when burdened with the feeling that he was God, he would search Scripture to find and take on a role that would satisfy his feeling that he was a divine being but without committing blasphemy. In my view, Jesus probably questioned his identity from an early date, i.e., from the first onset of a manic episode. The grandiose feelings of mania propelled Jesus into a desperate search for identity. Jesus assumes the role and title of different heavenly beings not as a normal human being intentionally playing particular roles[69] but with the intensity of sensation and feeling experienced by persons in a hypomanic/manic state.

It is interesting that many biblical scholars consider the titles afforded Jesus in John are the creations of the evangelist. Kysar lists a number of titles or roles but writes as if John invented them and applied them to Jesus in order to flesh out his own theological constructs concerning the divine nature of Jesus.[70] The titles attributed to Jesus in John are many: "Lamb of God," various titles of messiahship, "Messiah," "him about whom Moses and the prophets wrote," the "Chosen One," "King of Israel," "Son of God," and "Son of Man." There are other roles ascribed to Jesus in the Fourth Gospel. One important title of the Johannine Jesus is that of the "Good Shepherd." This may have been an even more defining role for Jesus than the Son of Man. I do not dispute that John may have used the titles to describe the divine character of Christ, but I think that Jesus got there first. He probably reflected on these many identities as defining his status in conversations with his disciples even before his last journey to Jerusalem. Jesus may well have accepted any or all of these at different times as descriptive of his identity.

We gain insight into Jesus's personality by referencing the poets considered manic-depressive by Jamison. These artists described themselves as housing many different selves.[71] Jamison describes Byron as a person of constantly shifting personalities, "a veritable city of selves." Keats observes that "the poetical character has no self—it is everything and nothing—It has no character. . . . It has as much delight in conceiving Iago as Imogen."[72] Custance writes, "I am in a sense identical with all spirits, from God to Satan."[73] Boison reports that one of his patients, Albert, identified at times

69. Van Os, *Psychological Analyses*, 174–75.

70. Kysar, *John*, 46–51.

71. Jamison, *Touched with Fire*, 151.

72. Jamison, *Touched with Fire*, 152.

73. Custance, "Universe of Bliss," 53.

as Jesus, St. Augustine, and the Christian martyrs;[74] at other times, as Judas or Jonah. These differing identifications with famous characters are not uncommon among manic-depressive patients. However, as Jamison puts it, "this does not mean that artists are delusional in the psychotic sense, although psychotic episodes with delusions do occur in Bipolar I disorders."[75] It must be emphasized that in manic depression, there is never a loss of memory from one role to another, as in the identity disorders.[76] The dissociative identity disorder (DID) patient experiences a "marked discontinuity in the sense of self." The second defining feature of DID is recurrent dissociative amnesia. There is a complete absence of memory for the alternate personalities in DID, but this is not the case in manic depression.[77]

The changes in personality in manic depression have quite often led to misdiagnoses. Identity disorders are often misdiagnosed as manic-depressive disorders.[78] But the personality and mood changes of manic depression are slower than those of DID. Most importantly, in DID, the alternate personas take over the person. This is not the case with manic depression.[79] The manic-depressive poet or artist is able to enter into characters, to understand and feel their identities, on the order of an experienced actor. As Jamison writes: while in a depressive state, "you experience how it must be to be old, to be old and sick, to be dying; to be slow of mind."[80] But the person suffering from the depressive or manic episode is never lost in the part. Custance states that "never in the midst of the wildest flights of grandiose ideas" has he allowed himself to forget that he is a "very ordinary man."[81]

In the ancient Jewish culture, the ideas behind the term Son of Man might have provided Jesus with a grounding, human identity, an identity that allowed him to realize his mortal status while experiencing at the same time a divine identity. The term Son of Man had two referents: one a divine person as described in Dan 7:13 but also a mortal human being as referenced by Ezekiel. This double meaning would have appealed to a Jesus, a poet and one given to double entendre, and would have allowed him to

74. Boison, *Exploration of Inner World*, 48.
75. Jamison, *Touched with Fire*, 52.
76. Barlow and Durand, *Abnormal Psychology*, 200–204.
77. APA, *Diagnostic and Statistical Manual*, 292–98.
78. APA, *Diagnostic and Statistical Manual*, 296.
79. Custance, "Universe of Bliss," 53–54.
80. Jamison, *Touched with Fire*, 24.
81. Custance, "Universe of Bliss," 54.

think of himself as a heavenly being but still prevent him from being overtaken by the heavenly aspect and losing his earthly persona.

I should note, however, that Jesus may not have completely resolved the identity issue; it is quite conceivable that, in his mind, he was both God and one of God's agents. This would be an example of combinatory thinking prevalent in mania.[82] He may have played the role of, and entered into the character of, the figure in Daniel, the Son of Man, the Messiah, the Son of God, Wisdom/Logos. Still, in all this, Jesus never seems to lose the idea that he is God. These feelings of identity with God come out in his manic episodes: the absolute "I am" statements are the expressions of his feeling that he is indeed *God simpliciter.*

It is Zechariah who may provide the key to much of Jesus's thinking as outlined in John, especially in the farewell discourses. The identity of the Good Shepherd provides the overall idea of an incarnate god who is stricken but returns to save his people (Zech 12:8ff). This is the theme of departure and return discussed by Dodd as providing the schema for the more specific elaborations of the Synoptics, the passion, or the parousia. Recall that at times Jesus actually feels as if he is both God and his Representative on earth. The book of Zechariah provides an especially vivid, graphic portrayal of a wounded God (the Lord) who returns to save his people. In Zech 12:8–10, it appears that God himself is pierced. God is wounded, but he is a wounded God who is also a man. In Zech 13:7, the Lord calls for a sword to strike against "My Shepherd . . . the Man who is My Companion. . . . Strike the Shepherd, and the sheep will be scattered." Jesus might have felt he was God or his companion and, realizing that he was a man, might well have thought that it was he who must be pierced. This could easily have transformed into the idea that he must court crucifixion. Further, Zech 14:9, which states that the Lord will ultimately triumph and "shall be King over the whole earth," may have provided Jesus with the basis for his assertions that the kingdom was imminent. The theme of dying and returning in Zechariah might well have provided Jesus with the hope that he would be vindicated after death. Finally, these ideas could well have been linked by Jesus with the ideas expressed in Isa 53. Thus, Jesus might well have decided that he would have to also assume the role of Isaiah's suffering servant (Isa 53), wounded for our transgressions.

Thus, the disparity between the interpretations of John by Bauckham and Robinson likely began with Jesus himself. It is not the author of John

82. Jamison, *Touched with Fire*, 128.

who for theological reasons assigns various personas and titles to Jesus.[83] It is Jesus who is the creative explorer of heaven, always within the bounds of Jewish Scripture. It is my hypothesis to the effect that Jesus was a great poet who suffered from the changeable moods and thought forms of manic depression. This allows us to say that Jesus did think of himself as God, the "I am" incarnate, and God's representative on earth. What of John the Evangelist? John, being privy to what were certainly many conversations about the identity of Jesus, absorbs these various possible arguments. John tries to express Jesus's christological identities by grounding them in Jesus's life situations as he remembers them.

Eschatology

A particularly vexing set of verses in the Gospel of John concerns the timing of Jesus's salvation. The eschatological verses are basically twofold: those that speak of "inaugurated eschatology" and those that speak of a future coming of the Lord.[84] John 5:25 combines present and future into one verse. It is particularly graphic: "Most assuredly, I say to you, the hour is coming, and now is, when the dead will hear the voice of the Son of God; and those who hear will live." This verse is perplexing until we recall that the reconciliation of opposites is a common characteristic of the manic state.[85] John contains many such contradictions. Kysar refers to John as one who loves paradox.[86] But John may only appear to love paradox; in fact, it is Jesus who does. Time and distance are two of the most common contradictory concepts expressed in manic states. For instance, Custance recalled that a particularly graphic hallucination appeared both infinitely far and infinitely close at the same time.[87] These space-time contradictions occur often in John, as they also do in the hypomania of manic thought processes. A classic time paradox is that concerning the resurrection of Lazarus. Martha says that she knows that Lazarus will be resurrected at the end of time; Jesus replies that he is the resurrection and the life (John 11:25). The future is in the future, and the future is now for Jesus. This is a common type of perceptual processing in a manic state. In my view, John

83. Kysar, *John*, 122.

84. Robinson, *Priority of John*, 340.

85. Jamison, *Touched with Fire*, 128.

86. Kysar, *John*, 55.

87. Custance, "Universe of Bliss," 50.

has accurately observed and recorded Jesus's mental processes, Jesus's poetic, often combinatory, flow of thought. Attributing a brilliant but normal mind, i.e., a normal way of thinking to Jesus, has left biblical scholars with great, even unsolvable, difficulties in understanding the Gospel of John. The presence of both futuristic and presentist eschatology in the same Gospel has led some to the conclusion that the evangelist himself put forth a presentist eschatology, and a later conservative redactor or redactors added the futuristic verses. Kysar has speculated that there may have been several such redactors.[88] Kysar also presents a different solution, one he refers to as dialectical eschatology. The author of John has presented both a present and future eschatology. That is, for John, the truth "is found in a dynamic interchange" between the presentist and futurist views. This comes down to accepting both views as true. God has already fulfilled some of his promises, but he has yet to complete them in their entirety.[89] However, such solutions sound overly complex. A poet such as Jesus with a fast and adroit mind in a hypomanic state would have no trouble holding both views, not as separate aspects of a now-and-not-yet eschatology but as a single concept outside of time. This is the mystic/manic poetic form of thought. This type of mental process may not appeal to the scientific/academic way of thinking, but it may come closer to Jesus's way of thinking than the more rational way. For Jesus, heaven is both now and in the future. This is not merely a foretaste of heaven.

The book of John presents a picture of reality much like that presented in Coleridge's poem, *The Rime of the Ancient Mariner*. Recall that Coleridge is considered manic-depressive by Jamison.[90] Reading the poem, one does not know whether the story told by the *Ancient Mariner* speaks of this world or a mythical one. The poem merges the two worlds. Jamison writes of Coleridge: "His thinking had an expansive and mystical quality associated with hypomanic and creative thought patterns."[91] These same qualities are present in the Gospel of John. In this world, this creative and poetic world, the normally contradictory concepts of near and far, now and future, life and death, are not oppositional. This is the combinatory thinking of hypomania when coupled with the poetic genius of a brilliant mind.[92] This is

88. Kysar, *John*, 122.

89. Kysar, *John*, 125.

90. Jamison, *Touched with Fire*, 219–24.

91. Jamison, *Touched with Fire*, 220.

92. Jamison, *Touched with Fire*, 107.

the divergent thinking suggested by Guilford: verbal and ideational fluency, including the ability to make broad associations and the ability to quickly switch from category to category.[93] Andreasen and Powers found that both "writers and manics tend to sort in large groups, change dimensions while in the process of sorting, arbitrarily change starting points, or use vague distantly related concepts as categorizing principles."[94] This should not be confused with schizophrenic processing. Andreasen and Powers included schizophrenics in their study but found that the thought patterns of schizophrenics did not show patterns similar to manic patients. In my view, this hypomanic and poetic mysticism and creativity displayed in Jesus's discourses is the thought-world of Jesus. John captures it, likely only in part but beautifully. Granted, the cognitive mechanism is that described by CAT, but this is the accommodation of a mind particularly attuned to Jesus.

The otherworldly style of Johannine discourses is not lost on biblical scholarship. Black writes of the sublime and evocative style of Jesus's speech in the recent provocative article subtitled "The Grandeur of Johannine Rhetoric." Black writes that the farewell discourses exhibit a style that Greek and Roman orators of the imperial period referred to as a "grand style." This grand style exhibits many concrete rhetorical features and, in addition, several major overriding features of a more general nature, the most important of which is the evocation of a sense of the divine. Black writes that the sublimity exhibited by Jesus in John contains "mysterious depths to be plumbed, reverberations of a dialogue between heaven and earth."[95] The sublime nature of Jesus's discourse is that of one who "even on earth is in heaven."[96] Black writes that Jesus does not just talk of or preach about God. The grand character of Jesus's rhetoric is "not merely that he orates of heaven and earth; he actually bestrides them."[97] The transcendent and ethereal quality of Jesus's speech in the farewell discourses does comport well with "the expansiveness and the often mystical quality associated with hypomanic and creative thought" of the manic-depressive artists discussed by Jamison.[98] Black began his article by inviting the reader to ponder the report of the temple police in John 7:46: "Never has anyone spoken like

93. Guilford, "Creativity."

94. Andreason and Powers, "Creativity and Psychosis," 72.

95. C. Black, "Words That You Gave," 228.

96. C. Black, "Words That You Gave," 229.

97. C. Black, "Words That You Gave," 229.

98. Jamison, *Touched with Fire*, 107.

this."[99] To me, this Johannine rhetoric was, in the main, Jesus's. As discussed earlier in this chapter, I think that much of the style and content of the Johannine sayings and discourses are in fact Jesus's. Certainly, John recalled Jesus through his own cognitive schemata, but not far behind that lies the grand, poetic thought and style of Christ.

In the Synoptics, the more commonplace logic prevails. Over time, Christ will return. This is not the thinking of the manic/mystic. The Synoptics have, for the most part, neutered the sublimity of Jesus's speech.

99. C. Black, "Words That You Gave," 220.

9

The Synoptic Gospels *and* Distributed Memory

Strauss envisioned a lengthy process of oral transmission for the Synoptics. This meant a slow accumulation of tradition, the specifics of which were based on Old Testament interpretations.[1] The form critics adopted this idea with some elaboration. For the form critics, transmission was conveyed by anonymous witnesses. The community invented scenarios and added a good deal to the original or earlier tradition in accordance with community needs. A modern update to Strauss and the form critics is the work of the Jesus Seminar, which considers oral tradition to be unreliable for the same reasons as those discussed by Strauss.[2] Nineham, a proponent of form criticism, notes that the Synoptic Gospels themselves provide evidence of long periods of oral transmission from one person or group to another. That is, the stories of Jesus are broad, stereotyped forms made so by community need.[3]

An opposing view has been put forth by Bauckham who argues that the fragments of Papias (an apostolic father, c. AD 60–130) available to us indicate that the early disciples of Jesus placed their highest confidence in known and named eyewitnesses.[4] In addition, in one of the fragments,

1. Strauss, *Life of Jesus*, 52–56; Schweitzer, *Quest of Historical Jesus*, 36.
2. Funk, *Acts of Jesus*, 2–8.
3. Nineham, "Eye-Witness Testimony, III."
4. Bauckham, *Jesus and the Eyewitnesses*, 21–38.

Papias writes that Mark acted as Peter's interpreter and wrote down many of the stories of Jesus as told to him by Peter.[5] There are two problems here. It is not clear whether Mark wrote down Peter's memories immediately, as Bauckham suggests, or at various times when circumstances allowed, perhaps even after Peter's death.[6] In addition, some scholars consider Papias to be an unreliable source. Neiderwimmer suggests that the claim that Peter was the source of the contents in Mark is inconsistent with the arguments of the form critics.[7] Regardless of these issues, it appears that the writings of Papias played an important role in shaping Bauckham's focus on eyewitness testimony. Depending in part on the Papias fragments, Bauckham suggests that it is a "genuine possibility that many Gospel pericopes owe their main features not to anonymous community formation but to their formulation by the eyewitnesses from whom they derive."[8] Bauckham, following Brewer's near copy theory of memory,[9] asserts that eyewitness memory is relatively veridical and that the early tradents' eyewitness memories would have been accurate except for small details. Large variations were intentional.[10] Bird asserts that there would have been many of these tradents and that they would have traveled throughout Galilee and beyond, acting as authorities to correct any mistakes made by various local villages. Bird further argues that the communities would likely have corrected any distortions and been ready to question anyone whose remembrance differed from theirs.[11]

However, neither the model put forth by the form critics nor the eyewitness approach of Bauckham and others is the most appropriate model for assessing the early oral tradition underlying the Synoptic gospels. Rather, I adopt and apply Hirst's conversational model of collective memory.[12] It seems likely that early tradition was founded on conversations among the disciples concerning events both before and after the crucifixion. These conversations would have taken place throughout Jesus's career but also within days and a few weeks after Jesus's death, certainly earlier than more

5. Bauckham, *Jesus and the Eyewitnesses*, 202–10; Bird, *Gospel of the Lord*, 59.

6. Bauckham, *Jesus and the Eyewitnesses*, 202–10.

7. Neiderwimmer, *Orthodoxy*, 184–89; cf. Bauckham, *Jesus and the Eyewitnesses*, 239.

8. Bird, *Gospel of the Lord*, 60.

9. Brewer, "What Is Autobiographical Memory," 43.

10. Bauckham, *Jesus and the Eyewitnesses*, 86–87.

11. Bird, *Gospel of the Lord*, 63–66.

12. Hirst et al., "Of Sins and Virtues," 146.

formal preaching or group discussions in the vein of Bailey's evening community gatherings.[13] They would have argued about and discussed what Christ said, what he did, and what these events meant, according to Scripture. Some conversations would have taken place before Jesus's death and some after. On this informal basis, the early traditions were formed. It has been shown that conversations are particularly given to the generation of metamemory, memory that references extraneous concepts or events.[14] Jesus's disciples most likely debated and discussed the meaning of his life, and as they did, so recalled Jewish Scripture in hopes of understanding these events. Jesus and his followers lived in a world full of ideas. They argued about apocalyptic and messianic concepts as well as wisdom.[15] The conversations of the greatest import likely occurred in Jerusalem after Jesus's crucifixion, primarily among members of two groups, the Galilean disciples and the Johannine circle.[16] These traditions would have been solidified long before any formal preaching or performances by the tradents. This would have been before the formation of Christian communities and, therefore, before any of the more formal methods of transmitting tradition, e.g., the approach described by Kenneth Bailey.[17]

As we have seen, several conditions have been shown to promote collective memory according to Hirst 2012. Three are particularly important: 1. cultural schemata, 2. dominant individuals, and 3. the existence of a social situations amenable to transmission of information throughout a general network.[18]

Cultural schemata. In the first place, as we have seen, these schematic narrative templates, or cultural schemata, can and often do promote the formation of collective memory. Quoting Bartlett, "this persistent framework helps provide those 'schemata' . . . ," which are the basis for the "imaginative reconstruction called memory."[19] The cultural background of ancient Israel, the Common Judaism of Galilee, provided an all-pervasive cultural narrative during Jesus's time. It was this scriptural narrative to which Jesus's

13. Bailey, "Informal Controlled Oral Tradition"; Bailey, "Middle Eastern Oral Tradition."

14. Hyman, "Conversational Remembering."

15. Patterson, *God of Jesus*, 46.

16. Cullmann, *Johannine Circle*, 39–56.

17. Bailey, "Middle Eastern Oral Tradition."

18. Hirst and Echterhoff, "Remembering in Conversations."

19. Hirst et al., "Of Sins and Virtues," 146.

followers turned to make sense of the events of Jesus's life, especially his crucifixion and resurrection. It may be hard to understand the influence and importance of the Jewish Scripture in the lives of the Jewish people. The extraordinary attention to the Bible over the centuries was based on the conviction that "every event and prospective or possible event must inevitably and necessarily be seen as reflection of what was contained in the spiritual writings."[20] Thus, the writings of the Old Testament provided very powerful cultural narratives that served as suggestive mechanisms to create and influence memory. These interpretative schemata "all grew out of the conviction that the events on earth are determined by what happens in heaven."[21] These Old Testament narratives and scriptural ideas were part of the cultural scene in Jesus's time. Patterson suggests that the disciples had conversations and dialogue about many of the ideas prevalent in the culture at the time and even that Jesus may have been attracted to some of them. Wisdom ideas, apocalyptic ideas, ascending/descending redeemer—all were present in the spirit of the times.[22]

These biblical ideas would have provided powerfully suggestive concepts, which in turn would have shaped the content of the disciples' recall. These Old Testament schemata could easily and quite reasonably be compared to the suggestive interviews given to participants in classical false memory experiments of cognitive psychology.[23] The suggestiveness of the Old Testament cultural schemata may be compared to that of the supposed indicators of child abuse discussed in various books and articles published during the "memory wars" of the 1980s.[24]

Dominant narrator. As we have seen, conversations are often led by a dominant narrator. This narrator may likely be an eyewitness to the event, but many factors determine who will dominate a conversation. If there is a dominant narrator, he will tend to contribute most of the unshared preconversational ideas to the group memory.[25]

According to many biblical scholars, Peter was among the more important disciples. Martin Hengel has written that Peter may have been the

20. Grant, *Jesus*, 18.

21. Grant, *Jesus*, 18.

22. Patterson, *God of Jesus*, 144–46.

23. Hyman and Billings, "False Memories"; Loftus and Ketchem, *Myth of Repressed Memory*; Schacter, *Searching for Memory*, 248–80.

24. Schacter, *Seven Sins of Memory*, 248–80.

25. Cuc et al, "Silence Is Not Golden."

single most influential person in terms of preserving and managing the Jesus movement shortly after Jesus's death. Hengel has argued that Peter was a dominant figure in the development of the Synoptics.[26] Peter played a decisive role in the development of the earliest kerygma, the apostolic preaching that Jesus is the Christ. Hengel's assertion is based on his reading and analysis of the Synoptic gospels and Acts.[27] Thus, in this vein of thought, Peter may be considered a dominant personality, whose presence was likely the overshadowing presence in the early conversational network. It is clear that Peter would have filled the shoes of the dominant person called for by Cuc et al. to promote the formation of collective memory and was the person who most likely shaped the conversational narrative of at least one large subdivision of followers, the Twelve, the Galilean group.[28]

General network. Bauckham has suggested that the Gospels were not written for individual communities but for all Christians of any community. Bauckham points out that early Christianity was not made up of isolated groups but consisted of a "network of communities with constant, close communication among themselves."[29] These early communities were spread across Palestine and into the entire Mediterranean. These communities then formed the basis of a general network of the type envisaged by Hirst, wherein secondary and later witnesses could communicate with original ones.

Overall, we see that all three of the cultural conditions that enhance the likelihood of forming collective memories, according to Hirst and colleagues—i.e., the existence of cultural schemata, a dominant narrator, and a general network—were in place in Jesus's time.

Individual Memory and Serial Retelling

First, it should be noted that Hirst's approach provides a structure that increases the likelihood that eyewitnesses' input will be used in shaping collective memory. It is the eyewitness who will probably dominate initial tellings and retellings of particular events. This would support Bauckham's views that the Gospels run close to source. However, Hirst's approach very much assumes that individual memory is subject to considerable distortion

26. Hengel, *Saint Peter*, 28–36.

27. Hengel, *Saint Peter*, 88.

28. Schröter, "Gospels as Eyewitness Testimony," 201; Cullmann, *Johannine Circle*, 93.

29. Bauckham, *Jesus and the Eyewitnesses*, 30.

over time via the so-called "sins of memory."[30] Furthermore, as we have seen, cognitive psychology does not support Brewer's copy theory of recollective theory, the theory referenced by Bauckham in support of his view that eyewitness memory is accurate.[31] Modern experimental psychology supports the idea that individual memory is not only subject to various sins—i.e., schematic processing with its corollary social contagion and RIF—but, more importantly, generally unconscious motivational, emotional processes.[32]

In addition, the experimental evidence indicates that when these processes operate over a succession of retellings, their effects cumulate with the number of retellings. Coman and Hirst showed that both practice effects and RIF effects cumulate as information is conveyed from one person to another in a serial retelling process.[33] In a later set of experiments, Yamashiro and Hirst investigated the influence of a prominent person, e.g., a politician or a journalist, on the public's recall of events.[34] Could such a person, referred to as a "Central Speaker" by the authors, produce a selective rendition of an event such that the public memory would be altered? It was found a central speaker could induce practice effects and RIF effects in listeners and, most importantly, that the RIF effect accumulated as the information was conveyed though a general or closed loop network. This meant that prominent people could indeed distort group memories through biased renditions of observed events and that subsequent conversations served to increase the percentage of people who remembered the story in a distorted fashion. In still another experiment, Meade and Roediger showed that the degree of distortion in a story increases with the number of retelling exchanges over time.[35] The memories of original witnesses do change with the number of retellings, even when the retellings are repeated by the same person.[36]

But perhaps the most important effect of sequential retelling is the continuous removal of atypical features and increased use of cultural

30. Hirst et al., "Of Sins and Virtues"; Schacter, *Searching for Memory*, 182–203.

31. Conway, "Memory and the Self"; Conway and Jobson, "On the Nature."

32. Conway, "Memory and the Self."

33. Coman and Hirst, "Cognition through Social Network."

34. Yamashiro and Hirst, "Convergence on Collective Memories," 475–77.

35. Meade and Roediger, "Explorations in Social Contagion," 1003–8.

36. Bartlett, *Remembering*, ch. 5; Meade and Roediger, "Explorations in Social Contagion."

stereotypes when stories are told and retold. This effect, discussed in chapter 5, is well known in the cognitive literature.[37] The effect is the same, whether the retellings are by the same or different people. The atypical is slowly removed and the typical added over time. Rubin cites the transmission of the "Ballad of Poor Pearl" over several years. The ballad tells the story of a young girl who was murdered and decapitated. The murder took place in 1896. Two men were involved in the murder. One was Pearl's cousin. Both of the men were convicted and hanged. They were hanged on the same gallows. However, according to Rubin, the pattern of the murdered girl genre involves only one murderer, her only lover. The body of the girl is simply abandoned, not mutilated. Cohen traced the evolution of the "Ballad of Poor Pearl" over the years. The changes did not all occur during any one time period. For instance, the girl was found headless in 49% of the ballad's variants prior to 1928, 28% prior to 1938, and none later than 1938. By 1938, all of the unique events had been removed from the ballad. The girl's body was not mutilated; there was only one murderer, not Pearl's cousin; and, of course, no double hanging.[38]

It is important to note that these observed effects are based on both linear chains of transmission and general networks. However, in a general network, information cycles back through the network, even to the first person. Thus, as the information is distorted and moves to a stereotypic format, it is recycled again to earlier people. This increases the likelihood that the considerable changes that occur in the later individuals will be recycled to those in the earlier regions of the network. In other words, the final stereotypes will likely be recycled to everyone and every community in the network. What is added in the transmission process and what is forgotten through RIF as the information is transmitted to later people or groups will be recycled to *all* in the network. Thus, a general network invites much more group cohesion than does a simple linear chain.[39]

Dennis Nineham, a well-known biblical scholar, has argued that it is the overly general, stereotypical form of the Synoptic texts themselves,[40] especially when combined with other factors, e.g., the many contradictions

37. Bartlett, *Remembering*, 93; Lyons and Kashima, "How Are Stereotypes Maintained."

38. Cohen (1973), as cited in Rubin, *Memory in Oral Traditions*, 280–82.

39. Hirst et al., "Of Sins and Virtues."

40. Kelber, *Oral and Written Gospel*, 44–51; Nineham, "Eye-Witness Testimony," I, II, and III.

and inconsistencies among the Gospels,[41] that makes the initial case against the Synoptics. Nineham argues that these factors indicate that the Synoptics are the product of successive oral retellings, retellings by one or many persons, over a lengthy time period. Cognitive psychology supports Nineham's assertion here. Empirical and experimental findings from cognitive psychology, particularly those of Kashima, Bartlett, and Rubin, demonstrate that successive retellings result in highly stereotypical forms. The process of adding typical cultural features and removing atypical ones continues with successive retellings. These empirical and experimental findings provide strong support for Nineham's assertion that the Synoptics are the result of a lengthy series of retellings.

An issue that produces some degree of confusion in the field concerns Rubin's observation that the changes observed in the psychology lab are often at odds with reality. This may be, once the atypical has been removed from the oral tradition. Before the subject of oral transmission reaches its generic form, even major unique features of events are very much subject to alteration or deletion from the story. The transmission of the "Ballad of Poor Pearl," as discussed by Rubin, offers a dramatic case in point.

Bauckham argues that general stereotypical schemata set in early, soon after witnessing events.[42] Thus, he argues that it need not take years to form generalities or more stories or events into more stereotypical forms. Bauckham's argument that schemata come into play early, soon after an event is witnessed, and that consequently the appearance of stereotypes in the Gospels need not be indicative of lengthy series retellings over many years, is faulty. Schemata do operate within seconds after an event occurs, but the process is a matter of degree. Not all unique detail is lost immediately; in fact, first-order witnesses are often quite detailed in their presentations, as are the eyewitness reports, as noted by the Swedish researchers.[43] But distortions increase dramatically with the number of retellings. Thus, I must agree with that group of scholars which maintains that the Synoptic Gospels are the result of a lengthy period of retellings.

41. Blomberg, *Historical Reliability of Gospels*, 31–37.

42. Bauckham, *Jesus and the Eyewitnesses*, 349.

43. Steller and Köhnkon, "Criteria Based Statement Analysis"; Volbert and Steller, "Is This Testimony Truthful."

Variations on the Johannine Tradition

We have seen that the Synoptic texts offer evidence on their face that indicates that they are based on a lengthy series of retellings,[44] that cognitive psychology supports this assertion, and that those conversations and retellings were likely dominated, at least in the beginning, by Peter. With these ideas as background, we can discuss several major concepts reported in the Synoptics and John and examine how the Synoptic versions may have grown out of the Johannine tradition.

Divinity

Contrary to the portrait of Jesus portrayed in John, the Synoptics do not portray a Jesus who considers himself God. Witherington says it well: "Material in the Synoptics suggests that Jesus had a transcendent self-image amounting to more than a unique awareness of the Divine," but nevertheless, "Jesus did not think of Himself as the whole or exclusive representation of the Godhead."[45]

James Dunn has written extensively on Christology and offers a similar viewpoint. According to Dunn, in his book *Christology in the Making*, Christ's view of himself as expressed in the Synoptics takes many facets. Jesus likely viewed himself as the figure of Dan 7, the Son of Man. He viewed himself as the one who would suffer and die and "be vindicated beyond his anticipated suffering and death and play the decisive role in the final judgement." He was conscious of being the Son of God. He viewed himself as the eschatological prophet, who would "announce and enact the good news of God's final rule and intervention." He may have claimed to speak as "the final envoy of wisdom."[46] According to Michael Grant, Jesus considered one of the major purposes of his mission to be that of the suffering servant as expressed in Isa 53.[47] Granted, these concepts express transcendent beings. But these ideas do not portray Jesus as a preexistent being equal to God. Then why, if Jesus thought of himself as true God as expressed in John, is the Synoptic version so culturally stereotypical, so circumspect, and

44. Nineham, "Eye-Witness Testimony," I, II, and III.

45. Witherington, *Christology of Jesus*, 276.

46. Dunn, *Christology in the Making*, 253.

47. Grant, *Saint Peter*, 53–73.

comparatively deficient in casting an aura of divinity about Jesus? What is the mechanism?

We have established that, according to John, Jesus saw himself as God; he talked as if he were God. As Bauckham says, the absolute "I ams" are pure monotheistic statements, not assertions of an agent of God.[48] How then is it that the Synoptics portray Jesus as a lesser being? Although Jesus probably talked as portrayed in John, his Galilean followers recast his speech in a form like the militant apocalyptic language of the Synoptic Gospels. This effect would increase with the number of retellings. This would fit the common tradition so important in Galilee.[49] Galilean peasants were practitioners of Common Judaism. Common Judaism may be described in terms of its focus on God, the temple, election, and Torah (the Pentateuch). Torah was part of a larger group: the Scriptures, i.e., the Law and the Prophets.[50] Common Judaism was the Judaism of the villages and most likely of Jesus and Peter. The Synoptic materials were the result of conversations and constant retellings within the culture of the Galilean villages. It has been shown that retellings over time are subject to the suggestive forces of predominant cultural frames.[51] These retellings are subject to the so-called "sins of memory," especially that of chunking information into broad cultural schemata. The cultural schemata of ancient Israel focused on the Law and the Prophets, including, Isaiah, Daniel, and Zechariah. Thus, it should not be surprising that the cultural schemata of Common Judaism would overtake the atypical content, language, and style of Jesus as expressed in the Gospel of John.

In addition to an analysis in which the anonymous cultural processes operate to remove the atypical concepts and events from stories, a second level of analysis is used in Hirst's approach. Hirst and his colleagues' experiments make it clear that collective memory is in great part formed on the basis of the personalities of dominant individuals. That being said, it should be emphasized that individual memories vary with clinical needs.[52] In addition to the universal memory sins (e.g., cultural schemata, RIF, etc.) as mechanisms of distortion, individual psychological makeup becomes

48. Bauckham, *Jesus and the Eyewitnesses*, 405.

49. Dunn, *Jesus Remembered*, 280–97.

50. Dunn, *Jesus Remembered*, 280–97.

51. Lee et al., "Serial Reproduction of Conflict"; Lyons and Kashima, "How Are Stereotypes Maintained"; Kashima et al., "Maintenance of Cultural Stereotypes."

52. Conway, "Memory and the Self."

relevant. One's worldview, how one sees the world, in terms of general emotional schemata becomes relevant. As Bartlett says, memory is personal, i.e., it depends on an interplay of appetites, instincts, interests, and ideals of the individual.[53] Psychological needs play a major part in determining one's attitudes towards particular events and thus one's memory for the events. And in conversational memory, it is the personality of the person who dominates the conversational matrix that guides the emergent collective memory. The dominant person in the conversational milieu of the Synoptics was likely Peter. According to Hengel, much of Peter's theology and Christology was based on the theological framework put forth in Isaiah, especially that of the suffering servant, the lamb without blemish whose stripes atone for "the many" (Isa 53:12). Peter's speeches in Acts 3 and 4 attest to this.[54]

At first, Peter could not accept the idea that Jesus must suffer and die (Matt 16:21–22). When Jesus was alive, Peter saw Jesus as the Messiah, in Peter's mind, a great worldly warrior who would free Israel and rule with supernatural power and authority.[55] He seems to have viewed Jesus as Messiah, Son of God, and Son of Man, perhaps all of them combined. As Grant puts it, "one might hazard the guess that the devoted Peter . . . would not have refused him the titles of Messiah, Son of Man, and Son of God in their most extreme significances."[56] Peter had not understood that the man whom he thought the Messiah was to suffer and die. But later, after Jesus's death, it was the idea of the suffering servant that formed the basis of Peter's thinking about Jesus.[57]

What caused this change in Peter's view of Jesus? Peter's views about Jesus changed after Jesus's death. But it was not just the death of Jesus that initiated a major shift in Peter's outlook. It was likely the fact that Peter had denied Jesus that provided the overwhelming impetus for Peter to accept Jesus as the suffering servant of Isa 53. The one who died for the sins of many. The idea that Jesus was indeed Isaiah's suffering servant could well have been triggered and brought to the front of Peter's consciousness by Peter's overwhelming need for forgiveness from Jesus.

53. Bartlett, *Remembering*, 205–8.

54. Hengel, *Saint Peter*, 86–87.

55. Grant, *Saint Peter*, 80–81.

56. Grant, *Saint Peter*, 81.

57. Hengel, *Saint Peter*, 87.

But did Jesus ever indicate that he was the suffering servant? The key may lie in the well-known (and controversial) Mark 10:45: "For even the Son of Man did not come to be served, but to serve, and give His life as a ransom for many." Peter may have recalled Jesus as having said something close to the writing in Mark 10:45. It makes little difference whether that saying is veridical. Peter's need for a resolution to his denial of Jesus may well have generated this reconstruction of the past, in any case. These memory constructions are unconscious memory processes. The shaping of memory to maintain self-integrity has been amply demonstrated in the experimental literature.[58] And it could well have happened here. This is the mechanism by which Peter adopts the relevant Scripture or cultural frame to maintain a coherent life story. Christ's suffering was preordained; history was being played out as Isaiah had predicted. But it is also the same mechanism that produces the memory of Christ's assertion in Mark 10:45 that indeed he had come as to give his life as ransom for the sins of many—including Peter's.

Peter's guilt was removed; but he must now bring people to Jesus. This is the initiating event of the Petrine gospel, preached in Acts 3 and 4, that of the suffering servant.[59] Conway argues that the working self strives to preserve the original goals of the individual, but will adopt new goals when necessary to maintain self-integrity.[60] After Jesus's death, Peter adopts a new set of self-maintenance goals, as did so many of Conway's patients. His goal structure has changed. Instead of acting as the viceroy to a militant Messiah, Peter will preach the forgiveness of sins to those who accept Jesus. And in so doing, bring people to Jesus. After Jesus's death, Peter would recall Jesus's life and sayings in the light of Isa 53.

The RIF Processes of Peter

Peter's intense focus on Isa 53 was probably very compelling and all-encompassing. As such, it could easily have worked to exclude Jesus's assertions of divinity from memory. Even before Jesus's death, Peter, steeped in Common Judaism, may not have deeply processed the dark/light language or the sublime quality of Jesus's speech as expressed in the Gospel of John.

58. Conway, "Memory and the Self."

59. Hengel, *Saint Peter*, 87.

60. Conway, "Memory and the Self."

As I have noted, attentional processes depend on already existing, personal, general schemata. For Peter, these cultural schemata were the Law and the words of the Prophets. He may have found it difficult to accommodate to the style of Jesus and to Jesus's assertions of divinity. Certainly, Peter witnessed such statements but likely considered them Jesus's unexplainable occurrences, all the while keeping Jesus as the Messiah and the Son of God. But now, after the crucifixion, Peter's entire mental outlook was centered on Jesus as the suffering servant of Isaiah whose suffering and death were designed by God to bring sinners to Jesus. The assertions of divinity, the "I am" statements, were simply not part of the story.

When telling people about Jesus, even before but certainly after Jesus's death, these likely manic episodes of Jesus (probably manic periods), particularly the "I am" assertions, were not fully attended to. Then when Peter retold the stories, likely omitting assertions of identity with God, then indeed these assertions would have been inhibited (via the RIF process) and omitted from later retellings. That this was the underlying process is supported by the attention experiments presenting out-of-schema events that are simply not recalled after being presented on screen; the gorilla in the room was simply not recalled, even when questioned within a few seconds after its presentation.[61] Against so-called common sense, it is not the oddities that are deeply processed or recalled but those that fit within common schemata. The out-of-schema nature of the "I am" statements would lead to their attenuation. This diminution of processing would have increased the likelihood of omitting expressions of identity with God at later retellings. In addition, Peter might have intentionally left them out of later conversations as simply too eccentric or even blasphemous to repeat. Intentional or not, omissions of content trigger RIF processes.

Certainly, under cross examination or cued recall, Peter might have recalled Jesus's oddities. But this is not cued recall. The oral tradition here is based on serial retellings, without forensic restraints. And most importantly, after a while, the omitted events, in Peter's own retellings and those of other witnesses, would undergo the RIF processes (WI-RIF for Peter and SS-RIF for listeners). Even before Jesus's death, Peter may have viewed Jesus only as a militant messianic figure. Peter's cultural perspective did not focus on Jesus as a preexistent being equal to God. Peter's messianic view of Jesus as God's representative, whether the Son of Man or the Son of God or

61. Neisser and Becklen, "Selective Looking."

his cultural resonance with Common Judaism in general,[62] was sufficient to block accommodation to Jesus's words of divinity.

But it was primarily after Jesus's death that Peter's feelings of guilt became overwhelmingly intense and thus provided an unconscious mechanism for the working self[63] to focus on retrieving Christ as the suffering servant. Jesus's assertions of divinity as in the absolute "I am" statements were removed from recall. The function of Peter's memory was to justify his denial of Jesus as part of God's plan for Isaiah's suffering servant.

The deletion or diminution of high Christology from the Synoptics was not committed with "fraudulent intention," as Strauss would say,[64] or part of a well-thought-out deceptive plan. I assume this is storytelling as in the Marsh and Tversky study.[65] The participants in Marsh and Tversky did make major distortions, additions, exaggerations, and omissions, depending on the audience and their motives. At times, these distortions were intentional. These distortions still functioned as part of the truth of the matter—much like the workings of midrash in ancient Israel,[66] although the workings were unconscious. Further, these unconscious constructions occurred[67] because of the intensely suggestive forces of Jewish Scripture, forces somewhat akin to the forces that generated false memories of parental abuse in recent times.[68] In the end, the storyteller, Peter, probably thought that his stories were for the most part accurate.[69]

In sum, the social memory approach, which avoids assessing the influence of particular individuals, would be sufficient to account for the deletion of Jesus's assertions of preexistence as a divine person identical with God from the Synoptic record. That is to say, eventually the anonymous cultural frame would override the style of Jesus. But reference to the individual makeup of particular individuals—in this case, Peter—provides more specific outcome. Peter's lack of understanding of Jesus, i.e., blocking his claims of divinity, perhaps combined with an intense and compelling focus on Jesus as the suffering servant to the exclusion of all other

62. Dunn, *Jesus Remembered*, 293–97.

63. Conway, "Memory and the Self."

64. Strauss, *Life of Jesus*, 83.

65. Marsh and Tversky, *Spinning*, 491–503.

66. Goulder, *Midrash and Lection*, 34–46.

67. Conway, "Memory and the Self."

68. Schacter, *Searching for Memory*, ch. 9.

69. Marsh and Tversky, *Spinning*, 491–503.

constructs, prevented him from viewing Jesus as God and allowed the slow but inevitable RIF processes to remove the assertions of divinity by Jesus from the Synoptic tradition.

But why did John, the Beloved Disciple, accommodate to Jesus's thought and speech while Peter did not? The two men were clearly two different personalities. Peter was more adept at shepherding and managing the church, whereas John was the more poetic and, as Bauckham suggested, the one who was chosen to convey Jesus's teachings.[70] Remember Jesus chose John: John was the one whom Jesus loved. Jesus thought that John understood him. It is reasonable to suggest that John accommodated to Jesus. It is reasonable to think that Peter thought in terms of agency and then, after Jesus's death, the suffering servant of Isaiah. All this is consistent with Pollard's view that Peter simply did not understand Jesus: "The Synoptics give an accurate picture of this failure on the part of the disciples to understand the personality and words and deeds of Jesus."[71] But in the end, it is the intense guilt of Peter, held in check by the thought of Jesus as the suffering servant, that provides relief to Peter and guides his memory.

Style and Vocabulary

We have seen that much of the language of Jesus in John closely reflects the voice of Jesus, and according to Dodd and Robinson,[72] predates the more militant apocalyptic vocabulary of the Synoptics. Some verses in the Synoptics bear close resemblance in style to Johannine phraseology and language. These form a group of verses in the Synoptics, common in meaning to both John and the Synoptics, that do not reflect the Synoptic style but rather reflect the mystical, grand style evident in John.[73]

Most striking in the Synoptics is the so-called "bolt from the Johannine sky" recorded in Matt 11:27 and Luke 10:22:[74] "All things have been delivered to Me by My Father, and no one knows who the Son is except the Father, and who the Father is except the Son, and the one to whom the Son wills to reveal Him." According to Dodd, Matt 11:27 "can be traced to the period before the formation of the common source of Matthew and Luke

70. Bauckham, *Jesus and the Eyewitnesses*, 399–402.

71. Robinson, *Priority of John*, 362.

72. Dodd, *Historical Tradition*, 420; Robinson, *Priority of John*, 300–322.

73. C. Black, "Words That You Gave."

74. Robinson, *Priority of John*, 315.

(Q)."[75] Another verse, Mark 13:32, is as close or even closer to Johannine vocabulary and style:[76] "But of that day and hour no one knows, not even the angels in heaven, nor the Son, but only the Father."

These Johannine-like verses stem from a group of verses common to John and the Synoptics which, Dodd suggests, predate the Synoptics (including Q) and John.[77] Robinson lists a number of other examples: John 12:25; 13:20; 16:23ff.[78] Such verses are a blend of Synoptic and Johannine styles and, according to Dodd,[79] may point back to a very early tradition and, as such, may be quite close to the language and voice of Jesus.[80] Thus, the Synoptics would seem to contain two languages, one much older than the other.[81] This is a picture similar to the one observed in the later retellings of "The War of the Ghosts."[82] The original style of the folk tale "The War of the Ghosts" is primitive and folklike, but after many retellings, the story, for the most part, becomes literary and quite English in character, although still, at times, interlaced with the more primitive vocabulary.

The mixing of the more apocalyptic/militant sayings together with the Johannine-like ones in the Synoptic Gospels gives every indication of a slow process of supplanting the poetic sublimity of Jesus's speech with the more familiar stereotypic style and concepts observed in the Synoptic Gospels. All this is quite consistent with the findings of Bartlett and more recent work of Kashima.[83] In fact, my view is that we are seeing in the Synoptics a gradual transformation of Jesus's speech from his grand poetic style, recorded in John, to that of Galilean Common Judaism, expressed in the relatively learned Greek in Matthew and Luke. This is reminiscent of the transformation of "The War of the Ghosts" from folklike poetry to a much more English literary style, the latter incorporating features of current events in the retellings. For instance, part of Bartlett's study was carried out during WWII. Thus, a fight among several villagers as expressed in

75. Dodd, *Historical Tradition*, 420.

76. Robinson, *Priority of John*, 316.

77. Dodd, *Historical Tradition*, 420.

78. Robinson, *Priority of John*, 315.

79. Dodd, *Historical Tradition*, 335–65.

80. Robinson, *Priority of John*, 316.

81. Robinson, *Priority of John*, 313.

82. Bartlett, *Remembering*, 63–94.

83. Lee et al., "Serial Reproduction of Conflict"; Lyons and Kashima, "How Are Stereotypes Maintained"; Kashima et al., "Maintenance of Cultural Stereotypes."

"The War of the Ghosts" became, after numerous retellings, "a great strategic battle."[84] As noted above, Bartlett referred to this transformation of the poetic primitive style to the more literary English style as a shift to the "general communication habits of a community."[85] This is "the conventionalization of language,"[86] a process I suggest occurred during the formation of the Synoptic Gospels.

Higgins has argued that perhaps Jesus talked both ways, sometimes with an apocalyptic/militant style, other times in a dark/light, Johannine style—that he changed his style depending on the audience.[87] This would certainly be consistent with Kelber. Kelber maintains that oral tradition is particularly audience sensitive.[88] Alternatively, it is possible that Jesus may have talked in a more literary fashion when in a normal or relatively low level of hypomania. However, if Jesus varied his style to so great a degree, why is this disparity never portrayed in John? A more parsimonious hypothesis is that Jesus generally talked something like that portrayed in John.

So, the Synoptic Gospels are not unities in themselves. They each consist of two traditions, one covering the other over but not covering quite all of it. Some of the early tradition is still observable. This early tradition, as Robinson and Dodd suggest, runs close to the voice of Jesus. Cognitive studies are supportive of this analysis.

Apocalyptic Sayings as in Mark 13

In the nineteenth century, one of the major controversies was whether Jesus was an apocalyptic prophet. Certainly, the Synoptic Gospels report that Jesus did make apocalyptic predictions, e.g., Mark 9:1; 13:30; Matt 10:23. Many of these apocalyptic verses include predictions that the Son of Man will appear at the end of time and judge the world. The question is whether these apocalyptic predictions are secondary, i.e., were invented by the early church. Did Jesus prophesy that he would return as the Son of Man described in Daniel, or are such prophesies secondary, i.e., imposed-on tradition by the early church? Most commonly, nineteenth-century scholarship considered Jesus a normal but extremely God-fearing person; it had to have

84. Bartlett, *Remembering*, 74.
85. Bartlett, *Remembering*, 86.
86. Bartlett, *Remembering*, 87.
87. Higgins, "Words of Jesus."
88. Kelber, *Oral and Written Gospel*, 14–17.

been the early church that conceived the coming Son of Man verses (e.g., Matt 10:23). Lurking in the background of this was the fear that to consider the coming Son of Man verses veridical and that Jesus thought of himself as the Son of Man of Dan 7 would be to admit that Jesus was mentally deranged.[89] Schweitzer put an end to the idea that Jesus was normal and would not have asserted that he would return as the Son of Man; Schweitzer insisted that Jesus was an apocalyptic prophet but was quite sane. Jesus was a prophet immersed in Jewish Scripture. This point of view held sway well into the twentieth century. Then, scholars of the Jesus Seminar again insisted that although Jesus was a talented preacher or extremely spiritual person, even in tune with an alternate world, a "spirit person,"[90] he was not demented. However, the controversy surfaced again some years later when Allison insisted that Schweitzer had been right.[91] These controversies were nicely addressed in Robert Miller's book *The Apocalyptic Jesus: A Debate.*[92] Here Allison squared off with three liberal scholars, Marcus Borg, Steven Patterson, and John Dominic Crossan. There appears to be no resolution to this in biblical scholarship as of now. The arguments as to whether Jesus thought the end of all things was imminent are based primarily on the Synoptic texts. The database for the Allison et al. debate did not include the Gospel of John.

Many scholars consider John's Gospel to be a brilliant theological invention and that although some of John may be true, it is not sufficiently credible to use as an independent witness. However, I consider John a credible Gospel. Given that John is a credible source, it is arguable that the Gospel provides a credible base, an originating schema, for the apocalyptic verses, e.g., the verses about the coming Son of Man[93] in the Synoptics. Robinson has stated that all of the apocalyptic themes mentioned in the Synoptics are also contained and mentioned in John, although in a different, more general style.[94] Throughout much of John are discourses that refer to a day when Christ will appear, believers will be gathered to him,

89. J. Miller, *Jesus at Thirty*, 103–9.

90. Capps, *Jesus*, 36.

91. Allison, *Constructing Jesus*, 651–58.

92. R. Miller, *Apocalyptic Jesus*, 1–15.

93. Borg, *Meeting Jesus*, 41.

94. Robinson, *Priority of John*, 305.

and the world will be judged.[95] References to the judgment at the last day are recorded in John 5:25–29; 6:39, 44, 54; 11:34; and 12:25.

Verses especially illustrative of an apocalyptic thinking in John are two parabolic sayings that speak of imminent disaster in personal terms. These parables of crisis not only convey a feeling of catastrophe, but they plead with the hearer that a decision must be made before the darkness engulfs them forever. The poetry is simple and intensely compelling. I cite both, using Hunter's titles for each. The verses are from the New English Bible:[96]

> *The Journeyer at Sunset*
>
> The light is still among you but not for long. Go on your way while you have the light, so that the darkness may not overtake you. He who journeys in the dark does not know where he is going. While you have the light trust the light, that you may become sons of light. (John 12:35–36 NEB)

Hunter suggests that in this parable, Jesus is saying that "the darkness of judgement is approaching. You still have time but not much, to make your decision, and escape the impending doom."[97]

> *The Benighted Traveler*
>
> Are there not twelve hours of daylight? If anyone walks at daytime he does not stumble because he sees the light of the world. But if he walks at night he stumbles, because the light fails him. (John 11:9 NEB)

Such parabolic sayings would seem to make impending judgment a critical factor in Jesus's message.

It is important to note that the Johannine Jesus speaks of judgment as occurring in the present as well as in the future (John 5:25). Jesus, as we have seen, is content to assert that the judgment is coming in the future and is now occurring in the present. Thus, his eschatology reflects the combinatorial thought patterns of hypomania.[98]

95. Robinson, *Priority of John*, 305.
96. Hunter, *According to John*, 83.
97. Hunter, *According to John*, 83.
98. Jamison, *Touched with Fire*, 107.

True, the Gospel of John contains most of the features of the Synoptic apocalypse. But can we say that the Gospel supports the concept of Jesus as an apocalyptic prophet when the timing of the in-breaking world is said to be occurring now and in the future? The refiguring of time in John, coupled with a pervading sense of imminent disaster, is difficult to explain in rational terms. As we have seen, much scholarship has been devoted to explaining the paradoxical thought patterns in John. But this combining of opposites is not unusual for a manic-depressive poet. Broad analogies and the combining of opposites are a notable feature of hypomanic/manic thought.[99]

If one insists that one must think in terms of a future but imminent in-breaking of God, of a new world, with no thought that the kingdom is now occurring, then no, the Johannine Jesus would not be an apocalyptic prophet. However, Jesus's warning that the time is short, the overriding urgency of his message, and the many verses that speak of Christ's future return[100] put him in the apocalyptic camp, although not as the Synoptics have it. The Synoptic assertions are generally too stereotypical. As Dodd states, in John, the return of Jesus is spoken of only in general terms.[101] The apocalyptic images in the Synoptics describing the resurrection or parousia are not contained in John. Cognitive research fully supports Dodd's suggestion that such stereotypical imagery was added later through the retelling process.[102] In the Gospel of John, it is the emotion, the urgency expressed in the parables of crisis, that is the key. This emotion, the sense that something catastrophic is about to happen, predominates in John. The feeling as expressed in the parabolic sayings is certainly apocalyptic. Manic-depressive patients are known for their recurrent feelings of the imminent occurrence of catastrophic events. The Synoptic Gospels simply verbalize and elaborate this feeling of imminent catastrophe over many retellings. This results in stereotypical apocalyptic imagery from Jewish cultural schema. But the apocalyptic thinking as expressed in the Synoptics begins with the old tradition that predates the Synoptics and Q.[103]

99. Jamison, *Touched with Fire*, 107.

100. Dodd, *Historical Tradition*, 416–20; Robinson, *Priority of John*, 305.

101. Dodd, *Historical Tradition*, 416.

102. Dodd, *Historical Tradition*, 420.

103. Dodd, *Historical Tradition*, 420.

Sense of Universal Benevolence

Perhaps the most intriguing aspect of manic stage of manic depression is that people in this stage often experience identification with God, a feeling of universal benevolence towards all people and a sense of communion with all of nature. As I noted earlier, these feelings of universal communion likely led to the sayings of Jesus in the Sermon on the Mount and elsewhere to the effect that one should love one's neighbor and indeed one's enemies. Jesus continually emphasized the necessity of loving our fellow humans. He emphasized that we should forgive one another, that we should turn the other cheek. He emphasized that humans should show mercy to one another. We should pray for those who persecute us. The idea that we should forgive one another and refrain from repaying evil with evil was not new to Jewish culture. But Jesus pursued and preached these ideas with unwavering intensity.[104]

We may look to Old Testament Scripture to find where Jesus may have obtained this idea or ideas. However, the Old Testament God is not always forgiving. In Exod 34:6, God is portrayed as gracious and forgiving but also punishing, visiting the sins of the fathers upon the sons to the fourth generation. The Old Testament does provide a story that teaches us to be kind to our enemies. This is a story about Oded the prophet, contained in 2 Chron 28. Here is the story: Israel (including Samaria), in conjunction with Syria, had conquered Judah. In so doing, Israel had slaughtered many men. Oded the prophet said they had sinned in the rage of battle and that God was angry at this. He then told them to return the captives. Then the Samaritans clothed the naked, dressed their wounds, put those who could not walk on donkeys, and took them to Jericho. The love of enemies could certainly have been generated from this story. Perhaps Jesus told it. It is a most striking story. It probably would not have been overlooked by Jesus. Jesus had all of Scripture to help him interpret feelings generated by the hypomanic state. Granted, a scholar would have known of the story of Oded who commanded good treatment of enemies, but he would not have had the energy of Jesus. Jesus's kindness of heart, when combined with the energy of manic depression, would have generated the consistent focus on compassion displayed in the Gospels.

It is important to note that this schema of universal benevolence exhibited in manic-depressive disorder is often accompanied by the idea that

104. Grant, *Saint Peter*, 73–84.

class barriers and social rankings are meaningless and are disruptive to the formation and experience of kindness and love among humans. Custance, while committed to a mental hospital for manic depression, states that he felt a "sense of communion . . . with all fellow creatures." He states that he had "no objection to being more or less herded together—as is inevitable in public mental hospitals—with men of all classes and condition. Class barriers cease to have any existence or meaning. I take particular pleasure in actual physical contact with my fellows, such as a sentimental holding of hands."[105] Compare these feeling with the sayings and actions of Jesus within the purity system of Israel, with its sharp social boundaries. Jesus touched lepers and hemorrhaging women. He entered a graveyard inhabited by a man possessed by demons. He ate at the table with outcasts. He was accused of eating with "tax collectors and sinners" and of being "a glutton and a drunkard and a friend of tax collectors and sinners." The followers of Jesus included women, untouchables, the poor, the maimed, but also some wealthy persons.[106] It should be noted that it is not just hypomania that produces these actions. A person's personality is not erased in mania/hypomania. This is the compassionate Jesus whose feelings are further ignited and elaborated by the manic processing of the true meaning behind the Law and the Prophets.

That manic processing has influenced the Gospels, John as well as the Synoptics, is indicated by the assertion in 1 John 4:8 that "God is love." Jesus's feelings of benevolence went beyond those of universal empathy. The assertion that "God is love" of 1 John 4:8 very probably began with Jesus. Recall that in the manic phase, many people not only experience universal benevolence but conceive of God in terms of love. As Custance says. "What I saw was the Power of Love . . . the Power that I knew somehow to have made all the universes, past, present and to come, to be utterly infinite."[107]

First John 4:7 reads: "Beloved, let us love one another." And 1 John 4:8: "He who does not love does not know God for God is love." This is a different idea of God than the personal God of the Old Testament. The Old Testament version of God provides that compassion is one characteristic of God but not the only one. As I have noted, Exod 34:6 reads that the Lord is gracious and forgiving but punishes iniquity and visits the sins of the fathers upon the children to the fourth generation. First John 4:8 expresses

105. Custance, "Universe of Bliss," 47.

106. Custance,"Universe of Bliss," 54–55.

107. Custance, "Universe of Bliss," 64.

a picture of God that is consistent with the elevated phases of manic depression. It is arguable that the Synoptics and in particular the verses from the Sermon on the Mount, preaching that humans should love even their enemies, are based on and derivative of the idea expressed in 1 John that God is love.

As we have seen, the Gospel of John contains many of the sayings of Jesus, and these were maintained in the Johannine community. It seems reasonable to argue, therefore, that the source of this saying that God is love in 1 John was Jesus, that he entertained the idea that God is love and that this concept was at the core of his focus on compassion throughout his life. Of course, 1 John may not have been written by the author of the Gospel of John, but the second- or tertiary-level authors would have maintained the basic concepts of the Beloved Disciple as core memories of the Christian community. Recall Hirst's findings on collective memory to the effect that the memories of dominant individuals form the greater part of the collective's traditions.[108] In this regard, it was likely the views and memories of the author of John, probably the Beloved Disciple, that would have formed the memory of the Johannine community. Even if the beloved disciple had died before the writing of 1 John, as long as it was written by a member of the community, the basic ideas would have been community ideas.

Still, the idea that God is love is revolutionary against a backdrop of the Old Testament God. Coincident with my hypotheses that Jesus was manic-depressive, it is reasonable that the image of God portrayed in 1 John 4:8 originated with Jesus and that this was the revolutionary idea upon which Jesus built his mission. It underlay the Sermon on the Mount and, as Borg might have it, the politics of compassion.[109] The feelings of universal benevolence are simply corollaries of this one proposition that God is love. This coincides with Custance's statements that, while in a manic episode, he felt that Love was "the power that created all the universes, past present and those to come."[110]

Finally, we may note that this feeling of universal benevolence runs counter to the criticism that the concept of love expressed in John was limited to members of the church or to those of the Johannine community. It is often argued that John encourages love, but only for the Christian

108. Cuc et al., "On the Formation."

109. Borg, *Meeting Jesus*, 46–61.

110. Custance,"Universe of Bliss," 50.

community.[111] However, note that manic-depressive experience is universal love. Thus, my hypothesis would predict that Jesus preached universal love, love of fellow man, not love restricted by community boundaries. Furthermore, it is likely that John (the Beloved Disciple), as the person Jesus chose to carry on his message, would also have preached a love extending beyond any class or group barrier.

It is simply not credible that the Johannine community would have restricted their love of brother to their own community and at the same time hold that God is love. In fact, Jesus probably felt, much as did Custance,[112] that the power of love was able to conquer hate. And thus, Jesus's command to love one another, even though addressed to his disciples in John, has the broadest possible meaning: to love one's fellow man. Other scholars have argued on the basis of extensive biblical exegesis that the Johannine community spoke in terms of universal fellowship. Schnackenburg has shown that, in a number of verses, namely 1 John 4:21 and 1 John 2:11, the term *brother* must refer to fellow man.[113] In view of analyses such as these, it does not seem reasonable to argue that the Johannine community limited Christian love to the community itself.

What of the Parables?

The Synoptic parables are often considered the most authentic of Jesus's sayings and are thought to closely reflect the voice of Jesus.[114] Even the Jesus Seminar[115] considers certain parts of many parables to be reliable. My own analysis suggests that the Synoptic parables were subject to cultural influences stemming from continuous retellings occurring over several decades.[116] In addition, the Hirst model of collective memory[117] supposes that the recollection of parables took place within a conversational framework, a situation that would have subjected the parables to constant revision over

111. Robinson, *Priority of John*, 329.

112. Custance, "Universe of Bliss," 50.

113. Schnackenburg, *Gospel*, 168.

114. Jeremias, *Parables of Jesus*, 1963.

115. Funk et al., *Parables of Jesus*, 16–18.

116. Bartlett, *Remembering*, 118–87, esp. 171–87; Lyons and Kashima, "How Are Stereotypes Maintained"; Kashima et al., "Maintenance of Cultural Stereotypes."

117. Hirst et al., "Of Sins and Virtues"; Vlasceanu et al., "Cognition in a Social Context," 32.

time. Cultural stereotypes would have played a much larger part in the formation of collective memory than might otherwise be expected.[118]

The traditional rabbinic parables cannot be dated earlier than the second century.[119] According to Young, Jesus's parables, those recorded in the Gospels, are of the same era as the "classical" variety of rabbinic parables, extant in the years before the time of the traditional rabbinic parables.[120] These earlier parables dealt with moral issues but were not exegetical teachings. Jesus's parables and the classical rabbinic ones show similar motifs and a continuity of expression between the two groups.[121] As Young puts it, "it seems more likely that the gospels preserve remnants of early Jewish instruction rather than the beginnings of a new *Gattung*."[122] Jesus did not invent the story-parable.[123]

A masterful parabalist draws from a ready repository of illustrations and images to communicate a particular message. As Scott puts it, such a teacher draws from a general "thesaurus" of themes and images.[124] An example of rabbinic and Gospel parables containing similar themes follows. For the theme "the wise and foolish," a rabbinic parable uses the theme to refer to wise and foolish servants; Jesus's parable in Matt 25:1–12 refers to wise and foolish virgins.[125] Young notes that the rabbinic parables are consistent with the style of Jesus. "Jesus' parables on the one hand, and the rabbinic parables on the other, contain similar illustrative motifs which show a continuity of expression."[126] Overall, then, it is certainly conceivable that Jesus's parables as recorded in the Synoptic Gospels were in no small part elaborated and edited by successive teachers or disciples over time. Goulder thinks that there would have been too few Christian teachers skilled in midrashic method to have serially produced the New Testament parables and that Matthew and Luke themselves wrote the parables that appear in their own Gospels.[127] I simply take the position that, although

118. Conway and Jobson, "On the Nature."

119. Blomberg, *Interpreting the Parables*, 68.

120. Young, *Jesus*, 106–9.

121. Young, *Jesus*, 34.

122. Young, *Jesus*, 35.

123. Young, *Jesus*, 108.

124. Scott, *Hear Then the Parable*, 18.

125. Young, *Jesus*, 35.

126. Young, *Jesus*, 4.

127. Goulder, *Midrash and Lection*, 33.

the evangelists may have finished the job, the parables in the main are the product of many retellings.

It is quite possible that unlearned disciples could have acquired the skills necessary to create the story-parable. Linguistic style is readily learned. Rubin's experiments show that student novices were able to write American ballads after only a short learning period.[128] The students were told only to try to imitate the ballads styles. They were not given specific instructions on the methods of ballad-making. During the learning phase, the students were instructed only to recall a set of ballads. They were not taught the specific rules of ballad formation and structure, i.e., that the ballad should contain four lines per verse, or that the last words of lines 2 and 4 should rhyme, or that nouns should be concrete, not abstract. If Young is correct that the classical type of rabbinic parable was extant during Jesus's day and contained many of the same motifs and the same type of moral inversions as illustrated in Jesus's parables,[129] it would not be difficult for teachers or motivated but unprofessional disciples to create parables from Jesus's poetry. Thus, the Synoptic parables may contain nuggets of Jesus's sayings, but in the main, they are probably the literary creations of either the evangelists or others using Jesus's teachings as they recalled them. Further, I have emphasized the dominance of personality and mood in memory. It would not be difficult to remember first the general antiestablishment perspective of Jesus, then to recreate a narrative *mashal* consistent with this general emotional framework of Jesus. It would not be hard, for example, to include references to and about the kingdom of God, as this concept was used often by Jesus. Overall, given the findings of Rubin,[130] I suggest that the parables of Jesus may in reality have been created by his disciples and followers over the decades that intervened between the writing of Synoptic Gospels and Jesus's life on earth. These revisions and elaborations operating during the process of serial retelling may have contributed to the creation of the Gospel parables to a much greater extent than envisioned even by the Jesus Seminar.

However, it is the hypotactic structure of the parables contained in Matthew and Luke that provides the most persuasive evidence that the Synoptic Gospels are the result of retelling processes. The prodigal son of Luke and the unmerciful steward of Matthew contain a large number of

128. Rubin, *Memory in Oral Traditions*, 289–93.

129. Young, *Jesus*, 36–40.

130. Rubin, *Memory in Oral Traditions*, 289–93.

hypotactic, subordinating participles. Speaking of the parables of Matthew and Luke, Black notes that "these parables are not direct literal translations of the Aramaic but they are literary creations."[131] As Black has noted, parataxis is "much more frequent in Aramaic than it is in Greek."[132] Black notes that parataxis occurs often in Mark and John but only in the sayings of Jesus in Matthew and Luke. Speaking of the parables of Matthew and Luke, Black notes that "these parables are not literal renderings of the Aramaic, but something more in the nature of literary reproductions of the Aramaic story."[133] Thus, the linguistic evidence shows that the parables as recorded are at best distant creations of Jesus's original sayings or stories. Whereas paratactic construction is characteristic of Mark and John, this is certainly not true of the parables of Matthew or Luke. These Synoptic parables were created by teachers likely versed in idiomatic Greek.[134] The linguistic evidence supports the conclusions of Goulder and Drury to the effect that the Synoptic parables, particularly those of Matthew and Luke, are creations of the early church or the Gospel writers.[135]

131. M. Black, *Aramaic Approach*, 46.

132. M. Black, *Aramaic Approach*, 44.

133. M. Black, *Aramaic Approach*, 46.

134. M. Black, *Aramaic Approach*, 46.

135. Goulder, *Midrash and Lection*, 64; Blomberg, *Interpeting the Parables*, 50.

10

Concluding Remarks

Nicea and Chalcedon

Returning again to Black's insightful article concerning the grandeur of Jesus's speech as expressed in John: near the end of the article, Black compares the thrust of the Synoptics with that of John. He notes that the Synoptics often offer homiletic counsel and contain paraenetic sayings but that John's Gospel in "both its theology and rhetoric are driven by a different engine: to preserve the living voice of the incarnate Word, whose glory the church has witnessed and in whose love it abides."[136] I think that the findings of modern cognitive psychology and clinical psychology support Black's assessment of the Fourth Gospel. I think that John has in large part accommodated to the language of Jesus and thus preserved it.

The Synoptic Gospels appear to be the result of many retellings over a good number of years. They have become suffused and overlaid with the predominant cultural framework of Common Judaism. These hypotheses are supported by recent data gathered from experiments in conversational memory. Most interesting, however, is Hirst's model of collective memory and also the social interactionist model of collective memory.[137] For Hirst, it is an individual's own psychological, idiosyncratic needs that form the basis of group memories. This means that the concepts of clinical psychology,

136. C. Black, "Words That You Gave," 233.

137. Hirst et al., "Of Sins and Virtues"; Vlasceanu et al., "Cognition in a Social Context," 32.

particularly as they are related to memory theory, come to the fore. In this regard, Conway's theory that autobiographical recall works to maintain the integrity of the conceptual self becomes important.[138] I suggest that the dominant person whose stamp is on the Synoptic Gospels is Peter. My views align with those of Bauckham in this regard, to the effect that Peter was chosen by Jesus to be the chief shepherd of the church, to spread the gospel throughout Israel.[139] According to Hengel, "Peter possessed a powerful Spirit-filled proclamation. . . . He was the first leader of the original Jerusalem community."[140] Peter's influence extends to all three of the Synoptic Gospels: "Traditions reported by Peter lie behind the Second Gospel and they motivate Luke and Matthew to base their work extensively on his gospel."[141] In sum, Peter's own set of needs, worked out in conjunction with Scripture as his schematic framework, generates the Synoptic perspective on Jesus.

As noted earlier, some scholars think that the Synoptics reflect eyewitness testimony.[142] I must take issue here, especially with McIver's ideas that the granular texture of the Synoptics illustrates eyewitness memory. McIver theorizes that the Synoptic modules are essentially personal event memories of the kind discussed by Pillemer.[143] However, PEMs are very detailed, unlike those posited by McIver.[144] The mark of eyewitness memory is specificity. The Synoptic Gospels are replete with short, brief pericopes that are lacking in context and in descriptive detail. Nineham's discussion of the Synoptics Gospels describes their stereotypical, ambiguous nature quite well.[145] This structure, as described by Nineham, accurately reflects the composition of serially retold stories as described in the experimental literature and as illustrated especially in the work of Kashima.[146] Kashima's work demonstrates a slow takeover of individuality by broad, overly general stereotypes. It certainly is not the generality of events that bespeaks of eyewitness testimony, as McIver's concept of granular structure would

138. Conway, "Memory and the Self."

139. Bauckham, *Jesus and the Eyewitnesses*, 395–96.

140. Hengel, *Saint Peter*, 34.

141. Hengel, *Saint Peter*, 101–2.

142. McIver, *Memory, Jesus*, 124.

143. Pillemer, *Momentous Events, Vivid Memories*, 50.

144. McIver, *Memory, Jesus*, 49, 124.

145. Nineham, "Eye-Witness Testimony, I."

146. Kashima et al., "Maintenance of Cultural Stereotypes."

suggest, but rather their specificity. First-order eyewitness evidence is specific, as attested to in many experiments.[147] The general makeup of the Synoptic Gospels provides compelling evidence that the Synoptic Gospels are based on successive retellings and not the testimony of an eyewitness or eyewitnesses. The Synoptics practically provide a compendium of examples illustrative of Bartlett's findings summarizing the results of serial retelling: the loss of setting, the conventionalization of language, the loss of individual style, and the utilization of cultural stereotypes.[148]

The Gospel of John is a different story. This Gospel provides evidence that it is the work of an eyewitness. Its precision with regard to spatial and chronological detail suffice to provide a framework for the conversations that take place in the various scenes. The eyewitness studies, especially the SVA studies, support the idea that the Gospel of John was written by an eyewitness to the events contained therein.[149] Communication accommodation studies[150] support the idea that John closely reflects Jesus's own linguistic style. Some biblical scholars have suggested that the words of Jesus in John are close to those of the historical Jesus. Communication accommodation theory (CAT) brings empirical studies to bear on the issue.

As we have seen, modern scholars disagree concerning whether John considered Jesus a preexistent divine person or a human being representing God's wisdom and character on earth. I maintain that the "I am" assertions of Jesus both with and without a predicate were uttered by Jesus.[151] John does not invent such statements; he records them. A manic-depressive Jesus could easily have thought of himself as a divine being and even, at times, God. The hypothesis that Jesus suffered from manic depression (bipolar I) suggests that Jesus not only thought of himself as a messenger of God but considered himself to be God simpliciter. He would have felt this in manic states and recalled the feeling in hypomanic states. This feeling in manic states would likely have generated the "I am" statements in his later hypomanic state of consciousness. We have seen that such grandiose thoughts are not uncommon among manic-depressives.[152]

147. Volbert and Steller, "Is This Testimony Truthful"; Vrij, "Criteria-Based Content Analysis," 33.

148. Bartlett, *Remembering*, 93–94.

149. Volbert and Steller, "Is This Testimony Truthful," 207, 220.

150. Giles et al., "Accommodation Theory."

151. Bauckham, *Jesus and the Eyewitnesses*, 239–52.

152. Custance, "Universe of Bliss."

The manic feeling is especially evident in John 8:58, wherein Jesus combines the "I am" assertion with a combinatory statement of time: "Before Abraham was, I am."

The Great Creeds of Nicea and Chalcedon

These great creeds express the core beliefs of Christianity, Catholic, and conservative Protestant. The Nicene and Chalcedonian Creeds assert essentially that Jesus was fully God and fully man. It is well known that the Gospel of John served as the foundation for these creeds.[153] But Robinson has argued that the Nicene Creed offers an erroneous interpretation of John. Robinson basically takes the position discussed earlier, that the author of the Forth Gospel views Jesus as a kind of representative of God.[154]

It is interesting that for almost three centuries after Christ, the early church affirmed the divinity of Christ. Discussions concerned the nature of his divinity, but it was generally agreed that Christ was "sovereign, existed before time and participated in Creation."[155] The arguments began to change color in the early fourth century and reached a flash point in Alexandria, the intellectual center of the times. Arius, a church presbyter in Alexandria, contended that God created Jesus and commissioned him to create the universe; Jesus was preexistent to the universe but not eternal. Alexander, the bishop of Alexandria, would have none of that, arguing that Christ was eternal and of the same substance as God. Alexander contended that Jesus was eternal, identical with God, and incarnated on earth.[156] The arguments continued, and finally Constantine called a council to convene at Nicea in 325. The council was not the purely academic gathering it is generally taken to be. The bishops had been persecuted and tortured for their faith. Many were permanently disabled. One had lost an eye. Others had lost their fingers; others had lost their limbs. The arguments about Christ's divine status evoked deep emotion in these men. When the Arian position was presented, some "were holding their hands over their ears and shouting for the blasphemies to stop."[157] For them, Christ was God come to

153. Robinson, *Priority of John*, 394.

154. Robinson, *Priority of John*, 394–97.

155. Komoszewski et al., *Reinventing Jesus*, 205.

156. Komoszewski et al., *Reinventing Jesus*, 208–15.

157. Komoszewski et al., *Reinventing Jesus*, 211.

earth, was crucified and ascended to heaven; his divinity was not secondary to the Father.

The issue was resolved at Nicea. That Jesus was fully God was expressed in the Nicene Creed. The Nicene Creed states that Jesus is true God, "begotten not made and from the substance as the Father through whom all things came into being."[158] It ends with a number of negative statements. These may be more informative than the positive assertions: "But for those who assert, There was when He was not, and, Before being born He was not, and that He came into existence out of nothing, or who assert that the Son of God is from a different hypostasis, or substance or is created, or is subject to alteration or change these—the Catholic Church anathematizes."[159] The Chalcedonian Creed of 451 made it clear that Jesus was truly human as well as preexistent divinity. It clearly stated that Jesus was "truly God and truly man."[160]

The Nicene and Chalcedonian Creeds are especially resonant with John. They express a high Christology, which is consistent with the high Christology expressed in the Gospel of John. The apostolic fathers who wrote the Nicene Creed interpreted John as presenting a Jesus who considered himself to be God, not merely his representative. This becomes clear in their rejection of the Arian view that Jesus was less a divinity than God.

Further and importantly, the creeds express the high Christology of Jesus. I say this because it is likely that the author of John appropriated the words and style of Jesus via cognitive accommodation processes. The "I am" statements were included in this accommodation process. Consider the following: Jesus offers fourteen "I am" assertions throughout the Gospel of John. Seven of these are those with a predicate, e.g. "I am the resurrection and the life" (John: 11:25). Seven are the so-called absolute "I am" sayings, those without a predicate. His best known of these occurs in John 8:58: "Truly, truly I say to you, before Abraham was, I am." Bauckham thinks that these absolute assertions identify "Jesus as truly God in the fullest sense."[161] My hypothesis that Jesus was manic-depressive supports the idea that Jesus did in fact utter these statements and that they are not contrivances of John. They are consistent with the manic phase of manic depression. Jesus

158. As quoted in Komoszewski et al., *Reinventing Jesus*, 213

159. As quoted in Komoszewski et al., *Reinventing Jesus*, 213.

160. Robinson, *Priority of John*, 394.

161. Bauckham, *Jesus and the Eyewitnesses*, 248.

thought of himself as fully God; the Nicene and Chalcedon Creeds simply affirm Jesus's own high Christology.

Since John reflects the words of Jesus, the creeds become more than just abstractions, more than something like hypothetical constructs concerning the nature of Christ. They embody the words of Christ. The bishops most likely thought that Jesus's words in John had been uttered by Jesus. The Nicene Creed summarizes and condenses the primary message of the Gospel of John: the words of Jesus, in particular, the "I am" assertions of John. For the bishops who had suffered torture at the hands of Rome and seen their friends put to death, Jesus was not merely a compassionate minister of the word; He was God incarnate, their saving Redeemer. This is the message of the Nicene Creed. It was not a mere abstraction.

C. Clifton Black considers the Fourth Gospel to be an expression of the "glorious diction of Jesus."[162] But does he mean the Johannine Jesus or the historical Jesus? For Black, the rhetoric itself illustrates the true light of God to a darkened world. Black maintains that "nothing could be more needful for today's church than to be grasped afresh by the grandeur of its own Gospel." I think that this is true, but rhetoric alone will not suffice. It is critical to realize that the rhetoric and the truths behind it are those of Jesus, not John.

It is entirely reasonable that the historical Jesus, the manic-depressive Jesus, uttered the high christological statements contained in the Gospel of John. The question then arises: does the hypothesis that Jesus was manic-depressive in any way subtract from the profundity and sublimity of Jesus's speech? Jamison addresses this problem when assessing the works of the great artists and writers, whom she considers to have suffered from manic depression.[163] She notes that historical as well as modern research "support a strong relationship between mood disorders and artistic creativity."[164] Creative thought is often triggered in already talented people by the onset of hypomanic states. William James, who himself was subject to extreme mood changes, wrote that "when a superior intellect and a psychopathic temperament coalesce . . . in the same individual we have the best possible condition for the kind of effective genius that gets into the biographical dictionaries."[165] In fact, it has been argued that the depths of depression in

162. C. Black, "Words That You Gave," 232.

163. Jamison, *Touched with Fire*, 92–99.

164. Jamison, *Touched with Fire*, 89.

165. James, *Varieties of Religious Experience*, 23–24.

manic depression may provide a person with more astute visions of reality than those that generally occur in normal people. In fact, the extreme depression that occurs in manic depression patients is not just a feeling, but rather an intellectual assessment of the human condition. Jamison writes that clinical-level depression forces one to look straight into the face of death and its finality.[166] This is the despair of the "dark night of the soul."[167] This is the despair that results in suicide. A not insubstantial number of poets and other artists have found refuge in their art. Some poets write that they found salvation in poetry. James Clarence Mangan, the poet, travels further; despair caused him to flee "for shelter to God."[168] This sort of desperate search for God may well portray Jesus. Jesus, however, probably had a more complex picture of God than do modern poets—that is to say, a more complex, deep, God-centered cultural schema than the modern poets, one that could envelope his mind and save it from despair.

As we have seen, a large number of artists and poets have suffered from manic depression. Does this subtract from their work? Jamison says of William Blake, as a case in point, "It does not render his work any the less extraordinary, or make him any less a great visionary or prophet."[169] So why would one say that the work of Jesus is diminished? His theology is complex and beautiful, enhanced by manic-depressive stages. Knowing despair but also the beauty of Scripture, his creativity enhanced, with Isaiah and Zechariah in hand, he attempted to provide comfort to humanity by means of the cross.

166. Jamison, *Touched with Fire*, 119.

167. Goodwin and Jamison, *Manic-Depressive Illness*, 360–64.

168. Mangan, "Nameless One."

169. Jamison, *Touched with Fire*, 94.

Appendix

The War of the Ghosts

Original Story

One night two young men from Egulac went down to the river to hunt seals, and while they were there, it became foggy and calm. Then they heard war cries, and they thought: "Maybe this is a war party." They escaped to the shore, and hid behind a log. Now canoes came up, and they heard the noise of paddles, and saw one canoe coming up to them. There were five men in the canoe, and they said:

"What do you think? We wish to take you along. We are going up the river to make war on the people."

One of the young men said: "I have no arrows."

"Arrows are in the canoe," they said.

"I will not go along. I might be killed. My relatives do not know where I have gone. But you," he said, turning to the other, "may go with them."

So one of the young men went, but the other returned home.

And the warriors went up the river to a town on the other side of Kalama. The people came down to the water, and they began to fight, and many were killed. But presently the young man heard one of the warriors say: "Quick, let us go home: that Indian has been hit." Now he thought: "Oh, they are ghosts." He did not feel sick, but they said he had been shot.

So the canoes went back to Egulac, and the young man went ashore to his house, and made a fire. And he told everybody and said: "Behold, I accompanied the ghosts, and we went to fight. Many of our fellows were killed, and many of those who attacked us were killed. They said I was hit, and I did not feel sick."

He told it all, and then he became quiet. When the sun rose he fell down. Something black came out of his mouth. His face became contorted. The people jumped up and cried.

He was dead.

Serial Reproduction 4

The War of the Ghosts

There were two young Indians of Malagua who were out seal-hunting on a calm, foggy day. Suddenly they saw five canoes emerge from the mist. A man in the foremost boat called out to them: "Come and help us fight the people who are beyond." And one answered: "I cannot, for it would pain my parents sore were I lost." Then said the other: "I cannot, for I have no arrows." "There are arrows in the bottom of the boat," said the warrior. Then the other spake: "I will"; and he came.

And they went to Kamama, and the strife waxed fierce between them and the foe. And the young man fell, pierced through the heart by an arrow. And he said to the warrior: "Take me back to Malagua, for that is my home." So the warrior brought him back, and the young man said: "I am wounded, but I am not sick, and feel no pain."

And he lived that night, and the next day, but at sunset his soul fled black from his mouth, and he grew stark and stiff. And when they came to lift him, they could not, for he was dead.

Bibliography

Allison, Dale C., Jr. *Constructing Jesus*. Grand Rapids: Baker Academic, 2010.

Anderson, Paul N. *The Fourth Gospel and the Quest for Jesus: Modern Foundations Reconsidered*. New York: Continuum, 2007.

Anderson, Michael C., et al. "Remembering Can Cause Forgetting: Retrieval Dynamics in Long-Term Memory." *Journal of Experimental Psychology: Learning, Memory, and Cognition* 20 (1994) 1063–87.

Andreason, Nancy J. C. "Creativity and Mental Illness: Prevalence Rates in Writers and Their First Degree Relatives." *American Journal of Psychiatry* 144 (1957) 1288–92.

———, and Pauline S. Powers. "Creativity and Psychosis." *Archives of General Psychiatry* 32 (1975) 70–73.

APA. *Diagnostic and Statistical Manual of Mental Disorders*. 5th ed. Washington, DC: American Psychiatric Association, 2013.

Ashcraft, Mark. *Cognition*. 3rd ed. Upper Saddle River, NJ: Prentice Hall, 2002.

Baddeley, Alan. "Reflections on Autobiographical Memory: Theories and Approaches." In *Understanding Autobiographical Memory: Theories and Approaches*, edited by Dorthe Berntsen and David C. Rubin, 70–88. Cambridge: Cambridge University Press, 2012.

———. "Working Memory: Theories, Models and Controversies." *Annual Review of Psychology* 63 (1) 1–29.

Bailey, Kenneth E. "Informal Controlled Oral Tradition and the Synoptic Gospels." *Themelios* 20 (1995) 4–11.

———. "Middle Eastern Oral Tradition and the Synoptic Gospels." *Journal of Experimental Theology* 106 (1995) 363–67.

Barclay, Craig R. "Autobiographical Remembering: Narrative Constraints on Objectified Selves." In *Remembering Our Past: Studies in Autobiographical Memory*, edited by David C. Rubin, rev. ed., 94–125. Cambridge: Cambridge University Press, 1999.

Barlow, David H., and V. Mark Durand. *Abnormal Psychology: An Integrated Approach*. 7th ed. Stamford, CT: Cengage Learning, 2015.

Barnstone, Willis. *The Poems of Jesus Christ*. New York: Norton and Co., 2012.

Bartlett, Frederic C. *Remembering: A Study in Experimental and Social Psychology*. Cambridge: Cambridge University Press, 1995.

Bass, Ellen, and Laura Davis. *The Courage to Heal: A Guide for Women Survivors of Child Sexual Abuse*. 3rd ed. New York: Harper Perennial, 1994.

Bauckham, Richard. *Jesus and the Eyewitnesses: The Gospels as Eyewitness Testimony*. Grand Rapids: Eerdmans, 2006.

———. *The Testimony of the Beloved Disciple: Narrative, History, and Theology in the Gospel of John*. Grand Rapids: Baker Academic, 2007.

Becker, Mark W., and Mark Leinenger. "Attentional Selection Is Biased toward Mood-Congruent Stimuli." *Emotion* 11 (2011) 1248–54. https://doi.org/10.1037/a0023524.

Bergman, Erik T., and Henry L. Roediger III. "Can Bartlett's Repeated Reproduction Experiments Be Replicated?" *Memory and Cognition* 27 (1999) 937–47.

Berntsen, Dorthe, and David C. Rubin. *Understanding Autobiographical Memory: Theories and Approaches*. Cambridge: Cambridge University Press, 2012.

Bird, Michael. *The Gospel of the Lord: How the Early Church Wrote the Story of Jesus*. Grand Rapids: Eerdmans, 2014.

Black, C. Clifton. "'The Words That You Gave to Me I Have Given to Them': The Grandeur of Johannine Rhetoric." In *Exploring the Gospel of John*, edited by R. Alan Culpepper and C. Clifton Black, 220–39. Louisville: Westminster John Knox, 1996.

Black, Matthew. *An Aramaic Approach to the Gospels and Acts*. 2nd ed. London: Oxford University Press, 1957.

Blomberg, Craig L. *The Historical Reliability of the Gospels*. 2nd ed. Downers Grove, IL: InterVarsity, 2007.

———. *Interpreting the Parables*. 2nd ed. Downers Grove, IL: IVP Academic, 2012.

Boison, Anton T. *The Exploration of the Inner World: A Study of Mental Disorder and Religious Experience*. Philadelphia: University of Pennsylvania Press, 1971.

Borg, Marcus. *Jesus in Contemporary Scholarship*. Valley Forge, PA: Trinity International, 1994.

———. *Meeting Jesus for the First Time*. San Francisco: Harper Collins, 1994.

Bower, Gordon H. "Mood and Memory." *American Psychologist* 36 (1981) 129–48.

Brewer, William F. "The Theoretical and Empirical Status of Flashbulb Memory." In *Affect and Accuracy in Recall: Studies of "Flashbulb" Memories*, edited by Eugene Winograd and Ulric Neisser, 274–306. Cambridge: Cambridge University Press, 1992.

———. "What Is Autobiographical Memory?" In *Autobiographical Memory*, edited by David C. Rubin, 25–49. Cambridge: Cambridge University Press, 1986.

———. "What Is Recollective Memory?" In *Remembering Our Past: Studies in Autobiographical Memory*, edited by David C. Rubin, rev. ed., 19–66. Cambridge: Cambridge University Press, 1999.

Brigham, J. C. "What Is Forensic Psychology Anyway?" *Law and Human Behavior* 23 (1999) 273–98.

Brown, Roger, and James Kulik. "Flashbulb Memories." *Cognition* 5 (1977) 73–99.

Bultmann, Rudolf. "The History of the Synoptic Tradition." In *Form Criticism: A New Method of New Testament Research*, edited by Frederick C. Grant, 93–111. Chicago: Willet, Clark and Co., 1934.

———. *The History of the Synoptic Tradition. Oxford: Blackwell, (1963) 4.*

Capps, Donald Eric. *Jesus: A Psychological Biography*. St Louis: Chalice, 2000.

Casey, Maurice. *Is John's Gospel True?* London: Routledge. 1996.

Cheney, Terri. *Manic: A Memoir*. New York: Harper Collins, 2009.

Coman, Alin, and William Hirst. "Cognition through a Social Network: The Propagation of Induced Forgetting and Practice Effects." *Journal of Experimental Psychology: General* 141 (2012) 321–36.

Coman, Alin, et al. "Mnemonic Convergence in Social Networks: The Emergent Properties of Cognition at a Collective Level." *Proceedings of the National Academy of Sciences* 113 (2016) 8171–76. https://doi.org/101073/pnas.1525569113.

Conway, Martin A. "Autobiographical Knowledge and Autobiographical Memories." In *Remembering Our Past: Studies in Autobiographical Memory*, edited by David C. Rubin, rev. ed., 67–93. Cambridge: Cambridge University Press, 1999.

———. "Memory and the Self." *Journal of Memory and Language* 53 (2005) 594–628.

Conway, Martin A., and Laura Jobson. "On the Nature of Autobiographical Memory." In *Understanding Autobiographical Memory: Theories and Approaches*, edited by Dorthe Berntsen and David C. Rubin, 54–69. Cambridge: Cambridge University Press, 2012.

Conway, Martin A., and C. W. Pleydell-Pearce. "The Construction of Autobiographical Memories in the Self-Memory System." *Psychological Review* 107 (2000) 261–88.

Conway, Martin A., and David Rubin. "The Structure of Autobiographical Memory." In *Theories of Memory*, edited by Alan F. Collins et al., 103–37. Hove, UK: Erlbaum, 1993.

Crossan, John Dominic. *The Birth of Christianity: Discovering What Happened in the Years Immediately after the Execution of Jesus*. San Francisco: Harper, 1998.

Cuc, Alexandru, et al. "On the Formation of Collective Memories: The Role of a Dominant Narrator." *Memory and Cognition* 34 (2006) 752–62.

———. "Silence Is Not Golden: A Case for Socially Shared Retrieval-Induced Forgetting." *Psychological Science* 18 (2007) 727–33.

Cullmann, Oscar. *The Johannine Circle*. Translated by John Bowden. Philadelphia: Westminster Press, 1976.

Custance, John. "The Universe of Bliss and the Universe of Horror: A Description of Manic-Depressive Psychosis." In *The Inner World of Mental Illness*, edited by B. Kaplan, 43–61. New York: Harper and Row, 1964.

Davies, Graham. "Statement Validity Analysis: An Art or a Science? Commentary on Bradford." *Child Abuse Review* 3 (1994) 104–6.

Davies, Steven L. *Jesus the Healer*. New York: Continuum, 1995.

DePaulo, Bella M., et al. "Lying in Everyday Life." *Journal of Personality and Social Psychology* 70 (1996) 979–95.

Dodd, Charles H. *Historical Tradition in the Fourth Gospel*. New York: Cambridge University Press, 1963.

Drayton, Michael. "Of Poets and Poesy." In *The Minor Poems of Michael Drayton*, edited by Cyril Brett, 108–13. Oxford, UK: Clarendon Press, 1907.

Dudukovic, Nicole, et al. "Telling a Story or Telling It Straight: The Effects of Entertaining versus Accurate Retelling on Memory." *Applied Cognitive Psychology* 18 (2004) 125–43.

Dunn, James G. *Christology in the Making*. 2nd ed. Grand Rapids: Eerdmans, 1989.

———. *Jesus Remembered*. Grand Rapids: Eerdmans, 2003.

———. "Let John Be John: A Gospel for its Time." In *The Gospel and the Gospels*, edited by Peter Stuhlmacher, 293–322. Grand Rapids, Eerdmans, 1991.

———. "On History, Memory and Eyewitnesses: In Response To Bengt Holmberg and Samuel Byrskog" JSNT 26 (2004) 483-84.

Eve, Eric. *Behind the Gospels: Understanding the Oral Tradition*. Minneapolis: Fortress, 2014.

Faber, David, et al. *Because of Romek: A Holocaust Survivor's Memoir*. El Cajon, CA: Granite Hills, 2005.

Feldman, Robert, et al. "Self-Presentation and Verbal Deception: Do Self-Presenters Lie More?" *Basic and Applied Social Psychology* 24 (2002) 163–70.

Fentress, James J., and Chris Wickham. *Social Memory.* New Perspectives on the Past. Ann Arbor: University of Michigan Press, 2008.

Ferrara, Kathleen. "Accommodation in Therapy." In Contexts of Accommodation: *Developments in Applied Sociolinguistics*, edited by Howard Giles et al., 187–222. New York: Cambridge University Press, 1991.

Frenda, Steven J., et al. "Current Issues and Advances in Misinformation Research." *Current Directions in Psychological Science* 20 (2011) 20–23. https://doi.org/10.1177/0963721410396620.

Funk, Robert W., ed. *The Acts of Jesus: The Search for the Authentic Deeds of Jesus.* San Francisco: Polebridge, 1998.

———,et al. *The Five Gospels: The Search for the Authentic Words of Jesus.* San Francisco: HarperCollins, 1993.

———, *The Parables of Jesus.* Jesus Seminar. Sonoma, CA: Polebridge, 1998.

Ganaway, George. "Some Additional Questions." *Journal of Psychology and Theology* 20 (1992) 201–5.

Gauld, A., and G. M. Stephenson. "Some Experiments Relating to Bartlett's Theory of Remembering." *British Journal of Psychology* 58 (1967) 39–49.

Giles, Howard, et al. "Accommodation Theory: Communication, Context, and Consequence." In Contexts of Accommodation: Development in Applied *Sociolinguistics*, edited by Howard Giles et al., 1–68. New York: Cambridge University Press, 1991.

Goodwin, Frederick K., and Kay Redfield Jamison. *Manic-Depressive Illness: Bipolar Disorders and Recurrent Depression.* 2nd ed. New York: Oxford University Press, 2007.

Goulder, Michael D. *Midrash and Lection in Matthew.* 2nd ed. Eugene, OR: Wipf and Stock, 2004.

Grant, Michael. *Jesus: An Historian's Review of the Gospels.* New York: Charles Scribner's Sons, 1977.

———.*Saint Peter: A Biography.* New York: Charles Scribner and Sons, 1994.

Guilford, J. P. "Creativity." *American Psychologist* 5 (1950) 444–54.

Haines, Richard F. "A Breakdown in Simultaneous Information Processing." In *Presbyopia Research: From Molecular Biology to Visual Adaptation*, edited by Gérard Obrecht and Lawrence W. Stark, 171–75. Boston: Springer, 1991.

Halbwachs, Maurice. *On Collective Memory.* Chicago: University of Chicago Press, 1992.

Harber, Kent D., and Dov. J Cohen. "The Emotional Broadcaster Theory of Social Sharing." *Journal of Language and Social Psychology* 24 (2005) 382–400. https://doi.org/ 10.1177/0261927x05281426.

Hazlitt, William. "On Going a Journey." Blupete, n.d. From *Table Talk: Essays on Men and Manners*, 1822. http://www.blupete.com/Literature/Essays/Hazlitt/TableTalk/GoingJourney.htm.

Heuer, Friderike, and Daniel Reisberg. "Vivid Memories of Emotional Events: The Accuracy of Remembered Minutiae." *Memory and Cognition* 18 (1990) 496–506.

Hengel, Martin. *Saint Peter: The Underestimated Apostle.* Grand Rapids: Eerdmans, 2010.

Hershman, D. Jablow, and Julien Lieb. *Manic Depression and Creativity.* Amherst, MA: Prometheus, 1998.

Higgins, A. J. B. "The Words of Jesus According to St. John." *Bulletin of the John Rylands Library* 49 (1967) 363–86.

Hirst, William, and Gerald Echterhoff. "Remembering in Conversations: The Social Sharing and Reshaping of Memories." *Annual Review of Psychology* 63 (2012) 55–79.

Hirst, William, and David Manier. "Remembering as Communication: A Family Recounts Its Past." In *Remembering Our Past: Studies in Autobiographical Memory*, edited by David C. Rubin, rev. ed., 271–90. Cambridge: Cambridge University Press, 1999.

Hirst, William, et al. "Of Sins and Virtues: Memory and Collective Identity." In *Understanding Autobiographical Memory: Theories and Approaches*, edited by Dorthe Berntsen and David C. Rubin, 141–59. Cambridge: Cambridge University Press, 2012.

Hoffman, Alice M., and Howard S. Hoffman. *Archives of Memory: A Soldier Recalls World War II*. Lexington: University of Kentucky Press, 2009.

Horsley, Richard. "Oral Tradition in New Testament Studies." *Oral Tradition* 18 (2003) 34–36.

Huebenthal, Sandra. *Reading Mark's Gospel as a Text from Collective Memory.* Grand Rapids: Eerdmans, 2020.

Hunter, Archibald M. *According to John: The New Look at the Fourth Gospel.* Philadelphia: Westminster, 1968.

Hyman, Ira E., Jr. "Conversational Remembering: Story Recall with a Peer versus for an Experimenter." *Applied Cognitive Psychology* 8 (1994) 49–66.

———, and F. J. Billings. "False Memories of Childhood Experiences." *Applied Cognitive Psychology* 9 (1995) 181–97.

James, William. "Memory." In *Principles of Psychology*, 1:270–90. New York: Dover, 1890.

———. *The Varieties of Religious Experience: A Study in Human Nature.* San Bernardino, CA: Seven Treasures, 2009.

Jamison, Kay R. *Touched with Fire: Manic-Depressive Illness and the Artistic Temperament.* New York: Free Press, 1993.

———. *An Unquiet Mind.* New York: Vintage, 1995.

Janoff-Bulman, Ronnie. "Assumptive Worlds and the Stress of Traumatic Events: Applications of the Schema Construct." *Social Cognition* 7 (1989) 113–36.

Jefferies, Elizabeth, et al. "Automatic and Controlled Processing in Sentence Recall: The Role of Long-Term and Working Memory." *Journal of Memory and Language* 51 (2004) 623–43.

Jeremias, Joachim. *The Parables of Jesus.* Upper Saddle River, NJ: Prentice-Hall, 1954.

Johnson, Marcia K., et al. "Phenomonal Characteristics of Memories for Perceived and Imagined Autobiographical Events." *Journal of Experimental Psychology: General* 117 (1988) 371–76.

Kashima, Yoshihisa. "Maintaining Cultural Stereotypes in the Serial Reproduction of Narratives." *Personality and Social Psychology Bulletin* 26 (2000) 594–604.

———, et al. "The Maintenance of Cultural Stereotypes in the Conversational Retelling of Narratives." *Asian Journal of Social Psychology* 16 (2013) 60–70.

Keener, Craig S. *Christobiography: Memory, History, and Reliability of the Gospels.* Grand Rapids: Eerdmans, 2019.

Kelber, Werner H. *The Oral and the Written Gospel.* Bloomington: Indiana University Press, 1997.

Kintsch, Walter. "Introduction." In *Remembering: A Study in Experimental and Social Psychology*, by Frederic L. Bartlett, xi–xv. Cambridge: Cambridge University Press, 1995.

Kirk, Alan. *Memory and the Jesus Tradition*. The Reception of Jesus in the First Three Centuries 2. New York: Bloomsbury, 2018.

Köhnken, Günter, and Max Steller. "The Evaluation of the Credibility of Child Witness Statements in the German Procedural System." *Issues in Criminological and Legal Psychology* 3 (1988) 37–45.

Koivisto, Mika, and Antti Revonsuo. "How Meaning Shapes Seeing." *Psychological Science* 10 (2007) 845–49.

Komoszewski, J. Ed, et al. *Reinventing Jesus: How Contemporary Skeptics Miss the Real Jesus and Mislead Popular Culture*. Grand Rapids: Kregel, 2006.

Kysar, Robert. *John: The Maverick Gospel*. 3rd ed. London: Westminster John Knox, 2007.

———. "John's Anti-Jewish Polemic." *Bible Review* 9 (1993). http://cojs.org/robert-kysar-johns-anti-jewish-polemic-bible-review-9-1-1993/.

Lee, Tiane L., et al. "The Serial Reproduction of Conflict: Third Parties Escalate Conflict through Communication Biases." *Journal of Experimental Social Psychology* 54 (2014) 68–72.

Lennard, Henry L. "Some Aspects of the Psychotherapeutic System." In *Research in Psychotherapy*, edited by Hans. H. Strupp and Lester Luborsky, 2:218–36. Washington, DC: American Psychological Association, 1962.

Linton, Marigold. "Ways of Searching and Contents of Memory." In *Autobiographical Memory*, edited by David C. Rubin, 50–67. Cambridge: Cambridge University Press, 1986.

Loftus, Elizabeth. "The Reality of Repressed Memories." *American Psychiatrist* (1993) 518–37.

———, and Katherine Ketchum. *The Myth of Repressed Memory: False Memories and Allegations of Sexual Abuse*. New York: St. Martin's, 1994.

———, et al. "Some Facts about Weapon Focus." *Law and Human Behavior* 11 (1987) 55–62.

Lyons, Anthony, and Yoshihisa Kashima. "How Are Stereotypes Maintained through Communication? The Influence of Stereotype Sharedness." *Journal of Personality and Social Psychology* 85 (2003) 989–1005.

———. "Maintaining Stereotypes in Communication: Investigating Memory Biases and Coherence-Seeking in Storytelling." *Asian Journal of Social Psychology* 9 (2006) 59–71.

Mandler, George, and David L. Watson. "Anxiety and the Interruption of Behavior." In *Anxiety and Behavior*, edited by Charles D. Spielberger, 263–87. New York: Academic, 1966.

Mangan, James Clarence. "The Nameless One." Poetry Nook, n.d. https://www.poetrynook.com/poem/nameless-one-1.

Marsh, Elizabeth J. "Retelling Is Not the Same as Recalling." *Current Directions in Psychological Science* 16 (2007) 16–20.

———, et al. "How Eyewitnesses Talk about Events: Implications for Memory." *Applied Cognitive Psychology* 19 (2005) 531–44.

McIver, Robert. *Memory, Jesus, and the Synoptic Gospels*. Atlanta: Society of Biblical Literature, 2011.

Meade, Michelle L., and Henry L. Roediger III. "Explorations in the Social Contagion of Memory." *Memory and Cognition* 30 (2002) 995–1009.

Meara, Naomi, et al. "Comparison of the Stylistic Complexity of the Language of the Counselor and Client across Three Theoretical Orientations." *Journal of Counseling Psychology* 26 (1979)181–89.

Miller, John W. *Jesus at Thirty: A Psychological and Historical Portrait.* Minneapolis: Fortress, 2007.

Miller, Robert J., ed. *The Apocalyptic Jesus: A Debate.* Santa Rosa, CA: Polebridge, 2001.

Myerson, Abraham, and Rosalie D. Boyle. "The Incidence of Manic-Depressive Psychosis in Certain Socially Important Families." *American Journal of Psychiatry* 98 (1941) 11–21.

Neisser, Ulric. "John Dean's Memory: A Case Study." *Cognition* 9 (1981) 102–15.

———, and Robert Becklen. "Selective Looking: Attending to Visually Specified Events." *Cognitive Psychology* 7 (1975) 480–94.

Nineham, Dennis E. "Eye-Witness Testimony and the Gospel Tradition, I." *Journal of Theological Studies* 9 (1958) 13–25.

———. "Eye-Witness Testimony and the Gospel Tradition, II." *Journal of Theological Studies* 9 (1958) 243–52.

———. "Eye-Witness Testimony and the Gospel Tradition, III." *Journal of Theological Studies* 11 (1960) 253–64.

Patterson, Steven J. *The God of Jesus: The Historical Jesus and the Search for Meaning.* Harrisburg, PA: Trinity, 1998.

Pichert, James W. and Richard C. Anderson. "Taking Different Perspectives on a Story." *Journal of Educational Psychology* 69 (1977) 309–15.

Pillemer, David B. *Momentous Events, Vivid Memories.* Boston: Harvard University Press, 2000.

Porter, Stephen, et al. "The Nature of Real, Implanted, and Fabricated Memories for Emotional Childhood Events: Implications for the Recovered Memory Debate." *Law and Human Behavior* 23 (1999) 517–37.

Radvansky, Gabriel A., and Mark H. Ashcraft. *Cognition.* 6th ed. Boston: Pearson, 2014.

Reisberg, Daniel, and Friderike Heuer. "Remembering the Details of Emotional Events." In *Affect and Accuracy in Recall: Studies of "Flashbulb" Memories*, edited by Eugene Winograd and Ulric Neisser, Emory Symposia in Cognition 4, 162–90. Cambridge: Cambridge University Press, 1992.

Robinson, John A. T. *The Priority of John.* Edited by J. F. Coakley. London: SCM, 1985.

Rubin, David C. *Memory in Oral Traditions: The Cognitive Psychology of Epic, Ballads, and Counting-Out Rhymes.* New York: Oxford University Press, 1995.

———, ed. *Remembering Our Past: Studies in Autobiographical Memory.* Rev. ed. Cambridge: Cambridge University Press, 1999.

Sachs, J. S. "Recognition Memory for Syntactic and Semantic Aspects of Connected Discourse." *Perception and Psychophysics* 2 (1967) 437–42.

Schacter, Daniel L. "Illusory Memories: A Cognitive Neuroscience Analysis." *Proceedings of the National Academy of Sciences* 93 (1996) 13527–33.

———. *Searching for Memory: The Brain, the Mind, and the Past.* New York: Basic, 1996.

———. *The Seven Sins of Memory: How the Mind Forgets and Remembers.* New York: Houghton Mifflin, 2001.

Schleiermacher, Friedrich. *The Life of Jesus.* Translated by S. M. Gilmour. Philadelphia: Fortress, 1975.

Schnackenburg, Rudolf. *The Gospel According to St. John.* New York: Seabury, 1970.

Schooler, Jonathon W., et al. "Qualities of the Unreal." *Journal of Experimental Psychology: Learning, Memory, and Cognition* 12 (1986) 171–81.

Schröter, Jens. "The Gospels as Eyewitness Testimony? A Critical Examination of Richard Bauckham's *Jesus and the Eyewitnesses*." *Journal for the Study of the New Testament* 31 (2008) 195–209.

Schweitzer, Albert. *The Psychiatric Study of Jesus*. Translated by C. R. Joy. Boston: Beacon, 2008.

———. *The Quest of the Historical Jesus: A Critical Study of Its Progress from Reimarus to Wrede*. Memphis: General, 2012.

Scott, Brandon B. *Hear Then the Parable: A Commentary on the Parables of Jesus*. Minneapolis: Fortress, 1990.

Simons, Daniel J., and Christopher F. Chabris. "Gorillas in Our Midst: Sustained Inattentional Blindness for Dynamic Events." *Perception* 28 (1999) 1059–74.

Steller, Max, and Günter Köhnken. "Criteria-Based Statement Analysis." In *Psychological Methods in Criminal Investigation and Evidence*, edited by David C. Raskin, 217–45. New York: Springer, 1989.

Stone, Charles B., et al. "Forgetting Our Personal Past: Socially Shared Retrieval-Induced Forgetting of Autobiographical Memories." *Journal of Experimental Psychology: General* 142 (2012) 1084–99. https://doi.org/10.1037/A0030739.

Strauss, David F. *The Life of Jesus Critically Examined*. Translated by George Eliot. New York: Cosimo, 2009. First published 1835–36.

Taylor, Vincent. *The Formation of the Gospel Tradition*. London: Macmillan, 1964.

Turner, Marilyn L., and Randall W Engle. "Is Working Memory Capacity Task Dependent?" *Journal of Memory and Language* 28 (1989) 127–54.

Tversky, Barbara, and Elizabeth J. Marsh. "Biased Retellings of Events Yield Biased Memories." *Cognitive Psychology* 40 (2000) 1–38.

Van Os, Bas. *Psychological Analyses and the Historical Jesus: New Ways to Explore Christian Origins*. Library of New Testament Studies 432. London: T&T Clark, 2012.

Vlasceanu, Madalina, et al. "Cognition in a Social Context: A Social-Interactionist Approach to Emergent Phenomena." *Current Directions in Psychological Science* 27 (2018) 369–77.

Volbert, Renate, and Max Steller. "Is This Testimony Truthful, Fabricated, or Based on False Memory? Credibility Assessment 25 Years after Steller and Köhnken." *European Psychologist* 19 (1989) 207–20.

Vrij, Aldert. "Criteria-Based Content Analysis: A Qualitative Review of the First 37 Studies." *Psychology, Public Policy, and Law* 11 (2005) 3–41.

Wagenaar, Willem A., and Jop Groeneweg. "The Memory of Concentration Camp Survivors." *Applied Cognitive Psychology* 4 (1990) 77–87.

Wakefield, Hollida, and Ralph Underwager. *Accusations of Child Abuse: In the Real World of Child Interrogations*. Springfield, IL: Thomas, 1988.

Waugh, Nancy C., and Norman, Donald A. "Primary Memory." *Psychological Review* 72, (1965) 89–104.

Weeden, Theodore J., Sr. "Kenneth Bailey's Theory of Oral Tradition: A Theory Contested by Its Evidence." *Journal for the Study of the Historical Jesus* 7 (2009) 3–43.

Witherington, Ben, III. *The Christology of Jesus*. Minneapolis: Fortress, 1989.

Wrede, William. *The Messianic Secret*. Translated by J. C. G. Greig. Greenwood, SC: Attic, 1976.

Yamashiro, Jeremy K., and William Hirst. "Convergence on Collective Memories: Central Speakers and Distributed Remembering." *Journal of Experimental Psychology: General* 149 (2020) 461–81.

Young, Brandon H. *Jesus and His Jewish Parables: Rediscovering the Roots of Jesus' Teaching.* New York: Paulist, (1989) 33-40.

Yuille, John C., and Judith L. Cutshall. "A Case Study of Eyewitness Memory of a Crime." *Journal of Applied Psychology* 7 (1986) 291–301.

Zaparniuk, Judy, et al. "Assessing the Credibility of True and False Statements." *International Journal of Law and Psychiatry* 18 (1995) 343–52.

Index

Index

Index

Index

Index

Scripture Index

Old Testament

New Testament